M

Your
Chinese
Horoscope
2016

MAR 0 9 2016

133.59251
Somer. N

MAR 0 9 2016

Neil Somerville

What the Year of the Monkey holds in store for you

Your Chinese Horoscope 2016

Thorsons

Thorsons
An Imprint of HarperCollins*Publishers*
1 London Bridge Street
London SE1 9GF

www.harpercollins.co.uk

First published by Thorsons 2015

1 3 5 7 9 10 8 6 4 2

© Neil Somerville 2015

Neil Somerville asserts the moral right to
be identified as the author of this work

A catalogue record of this book is
available from the British Library

ISBN 978-0-00-758825-1

Printed and bound in the United States of America by
RR Donnelley

All rights reserved. No part of this publication may be
reproduced, stored in a retrieval system or transmitted,
in any form or by any means, electronic, mechanical,
photocopying, recording or otherwise, without the
prior written permission of the publishers.

About the Author

Neil Somerville is one of the leading writers in the West on Chinese horoscopes. He has been interested in Eastern forms of divination for many years and believes that much can be learned from the ancient wisdom of the East. His annual book on Chinese horoscopes has built up an international following and he is also the author of *What's your Chinese Love Sign?* (Thorsons, 2000; HarperElement, 2013), *Chinese Success Signs* (Thorsons, 2001) and *The Answers* (Element, 2004).

Neil Somerville was born in the year of the Water Snake. His wife was born under the sign of the Monkey, his son is an Ox and daughter a Horse.

TO ROS, RICHARD AND EMILY

As we march into a new year,
we each have our hopes, our ambitions and our dreams.

Sometimes fate and circumstance will assist us,
sometimes we will struggle and despair,
but march we must.

For it is those who keep going,
and who keep their aspirations alive,
who stand the greatest chance of securing what they want.

March determinedly,
and your determination will, in some way, be rewarded.

Neil Somerville

Contents

Acknowledgements

In writing *Your Chinese Horoscope 2016* I am grateful for the assistance and invaluable support that those around me have given.

I would also like to acknowledge Theodora Lau's *The Handbook of Chinese Horoscopes* (Harper & Row, 1979; Arrow, 1981), which was particularly useful to me in my research.

In addition to Ms Lau's work, I commend the following books to those who wish to find out more about Chinese horoscopes: Kristyna Arcarti, *Chinese Horoscopes for Beginners* (Headway, 1995); Catherine Aubier, *Chinese Zodiac Signs* (Arrow, 1984), series of 12 books; E. A. Crawford and Teresa Kennedy, *Chinese Elemental Astrology* (Piatkus Books, 1992); Paula Delsol, *Chinese Horoscopes* (Pan, 1973); Barry Fantoni, *Barry Fantoni's Chinese Horoscopes* (Warner, 1994); Bridget Giles and the Diagram Group, *Chinese Astrology* (HarperCollins*Publishers*, 1996); Kwok Man-Ho, *Complete Chinese Horoscopes* (Sunburst Books, 1995); Lori Reid, *The Complete Book of Chinese Horoscopes* (Element Books, 1997); Paul Rigby and Harvey Bean, *Chinese Astrologics* (Publications Division, South China Morning Post Ltd, 1981); Ruth Q. Sun, *The Asian Animal Zodiac* (Charles E. Tuttle Company, Inc., 1996); Derek Walters, *Ming Shu* (Pagoda Books, 1987) and *The Chinese Astrology Workbook* (The Aquarian Press, 1988); Suzanne White, *The New Astrology* (Pan, 1987), *The New Chinese Astrology* (Pan, 1994) and *Chinese Astrology Plain and Simple* (Eden Grove Editions, 1998).

Introduction

The origins of Chinese horoscopes have been lost in the mists of time. It is known, however, that oriental astrologers practised their art many thousands of years ago and even today Chinese astrology continues to fascinate and intrigue.

In Chinese astrology there are 12 signs named after 12 different animals. No one quite knows how the signs acquired their names, but there is one legend that offers an explanation. According to this legend, one Chinese New Year the Buddha invited all the animals in his kingdom to come before him. Unfortunately, for reasons best known to the animals, only 12 turned up. The first to arrive was the Rat, followed by the Ox, Tiger, Rabbit, Dragon, Snake, Horse, Goat, Monkey, Rooster, Dog and finally Pig. In gratitude, the Buddha decided to name a year after each of the animals and that those born during that year would inherit some of the personality of that animal. Therefore those born in the year of the Ox would be hardworking, resolute and stubborn, just like the Ox, while those born in the year of the Dog would be loyal and faithful, just like the Dog. While it is not possible that everyone born in a particular year can have all the characteristics of the sign, it is incredible what similarities do occur, and this is partly where the fascination of Chinese horoscopes lies.

In addition to the 12 signs of the Chinese zodiac there are five elements and these have a strengthening or moderating influence upon the signs. Details about the effects of the elements are given in each of the chapters on the signs.

To find out which sign you were born under, refer to the tables on the following pages. As the Chinese year is based on the lunar year and does not start until late January or early February, it is particularly important for anyone born in those two months to check carefully the dates of the Chinese year in which they were born.

Also included, in the appendix, are two charts showing the compatibility between the signs for personal and business relationships and details about the signs ruling the different hours of the day. From this it is possible to locate your ascendant and, as in Western astrology, this has a significant influence on your personality.

In writing this book I have taken the unusual step of combining the intriguing nature of Chinese horoscopes with the Western desire to know what the future holds, and have based my interpretations upon various factors relating to each of the signs. Over the years in which *Your Chinese Horoscope* has been published I have been pleased that so many have found the sections on the forthcoming year of interest and hope that the horoscope has been constructive and useful. Remember, though, that at all times you are master of your own destiny.

I sincerely hope that *Your Chinese Horoscope 2016* will prove interesting and helpful for the year ahead.

The Chinese Years

Rabbit	14 February	1915	to	2 February	1916
Dragon	3 February	1916	to	22 January	1917
Snake	23 January	1917	to	10 February	1918
Horse	11 February	1918	to	31 January	1919
Goat	1 February	1919	to	19 February	1920
Monkey	20 February	1920	to	7 February	1921
Rooster	8 February	1921	to	27 January	1922
Dog	28 January	1922	to	15 February	1923
Pig	16 February	1923	to	4 February	1924
Rat	5 February	1924	to	23 January	1925
Ox	24 January	1925	to	12 February	1926
Tiger	13 February	1926	to	1 February	1927
Rabbit	2 February	1927	to	22 January	1928
Dragon	23 January	1928	to	9 February	1929
Snake	10 February	1929	to	29 January	1930
Horse	30 January	1930	to	16 February	1931
Goat	17 February	1931	to	5 February	1932
Monkey	6 February	1932	to	25 January	1933
Rooster	26 January	1933	to	13 February	1934
Dog	14 February	1934	to	3 February	1935
Pig	4 February	1935	to	23 January	1936
Rat	24 January	1936	to	10 February	1937
Ox	11 February	1937	to	30 January	1938
Tiger	31 January	1938	to	18 February	1939
Rabbit	19 February	1939	to	7 February	1940
Dragon	8 February	1940	to	26 January	1941
Snake	27 January	1941	to	14 February	1942
Horse	15 February	1942	to	4 February	1943

Goat	5 February	1943	to	24 January	1944
Monkey	25 January	1944	to	12 February	1945
Rooster	13 February	1945	to	1 February	1946
Dog	2 February	1946	to	21 January	1947
Pig	22 January	1947	to	9 February	1948
Rat	10 February	1948	to	28 January	1949
Ox	29 January	1949	to	16 February	1950
Tiger	17 February	1950	to	5 February	1951
Rabbit	6 February	1951	to	26 January	1952
Dragon	27 January	1952	to	13 February	1953
Snake	14 February	1953	to	2 February	1954
Horse	3 February	1954	to	23 January	1955
Goat	24 January	1955	to	11 February	1956
Monkey	12 February	1956	to	30 January	1957
Rooster	31 January	1957	to	17 February	1958
Dog	18 February	1958	to	7 February	1959
Pig	8 February	1959	to	27 January	1960
Rat	28 January	1960	to	14 February	1961
Ox	15 February	1961	to	4 February	1962
Tiger	5 February	1962	to	24 January	1963
Rabbit	25 January	1963	to	12 February	1964
Dragon	13 February	1964	to	1 February	1965
Snake	2 February	1965	to	20 January	1966
Horse	21 January	1966	to	8 February	1967
Goat	9 February	1967	to	29 January	1968
Monkey	30 January	1968	to	16 February	1969
Rooster	17 February	1969	to	5 February	1970
Dog	6 February	1970	to	26 January	1971
Pig	27 January	1971	to	14 February	1972
Rat	15 February	1972	to	2 February	1973
Ox	3 February	1973	to	22 January	1974
Tiger	23 January	1974	to	10 February	1975
Rabbit	11 February	1975	to	30 January	1976
Dragon	31 January	1976	to	17 February	1977
Snake	18 February	1977	to	6 February	1978

Horse	7 February	1978	to	27 January	1979
Goat	28 January	1979	to	15 February	1980
Monkey	16 February	1980	to	4 February	1981
Rooster	5 February	1981	to	24 January	1982
Dog	25 January	1982	to	12 February	1983
Pig	13 February	1983	to	1 February	1984
Rat	2 February	1984	to	19 February	1985
Ox	20 February	1985	to	8 February	1986
Tiger	9 February	1986	to	28 January	1987
Rabbit	29 January	1987	to	16 February	1988
Dragon	17 February	1988	to	5 February	1989
Snake	6 February	1989	to	26 January	1990
Horse	27 January	1990	to	14 February	1991
Goat	15 February	1991	to	3 February	1992
Monkey	4 February	1992	to	22 January	1993
Rooster	23 January	1993	to	9 February	1994
Dog	10 February	1994	to	30 January	1995
Pig	31 January	1995	to	18 February	1996
Rat	19 February	1996	to	6 February	1997
Ox	7 February	1997	to	27 January	1998
Tiger	28 January	1998	to	15 February	1999
Rabbit	16 February	1999	to	4 February	2000
Dragon	5 February	2000	to	23 January	2001
Snake	24 January	2001	to	11 February	2002
Horse	12 February	2002	to	31 January	2003
Goat	1 February	2003	to	21 January	2004
Monkey	22 January	2004	to	8 February	2005
Rooster	9 February	2005	to	28 January	2006
Dog	29 January	2006	to	17 February	2007
Pig	18 February	2007	to	6 February	2008
Rat	7 February	2008	to	25 January	2009
Ox	26 January	2009	to	13 February	2010
Tiger	14 February	2010	to	2 February	2011
Rabbit	3 February	2011	to	22 January	2012
Dragon	23 January	2012	to	9 February	2013

Snake	10 February	2013	to	30 January	2014
Horse	31 January	2014	to	18 February	2015
Goat	19 February	2015	to	7 February	2016
Monkey	8 February	2016	to	27 January	2017

Note

The names of the signs in the Chinese zodiac occasionally differ, although the characteristics of the signs remain the same. In some books the Ox is referred to as the Buffalo or Bull, the Rabbit as the Hare or Cat, the Goat as the Sheep and the Pig as the Boar.

For the sake of convenience, the male gender is used throughout this book. Unless otherwise stated, the characteristics of the signs apply to both sexes.

Welcome to the
Year of the Monkey

Whether swinging from branch to branch, playing chase with other Monkeys or observing his surroundings, the Monkey has great character and verve. And his energy can be seen in his own year.

Almost as soon as the Monkey year starts, its exciting and innovative nature will be apparent. On the world stage, events will erupt which will take some authorities by surprise. Factions and minorities will strive to be heard and their actions will lead to change. Particularly in more authoritarian areas, developments this year can be significant, even changing the geographical borders of some regions.

In view of the volatility that is being seen, throughout the year world leaders will frequently confer and in some cases put past animosities behind them and forge new alliances. Monkey years can be dramatic both politically and culturally. Past Monkey years have seen the birth of the Polish Solidarity movement, which ultimately led to so much change in Europe, students taking to the streets in Paris, rioting in Los Angeles and revolution in Hungary. This Monkey year will continue to shape history and leave a far-reaching legacy.

The United States celebrated the start of its nationhood in 1776, a previous Year of the Fire Monkey, and in this one, much attention will be focused on the presidential election. There will be great debate over the direction of domestic and foreign policy as well as increasing focus on American identity, and the campaign will be passionately fought, with some issues proving divisive and sometimes even causing rifts between party supporters. The campaign – its significance, its drama, but also its hope – will be an ongoing feature of 2016 and ultimately the newly elected president will promise ambitious reform.

The year's political gyrations will also have an effect on stock markets around the world. There will be some major swings and some dramatic currency fluctuations. It was in a Monkey year that Black Wednesday occurred, an event forever marked in the annals of British fiscal history. Investors this year will require strong nerves, but despite the fluctuations, there will be major success stories and significant fortunes to be made.

Helping drive growth will be the launch of innovative products and inventions. Monkey years favour progress and this one will see some industries abuzz with new ideas. It has been said that Monkey years are times when anything can happen, and certainly in business, events will proceed at a swift pace.

The areas of science, technology and communication will be particularly prominent. Interestingly, it was in a Monkey year that Marconi launched the first public broadcasting service, which helped pave the way to much of the communication we enjoy today. Monkey years are pioneering and, perhaps surprisingly, it was only 12 years ago that Facebook was launched, an event which helped give rise to the social networking phenomenon.

In space, too, pioneering developments will take place. More will be discovered about the universe as probes reach new areas and reveal more about distant planets and galaxies. Again, humanity's quest for knowledge will be greatly advanced this year.

Monkey years are also trendsetting. In fashion, bright new styles could catch the imagination of many, while in entertainment, music and cinematography there will be exciting developments. It was in a Monkey year that Elvis Presley came to prominence with 'Heartbreak Hotel' and in the process opened up a new musical genre. This year will again witness pivotal cultural moments.

Sadly, however, no year can escape tragedy, and this one will be no exception. The vagaries of weather systems will continue to cause havoc, with the year being marked by some horrendous disasters. Some of what occurs will lead to even greater attention being given to climate change and new actions will be agreed. But not all misfortune will be the result of natural catastrophe. Unfortunately, Monkey years have been marked by violence and some high-profile assassinations. These include those of President Doumer of France, Senator Robert Kennedy, Martin Luther

King, Archbishop Romero and John Lennon, and while it is hoped that 2016 will be free of such acts, the portents are not promising.

A major event of the year will be the summer Olympics held in Brazil. The games will be colourful and a visual feast. For a few weeks at least, billions around the world will enjoy following the fortunes of athletes as well as marvel at some mesmerizing performances. Quite a few long-standing records will be broken.

For the individual, Monkey years can be regarded as times of great possibility. They favour enterprise and progress. They also contain the seeds of personal growth and making more of the potential that lies within. Each of us has the ability to put our talents to greater use. In the Monkey year, aim to make this year special – whether by nurturing your talents, working on an idea or contributing more in some way. Monkey years have energy and opportunity for us all. Enjoy what this year brings.

Good luck and good fortune.

Your Chinese Horoscope 2016

5 February 1924 to 23 January 1925 — *Wood Rat*

24 January 1936 to 10 February 1937 — *Fire Rat*

10 February 1948 to 28 January 1949 — *Earth Rat*

28 January 1960 to 14 February 1961 — *Metal Rat*

15 February 1972 to 2 February 1973 — *Water Rat*

2 February 1984 to 19 February 1985 — *Wood Rat*

19 February 1996 to 6 February 1997 — *Fire Rat*

7 February 2008 to 25 January 2009 — *Earth Rat*

The Rat

The Personality of the Rat

To see,
and to see what others do not see.
That is true vision.

The Rat is born under the sign of charm. He is intelligent, popular and loves attending parties and large social gatherings. He is able to establish friendships with remarkable ease and people generally feel relaxed in his company. He is a very social creature and is genuinely interested in the welfare and activities of others. He has a good understanding of human nature and his advice and opinions are often sought.

The Rat is a hard and diligent worker. He is also very imaginative and is never short of ideas. However, he does sometimes lack the confidence to promote his ideas and this can often prevent him from securing the recognition he deserves.

The Rat is very observant and many Rats have made excellent writers and journalists. The Rat also excels at personnel and PR work and any job that brings him into contact with people and the media. His skills are particularly appreciated in times of crisis, for the Rat has an incredibly strong sense of self-preservation. When it comes to finding a way out of an awkward situation, he is certain to be the one who comes up with a solution.

The Rat loves to be where there is a lot of action, but should he ever find himself in a very bureaucratic or restrictive environment he can become a stickler for discipline and routine. He is also something of an opportunist and is constantly on the lookout for ways in which he can improve his wealth and lifestyle. He rarely lets an opportunity go by and can become involved in so many plans and schemes that he sometimes squanders his energies and achieves very little as a result. He is also rather gullible and can be taken in by those less scrupulous than himself.

Another characteristic of the Rat is his attitude towards money. He is very thrifty and to some he may appear a little mean. The reason for this is purely that he likes to keep his money within his family. He can be most generous to his partner, his children and close friends and relatives. He can also be generous to himself, for he often finds it impossible to deprive himself of any luxury or object he fancies. He is very acquisitive and can be a notorious hoarder. He also hates waste and is rarely prepared to throw anything away. He can be rather greedy and will rarely refuse an invitation to a free meal or a complimentary ticket to a lavish function.

The Rat is a good conversationalist, although he can occasionally be a little indiscreet. He can be highly critical of others – for an honest and unbiased opinion, the Rat is a superb critic – and will sometimes use confidential information to his own advantage. However, as he has such a bright and irresistible nature, most people are prepared to forgive him his slight indiscretions.

Throughout his long and eventful life the Rat will make many friends and will find that he is especially well suited to those born under his own sign and those of the Ox, Dragon and Monkey. He can also get on well with those born under the signs of the Tiger, Snake, Rooster, Dog and Pig, but the rather sensitive Rabbit and Goat will find him a little too critical and blunt for their liking. The Horse and Rat will also find it difficult to get on with each other – the Rat craves security and will find the Horse's changeable moods and rather independent nature a little unsettling.

The Rat is very family orientated and will do anything to please his nearest and dearest. He is exceptionally loyal to his parents and can himself be a very caring and loving parent. He will take an interest in all his children's activities and see that they want for nothing. He usually has a large family.

The female Rat has a kindly, outgoing nature and involves herself in a multitude of different activities. She has a wide circle of friends, enjoys entertaining and is an attentive hostess. She is also conscientious about the upkeep of her home and has good taste in home furnishings. She is most supportive to the other members of her family and, due to her resourceful, friendly and persevering nature, can do well in practically any career she chooses.

Although the Rat is essentially outgoing, he is also a very private individual. He tends to keep his feelings to himself and while he is not averse to learning what other people are doing, he resents anyone prying too closely into his own affairs. He also does not like solitude and if he is alone for any length of time he can easily get depressed.

The Rat is undoubtedly very talented, but he does sometimes fail to capitalize on his many abilities. He has a tendency to become involved in too many schemes and chase after too many opportunities at once. If he can slow down and concentrate on one thing at a time, he can become very successful. If not, success and wealth can elude him. But, with his tremendous ability to charm, he will rarely, if ever, be without friends.

The Five Different Types of Rat

In addition to the 12 signs of the Chinese zodiac there are five elements and these have a strengthening or moderating influence on the signs. The effects of the elements on the Rat are described below, together with the years in which they were exercising their influence. Therefore Rats born in 1960 are Metal Rats, Rats born in 1972 are Water Rats, and so on.

Metal Rat: 1960

This Rat has excellent taste and certainly knows how to appreciate the finer things in life. His home is comfortable and nicely decorated and he likes to entertain and mix in fashionable circles. He has considerable financial acumen and invests his money well. On the surface he appears cheerful and confident, but deep down he can be troubled by worries that are quite often of his own making. He is exceptionally loyal to his family and friends.

Water Rat: 1972

The Water Rat is intelligent and very astute. He is a deep thinker and can express his thoughts clearly and persuasively. He is always eager to learn and is talented in many different areas. He is usually very popular, but his fear of loneliness can sometimes lead him into mixing with the wrong sort of company. He is a particularly skilful writer, but can get sidetracked very easily and should try to concentrate on just one thing at a time.

Wood Rat: 1924, 1984

The Wood Rat has a friendly, outgoing personality and is popular with his colleagues and friends. He has a quick, agile brain and likes to turn his hand to anything he thinks may be useful. His one fear is insecurity, but given his intelligence and capabilities, this fear is usually unfounded. He has a good sense of humour, enjoys travel and, due to his highly imaginative nature, can be a gifted writer or artist.

Fire Rat: 1936, 1996

The Fire Rat is rarely still and seems to have a never-ending supply of energy and enthusiasm. He loves being involved in some form of action, be it travel, following up new ideas or campaigning for a cause in which he fervently believes. He is an original thinker and hates being bound by petty restrictions or the dictates of others. He can be forthright in his views but can sometimes get carried away in the excitement of the moment and commit himself to various undertakings without thinking through all the implications. Yet he has a resilient nature and with the right support can go far in life.

Earth Rat: 1948, 2008

This Rat is astute and very level-headed. He rarely takes unnecessary chances and while he is constantly trying to improve his financial status, he is prepared to proceed slowly and leave nothing to chance. He is probably not as adventurous as the other types of Rat and prefers to remain in familiar territory rather than rush headlong into something he knows little about. He is talented, conscientious and caring towards his loved ones, but at the same time can be self-conscious and worry a little too much about the image he is trying to project.

Prospects for the Rat in 2016

Whether introducing changes to his lifestyle, making alterations to his work or pursuing his interests, the Rat will have made the Year of the Goat (19 February 2015–7 February 2016) an active one. In its closing stages he will continue to be involved in a great many activities and will need to remain well-organized and decide on priorities, otherwise some weeks may seem a whirl and he may not always use his time in the most effective way.

This is particularly the case in his work. New demands, busy schedules and interruptions could frequently occur and the Rat will need to focus and beware of distractions or wasting time on unimportant matters. However, amid the activity, there will still be the chance to contribute and make an impact. For Rats seeking work or hoping for promotion, August and October could be significant.

The Rat will also have many outgoings at the end of the Goat year and should watch his spending levels and plan out his more substantial purchases.

Domestically and socially, he will be in demand, with many chances to enjoy parties and other occasions and spend time with family and friends. In his home life, if there are certain tasks he would like to get done, he will find that by talking these over with those around him, he may not only be able to get them started but also finished by the year's end.

Goat years favour new friendships and romance, and over the course of this one, unattached Rats could meet someone who could become important over the next 12 months. August, September and early 2016 could be significant and lively times.

Overall, the Goat year will have been a busy one for the Rat, but while it will have brought its pressures, there will also have been many achievements that the Rat can now build on. His prospects are on the up!

*   *   *

One of the strengths of the Rat is his resourceful nature. When he spots an opportunity (which he does often), he invariably makes the most of it. And the Monkey year will contain opportunities aplenty. This is a favourable year for the Rat and will offer him the chance to make more of his potential and enjoy some deserved success.

The Year of the Monkey starts on 8 February and almost at once the Rat could be blessed with some surprising good fortune. Whether acquiring something he has been wanting for some time, receiving an encouraging response to an enquiry or application, or being enthused by an idea, he can find the Monkey year getting off to a promising start. And in true Rat style, he should aim to make the most of it. Events can happen quickly in the Monkey year and chances need to be seized before the moment is lost.

This will particularly be the case in the Rat's work. Many organizations will be implementing changes as well as adapting to new markets and conditions, and by being involved and aware, the Rat will often be well-placed to benefit. When openings occur in his place of work, or his industry as a whole, his experience can stand him in good stead. There will be excellent chances to take on greater and more remunerative responsibilities this year. Especially for Rats who have been in the same position for some time, this is a year to move forward, and as soon as the Rat learns of an opening, he should be quick to follow it up. Speed and initiative count for a lot this year.

Late February, March, June, October and November could see encouraging developments and such is the nature of the year that new responsibilities taken on in the early months (even if initially offered on a temporary basis) could pave the way to something more substantial later on.

For Rats who are unfulfilled in their present position and those seeking work, the prospects are also encouraging. However, to benefit, these Rats should not be too restrictive in the type of work they consider. By widening their options they may discover a position which not only suits them but also offers potential for the future.

In addition, there could be increased opportunities for the Rat to travel in connection with his work this year, or possibly relocate. Also, with this being a year favouring self-development, if there are chances for him to go on training courses or set time aside for study, his efforts could reward him handsomely. For Rats currently on educational courses, this is a time when commitment and hard work can lead to good results which can be built upon in the future.

Although the Rat will be involved in a great many activities this year, it is also important he makes time to enjoy recreational pursuits. If there are interests he is keen to develop, he should allow himself chance to do so. Regular 'me time' can enrich his lifestyle.

Travel is also favourably aspected, and if he is able, the Rat should aim to take a holiday this year. To enjoy his time away even more, he will find it helpful to read about his destination prior to leaving. Travel, including short breaks and weekends away, can give rise to some particular delights, notably in the summer.

The Rat's progress at work may help financially and many Rats will now have the opportunity to proceed with some plans and acquisitions for the home. However, the Rat would do well to consider his purchases carefully rather than rush. Also, any provision he can make for the future could be something he is grateful for at a later date. This generally favourable year rewards good management and control.

On a personal level, the Rat will be kept busy. For the unattached Rat, the Monkey year will contain many social opportunities, with good chances to meet others, make friends and, for quite a few, find romance. Rats already enjoying romance could find this becoming more significant, and some will marry or settle down together. Monkey years favour relationships and the sociable Rat will enjoy the good times this one offers. March, May, August and November could be busy months for meeting others.

The Rat's home life will also be active. His home is important to him and he is always looking for ways to improve it. However, while he may be a driving force in making changes, he does need to discuss his ideas and be mindful of the suggestions of others, especially where choices and potentially disruptive projects are concerned.

Similarly, with the changes in working patterns that the Rat and other family members may experience this year, there needs to be some flexibility from all concerned. The Monkey year is a time for dialogue as well as for enjoying quality time with others. But the Rat's thoughtfulness will make a difference in many a home this year.

In general, the Monkey year holds encouraging prospects for the Rat. In his work, this is a year favouring growth, while his social life can bring him considerable pleasure and his home life can be gratifying, especially when he joins with others to see through projects and enjoy personal and family successes. To make things happen, however, he does need to set his ideas in motion. To drift or hold back could lead to him missing some fine opportunities. By being active and involved, however, the Rat can reap some good rewards this year.

The Metal Rat

The Metal Rat is a redoubtable figure. Not only is he determined and conscientious, but also resourceful. When he senses an opportunity, he is prepared to follow it up and see what transpires. His strengths and qualities can serve him well this year.

In almost all areas of his life he can look forward to positive developments, and if there are particular plans he would like to carry out, now is the time. Throughout the year, he will find those around him helpful, and with backing, and in some instances combined effort, a lot can happen for him.

At work, the aspects are especially encouraging. Although many Metal Rats will have made progress in recent years, in the Monkey year they will be given the opportunity to build on what they do. Some could find themselves offered a more specialist role or project, while others will be favourably placed for promotion. This is a year favouring progress and there will be opportunities for the Metal Rat to build on his expertise.

The majority of Metal Rats will remain with their current employer over the year, but some may be tempted elsewhere, perhaps drawn by a new challenge as well as better remuneration. By remaining alert for openings and talking to contacts in their industry, quite a few will make the change they want. In some instances, this could involve a considerable change of duties, and even relocation. However, these Metal Rats will feel more motivated than they have for some while.

The aspects are also encouraging for Metal Rats seeking work. As well as keeping alert for vacancies, they could find it helpful to talk to employment advisers, friends and contacts. They could be informed of a suitable position or given an idea worth pursuing.

Events can happen quickly in the Monkey year and in some instances an application could swiftly be followed up, or an opening found and offer made within a matter of days. Opportunities could arise at almost any time, but late February, March, June, October and November could be key months.

Progress at work can also help financially. Many Metal Rats will increase their income over the year and some will also receive funds from another source or put an enterprising idea to profitable use. As a result, the Metal Rat may decide it is time to make additions to his home, update equipment and treat himself and his loved ones to special occasions or trips. However, he should be wary of rush. If he considers his options carefully, he will not only make better decisions but also be more likely to identify favourable purchasing opportunities.

The Metal Rat has an enquiring mind and will again take pleasure in furthering his interests. Sometimes new equipment and knowledge and shared pursuits will make his activities even more fulfilling. With travel favourably aspected, he could also find his interests taking him out more, perhaps to special events.

The Metal Rat can also look forward to a rewarding social life and his circle of acquaintances and contacts is set to grow. For Metal Rats who are unattached and would welcome new friendships, joining groups and pursuing interests can be excellent ways of meeting others. For some, significant romance can beckon. March, May, August and mid-October to November could see the most social opportunities.

The busy nature of the year will also extend to the Metal Rat's domestic life and it is important that there is good co-operation between all in his household. That way, a lot can be undertaken and some ambitious projects carried through.

Over the year there could also be a major family occasion taking place, most likely involving a younger family member. The Metal Rat will be keen to be involved and will once again provide helpful input. The summer could be a particularly busy and rewarding time and further good news could come near the year's end.

The Year of the Monkey is one of opportunity for the Metal Rat, and with a sense of purpose and his engaging personal qualities, he can fare well. This is a time for looking to move forward. For the determined and enterprising, much can be accomplished and enjoyed.

Tip for the Year
Act with determination. You have much in your favour this year, but the initiative rests with you. Believe in yourself and go forward.

The Water Rat

One of the hallmarks of the Water Rat's personality is his keen and enterprising nature. This year some important opportunities will open up for him and if there are particular ambitions he is keen to realize or plans he wants to set in motion, this is very much a time for action. By making a start – ideally early on in the year – not only can he see certain activities and hopes gather momentum but also lead to further and sometimes unanticipated opportunities. Luck will favour the bold and enterprising.

In the Water Rat's work this will be a year of important developments. In view of the expertise he has built up, his current employer could look to him to take on new responsibilities. Particularly if he is in a creative and/or sales environment, he could find his ideas encouraged and his input potentially significant. Another factor to his advantage will be the good working relations he enjoys with many of those around him. The respect he has earned and his ability to communicate effectively can lead to him taking a greater role. This is a year when he can make his strengths count and in the process move his career forward.

While many Water Rats will make (often substantial) progress with their current employer, some will be tempted by better prospects elsewhere. Again, once enquiries and applications are made, interesting developments could quickly follow in this encouraging year.

The favourable aspects also apply to Water Rats currently seeking work. These Water Rats should be open to considering different types of work and acquiring new skills. Much can be achieved this year and many will have the chance to prove themselves in an often new and greater capacity.

From the beginning of the Monkey year to early April and June, October and November could be key times for work matters.

Progress made at work will improve the income of many Water Rats this year and quite a few will benefit from an additional payment or gift. Financially, the aspects are encouraging, although money matters do require discipline, otherwise any extra earnings could quickly be spent, and not always in the best way. Ideally, if there are major purchases the Water Rat would like to make, he should make early provision for these as well as take the time to compare options. With advice and good management, he could be particularly pleased with some of his acquisitions, especially new equipment.

With this a year for action, a few Water Rats will decide to move house. Again, once they start to make enquiries, they could quickly get the process underway. At all times the Water Rat will need to be mindful of costs and other implications, and seek advice as necessary, but this is a year when a lot can be accomplished.

Travel, too, could feature on the agenda of many Water Rats. In addition to any holiday taken with loved ones, there could be travel opportunities involving work or key interests. During the year many Water Rats will travel more than usual and enjoy visiting some impressive places.

Another encouraging aspect of the year concerns the Water Rat's own interests. Something he hears or sees could whet his curiosity and reawaken a former interest or tempt him to try something new. A key aspect of the Monkey year is opportunity, and by being aware and game, the Water Rat can derive much pleasure from the activities he pursues. In addition, those who enjoy writing and other creative pursuits should consider putting their talents to greater use and promote anything they produce. There could be surprises in store in this encouraging year.

With his interest in others and good conversational skills, the Water Rat enjoys good relations with many people and can look forward to a variety of pleasing social occasions over the year. Whether going to parties, meeting friends or attending other gatherings, he will find new contacts can be made and friendships forged. For the unattached, a chance meeting can quickly blossom into romance. In many respects, the Monkey year is one that will surprise and delight the Water Rat. Also, if at any time he is in a dilemma or just wants to run his thoughts past another person, there will be many who are ready and willing to help. March, May, August and November could see the most social opportunity.

The progressive nature of the Monkey year will also filter through to the Water Rat's home life. In addition to assisting family members, he will have several plans he will be keen to get underway. Again, once these are started, a lot will happen quickly, and initially modest undertakings may become more extensive. The more that can be undertaken jointly, the more gratifying the outcome will be. Domestically, this can be a busy and rewarding year. Change could also be on the cards for several family members, especially involving their education or work. The summer and end of the year could be especially active.

By the time the Monkey year draws to a close, many Water Rats will be taken aback by all that has taken place. There will have been many changes and some important ambitions will have been realized. Certain plans will have taken different courses than expected, but in true Water Rat fashion, the Water Rat will have made the most of what has opened up. This will be a busy year, but it is one for building, for moving forward and making the most of ideas and strengths. And as well as surprises, it can bring the Water Rat some well-deserved success.

Tip for the Year
Be ready: events can happen quickly this year. To benefit, you will need to seize the moment. Look to move forward. You have much to offer.

The Wood Rat

This will be an eventful year for the Wood Rat, with a lot going in his favour. However, while he may have particular ambitions he would like to realize, he will need to be flexible. Circumstances can change and he will need to modify his thinking and actions accordingly. Also, he would do well to draw on the assistance of others. With their backing, advice and support, he can make this a full and potentially rewarding 12 months.

For Wood Rats with a partner, this is a year for taking decisions and moving forward. Some may see an addition to their family, some may move and some will have ambitious plans for their current home. Whatever they choose to do, this is a year when many will see their hopes realized and share wonderful moments.

As many Wood Rats will find, once plans are set in motion, encouraging developments can quickly follow on. This is a year when serendipity can often come into play. Where more practical plans are concerned, however, the Wood Rat (and others) should be mindful of other possibilities and obtain expert advice when necessary. Whether purchasing equipment, carrying out modifications or moving house, the Wood Rat could find some guidance of particular value. More senior relations will be keen to assist and some could have considerable experience behind them. If the Wood Rat is willing to talk over his ideas and plans, he could receive help in sometimes unexpected ways. March, July, August and December could be domestically busy and often special months.

With the Wood Rat's wide social circle, together with his current activities, he will also have some good social opportunities this year. In addition to regularly meeting up with his friends, he could be invited to various parties and celebrations as well as events related to his interests. The Monkey year promises some fun and lively times and, particularly for those who are unattached or have had recent personal difficulty, can see a considerable transformation taking place. Sometimes new interests could lead to these Wood Rats building an important new network of friends, and for quite a few, affairs of the heart will make the year all the more special. Some Wood Rats will meet their future partner, often in a curious way. Chance will play a big part this year. March, May, August and mid-October to the end of November are likely to see the most social activity.

Although the Wood Rat will have many demands on his resources, particularly with possible deposits to put down and expensive purchases to make, if possible he should try to take a holiday this year. A change of scene can do him a lot of good as well as give him the opportunity to explore new areas. Last-minute offers could be tempting and the unexpectedness will add to the fun.

The Monkey year can also bring important developments work-wise. In recent years many Wood Rats will have built up experience in a particular area of work and this year will give them the chance to take their knowledge further. Many of those employed in large organizations will benefit from internal openings, securing promotion and the chance to prove themselves in a new capacity. Should opportunities be limited in his present place of work, the Wood Rat should explore possibilities elsewhere. This is a year for progress. Late February, March, June, October and November could be significant months, although whenever the Wood Rat sees a position of possible interest, he should be quick to follow it up. Speed is of the essence this year.

Similarly, for Wood Rats seeking work, the Monkey year can have important developments in store. Although the job-seeking process can be wearying, these Wood Rats should have faith in themselves and actively explore possibilities. If they find out more about particular vacancies and the companies offering them, their thoroughness can impress and often lead to success.

The Wood Rat will have many demands on his time this year and it is important he does not allow his recreational pursuits to suffer. This may be a successful year, but his lifestyle does need balance and the preservation of some 'me time'. Also, as the aspects are favourable for self-development, if there is a skill he would like to become more proficient in or a particular subject that appeals to him, he should set time aside for research, practice and, if applicable, a course. This can be both satisfying and beneficial in other ways.

Many Wood Rats will enjoy a noticeable increase in income over the year. However, to benefit fully, the Wood Rat will need to keep careful control over spending. With personal plans, expensive purchases, commitments and possible deposits to consider, provision needs to be made for present and forthcoming requirements. Also, when considering major commitments, the Wood Rat would do well to seek advice and not rush decisions. This can be an improved year financially, but it is one for vigilance *and* good management.

By nature the Wood Rat is both keen and ambitious, and by putting himself forward and making the most of his opportunities, he can enjoy some good successes this year. Much of what he achieves now will shape the next few years, especially work-wise. His personal interests, too, can be meaningful, and whether with a partner or enjoying the company of friends, he will enjoy sharing his time with others. This can be a good and often fortuitous year for him.

Tip for the Year
Follow your ambitions. You have much in your favour this year and with purpose, belief and the support of others, you can accomplish a great deal. This is a year for action – make things happen!

The Fire Rat

The fire element adds to the drive and determination of a sign, and this, combined with the favourable aspects of the Monkey year, will make this an important and successful time for the Fire Rat. With resolve and initiative, he can fare well and enjoy himself in the process.

One important aspect of the Monkey year is the way it encourages the Fire Rat to broaden his skills and interests. No matter what his present situation may be, during the year he will be introduced to something new. By being willing to explore and learn, rather than close his mind, he will find that what results can often be to his long-term benefit.

For the many Fire Rats in education, there will be much to learn. However, by remaining focused and working consistently, many of these

Fire Rats will make important headway and secure skills and qualifications they can build on in the future. Over the year their studies can develop in an interesting manner and perhaps open up subject areas they will be keen to take further or alert them to other possibilities, including particular vocations. The Monkey year is a time for learning *and* discovery.

This also applies to more personal interests and if there is a particular skill or hobby the Fire Rat is keen to make more of, he should look to develop this. If applicable, further guidance could help take his skills to new levels. Whether he prefers practical, creative or sporting pursuits, his recreational activities can be both satisfying and inspiring this year.

Many of the Fire Rat's activities will have a good social element too, and he will often be helped by sharing his thoughts and talking over his ideas. New friendships can be made over the year and these can become valuable during this and following years.

The aspects also favour romance, and for Fire Rats already in love, or who find love, the year will contain exciting times. The vibrant personality and verve of many Fire Rats will make them attractive company.

Admittedly, amid all the activity there could be some fraught moments – perhaps a disagreement may arise or a hope not materialize – but these are part of life's learning experiences. Whenever problems do emerge, it is important the Fire Rat does not feel alone but talks matters over with close friends and family. A worry shared can often be one considerably eased.

At most times of the year the Fire Rat will have chances to go out, but March, May, August and mid-October to the end of November could be particularly pleasing and eventful months socially. Also, with this being their twentieth year, many Fire Rats will celebrate the start of a new decade in style, with family members and close friends demonstrating their affection and support. Some Fire Rats may receive generous gifts, including equipment to advance an interest.

The Monkey year can also be significant work-wise. For Fire Rats already in a position, new opportunities can present themselves. If in a large organization, the Fire Rat could be offered training or be tempted by a vacancy in another sector. If opportunities are limited where he is, he should investigate openings elsewhere. By keeping alert, many Fire Rats will not only take on a greater role over the year but also acquire new skills and strengthen their prospects for the future.

The aspects are also encouraging for those seeking work. By considering a variety of possibilities, many could obtain a position which builds on their particular strengths. With commitment, this can prove a significant time, with late February, March, June, October and November particularly likely to see encouraging developments.

With his many interests and lively social life, the Fire Rat will, however, need to be disciplined in spending. With care, he can do a lot, but if he proceeds in an ad hoc way, some plans may need to be scaled back. Travel may be particularly appealing, but here again the Fire Rat would do well to budget in advance. The year requires good management of resources.

This Monkey year marks the start of a new decade in the Fire Rat's life and he will be determined to make the most of it. And it can be both exciting and significant. This is a time for discovering more about himself and his capabilities. He knows he has much to offer, and by making the most of his opportunities and resources, he will find his efforts rewarding him with a firm base he can build on in the future.

Tip for the Year

Focus on what you want. Progress made now will prepare the way for future opportunities. Also, enjoy your special talents and look to develop them. You have much in your favour this year. Use it well, for its legacy can be far-reaching.

The Earth Rat

The Monkey year offers considerable scope for the Earth Rat, although to make the most of the favourable aspects, he needs to seize his opportunities and act on his ideas. With purpose, however, he can accomplish a great deal.

The Earth Rat's domestic life can be especially meaningful. Family celebrations and happy times are in store for many. Whether seeing their family grow in numbers and/or a wedding, graduation or the success of someone close, these Earth Rats will have several occasions to feel proud. Throughout the year, the Earth Rat will also be glad to assist others in their various activities and plans. His thoughtfulness and ability to sense the best way forward will be particularly valued, with younger relations especially grateful. July, August and December could be busy times in many an Earth Rat household.

In addition to assisting others, the Earth Rat will be keen to go ahead with some of his own plans. Often these will relate to his home. Some Earth Rats will have a purge on clutter and decide to smarten certain rooms and one project may soon lead to another and practical activities mushroom. However, while some undertakings will become more extensive than initially envisaged, the Earth Rat (and others) will often delight in the results.

The Earth Rat may also be fortunate in some acquisitions made over the year. If considering new equipment or wanting something specific for the home, he will find that taking the time to consider his options could result in some shrewd purchases. His thoroughness and care can serve him well this year.

Travel, too, is favourably aspected, and if possible, the Earth Rat should try to go away for a holiday over the year. Local attractions could also appeal, but the Monkey year encourages venturing out and discovering places new.

The Earth Rat's personal interests can also develop well. Some Earth Rats will set themselves a challenge that will allow them to use their knowledge in a new and purposeful way. For any who may feel unfulfilled or perhaps jaded, it could be to their advantage to see what is available in their area and consider enrolling on a course or joining a group. With the aspects as they are, positive action can prove surprisingly rewarding.

The Earth Rat will also enjoy meeting up with his friends. Being interested in many subjects and a talented communicator, he will revel in some of the lively times (and debates) of the year. There will be chances to meet quite a few new people too, and for the unattached, romance could beckon. On a personal level, this can be an interesting year, and the Earth Rat should make the most of his social opportunities. March, May, August and mid-October to the end of November could be particularly stimulating months.

With home projects and purchases, family expenses, travel and personal interests, the Earth Rat's spending will be considerable. However, with care, he will be able to proceed with most of his plans. Some Earth Rats may also enjoy some financial luck, possibly through selling items they no longer require and receiving more than anticipated. Certain skills or a competition win may also bring them something extra. Monkey years have an element of good fortune to them.

In most respects, this will be an encouraging year for the Earth Rat, but, as is always the case, problems will sometimes arise. When they do, it is important the Earth Rat talks to others and, if necessary, seeks an expert opinion. To keep concerns to himself may compound problems and cause him to worry more than necessary. Earth Rats, remember, advice is available.

For the most part, however, this will be a practical and satisfying year for the Earth Rat. It is a time to act upon his ideas. Once he has made a start, a lot can follow on, with luck often helping along the way. For many Earth Rats there will be family successes to enjoy and the Earth Rat will also make the most of his social life and enjoy the interests he is able to share. Overall, an active and personally rewarding year.

Tip for the Year
Once plans are underway, other possibilities can often arise in this encouraging year. Be alert for these, as they may be better than what you originally had in mind. Also, enjoy your good relations with those around you.

Famous Rats

Ben Affleck, Ursula Andress, Louis Armstrong, Lauren Bacall, Dame Shirley Bassey, Kathy Bates, Irving Berlin, Kenneth Branagh, Marlon Brando, Charlotte Brontë, Jackson Browne, George H. W. Bush, Glen Campbell, Jimmy Carter, Jeremy Clarkson, Aaron Copland, Cameron Diaz, David Duchovny, Duffy, T. S. Eliot, Eminem, Colin Firth, Pope Francis I, Clark Gable, Neil Gaiman, Al Gore, Hugh Grant, Lewis Hamilton, Thomas Hardy, Prince Harry, Charlton Heston, Buddy Holly, Mick Hucknall, Henrik Ibsen, Jeremy Irons, Samuel L. Jackson, LeBron James, Jean-Michel Jarre, Scarlett Johansson, Gene Kelly, Avril Lavigne, Jude Law, Gary Lineker, Lord Andrew Lloyd Webber, Ian McEwan, Katie Melua, Claude Monet, Olly Murs, Richard Nixon, Ozzy Osbourne, Brad Paisley, Sean Penn, Katy Perry, Philippe I, King of the Belgians, Sir Terry Pratchett, Ian Rankin, Burt Reynolds, Rossini, William Shakespeare, James Taylor, Leo Tolstoy, Henri Toulouse-Lautrec, Spencer Tracy, the Prince of Wales, George Washington, the Duke of York, Emile Zola.

24 January 1925 to 12 February 1926 — *Wood Ox*

11 February 1937 to 30 January 1938 — *Fire Ox*

29 January 1949 to 16 February 1950 — *Earth Ox*

15 February 1961 to 4 February 1962 — *Metal Ox*

3 February 1973 to 22 January 1974 — *Water Ox*

20 February 1985 to 8 February 1986 — *Wood Ox*

7 February 1997 to 27 January 1998 — *Fire Ox*

26 January 2009 to 13 February 2010 — *Earth Ox*

The Ox

The Personality of the Ox

The more considered the way,
the more considerable the journey.

The Ox is born under the signs of equilibrium and tenacity. He is a hard and conscientious worker and sets about everything he does in a resolute, methodical and determined manner. He has considerable leadership qualities and is often admired for his tough and uncompromising nature. He knows what he wants to achieve in life and, as far as possible, will not be deflected from his ultimate objective.

The Ox takes his responsibilities and duties very seriously. He is decisive and quick to take advantage of any opportunity that comes his way. He is also sincere and places a great deal of trust in his friends and colleagues. He is, nevertheless, something of a loner. He is a quiet and private individual and often keeps his thoughts to himself. He also cherishes his independence and prefers to set about things in his own way rather than be bound by the dictates of others or influenced by outside pressures.

The Ox tends to have a calm and tranquil nature, but if something angers him or he feels that someone has let him down, he can have a fearsome temper. He can also be stubborn and obstinate and this can lead him into conflict with others. Usually he will succeed in getting his own way, but should things go against him he is a poor loser and will take any defeat or setback extremely badly.

The Ox is often a deep thinker and rather studious. He is not particularly renowned for his sense of humour and does not take kindly to new gimmicks or anything too innovative. He is too solid and traditional for that and prefers to stick to the more conventional norm.

His home is very important to him and in some respects he treats it as a private sanctuary. His family tends to be closely knit and the Ox will make sure that each member does their fair share around the house. He tends to be a hoarder, but he is always well organized and neat. He also places great importance on punctuality and there is nothing that infuriates him more than to be kept waiting, particularly if it is due to someone's inefficiency. The Ox can be a hard taskmaster!

Once settled in a job or house, the Ox will quite happily remain there for many years. He does not like change and he is also not particularly keen on travel. He does, however, enjoy gardening and other outdoor pursuits and he will often spend much of his spare time out of doors. He is usually an excellent gardener and whenever possible will make sure he has a large area of ground to maintain. He usually prefers to live in the country rather than the town.

Due to his dedicated and dependable nature, the Ox will usually do well in his chosen career, providing he is given enough freedom to act on his own initiative. He invariably does well in politics, agriculture and careers that need specialized training. He is also very gifted artistically and many Oxen have enjoyed considerable success as musicians or composers.

The Ox is not as outgoing as some and it often takes him a long time to establish friendships and feel relaxed in another person's company. His courtships are likely to be long, but once he is settled, he will remain devoted and loyal to his partner. He is particularly well suited to those born under the signs of the Rat, Rabbit, Snake and Rooster. He can also establish a good relationship with the Monkey, Dog, Pig and another Ox, but he will find that he has little in common with the whimsical and sensitive Goat. He will also find it difficult to get on with the Horse, Dragon and Tiger – the Ox prefers a quiet and peaceful existence and those born under these three signs tend to be a little too lively and impulsive for his liking.

The female Ox has a kind and caring nature and her home and family are very much her pride and joy. She always tries to do her best for her partner and can be a most conscientious and loving parent. She is an excellent organizer and a very determined person who will often succeed in getting what she wants in life. She usually has a deep interest in the arts and is often a talented artist or musician.

The Ox is a very down-to-earth character. He is sincere, loyal and unpretentious. He can, however, be rather reserved and to some he may appear distant and aloof. He has a quiet nature, but underneath he is very strong-willed and ambitious. He has the courage of his convictions and is often prepared to stand up for what he believes to be right, regardless of the consequences. He inspires confidence and trust and throughout his life he will rarely be short of people who are ready to support him.

The Five Different Types of Ox

In addition to the 12 signs of the Chinese zodiac there are five elements and these have a strengthening or moderating influence on the signs. The effects of the elements on the Ox are described below, together with the years in which they were exercising their influence. Therefore Oxen born in 1961 are Metal Oxen, Oxen born in 1913 and 1973 are Water Oxen, and so on.

Metal Ox: 1961

This Ox is confident and very strong-willed. He can be blunt and forthright in his views and is not afraid of speaking his mind. He sets about his objectives with a dogged determination, but he can become so involved in his various activities that he can be oblivious to the thoughts and feelings of those around him, and this can sometimes be to his detriment. He is honest and dependable and will never promise more than he can deliver. He has a good appreciation of the arts and usually a small circle of very good and loyal friends.

Water Ox: 1973

This Ox has a sharp and penetrating mind. He is a good organizer and sets about his work in a methodical manner. He is not as narrow-minded as some of the other types of Ox and is more willing to involve others in his plans and aspirations. He usually has very high moral standards and is often attracted to careers in public service. He is a good judge of character and has such a friendly and persuasive manner that he usually

experiences little difficulty in securing his objectives. He is popular and
has an excellent way with children.

Wood Ox: 1925, 1985

The Wood Ox conducts himself with an air of dignity and authority and
will often take a leading role in any enterprise in which he becomes
involved. He is very self-confident and is direct in his dealings with
others. He does, however, have a quick temper and has no hesitation in
speaking his mind. He has tremendous drive and willpower and an
extremely good memory. He is particularly loyal and devoted to the
members of his family and has a most caring nature.

Fire Ox: 1937, 1997

The Fire Ox has a powerful and assertive personality and is a hard and
conscientious worker. He holds strong views and has very little patience
when things do not go his way. He can also get carried away in the
excitement of the moment and does not always take into account the
views of those around him. He nevertheless has many leadership qualities and will often reach positions of power, eminence and wealth. He
usually has a small group of loyal and close friends and is very devoted
to his family.

Earth Ox: 1949, 2009

This Ox sets about everything he does in a sensible and level-headed
manner. He is ambitious but also realistic in his aims and is often
prepared to work long hours to secure his objectives. He is shrewd in
financial and business matters and is a very good judge of character. He
has a quiet nature and is greatly admired for his sincerity and integrity.
He is also very loyal to his family and friends and his views are often
sought.

Prospects for the Ox in 2016

The Year of the Goat (19 February 2015–7 February 2016) will have been a tricky one for the Ox and in what remains of it he will need to keep his wits about him. The Ox likes certainty and the volatility of some situations will exasperate him in the closing months of the year.

At work, he could feel unsettled, as extra demands are placed upon him. Also, he may not always be in full accord with certain colleagues. However, it will be a case of knuckling down and concentrating on specific duties, and remaining wary of distractions and time-consuming trifles. Although great effort will be required, impressive results *can* still be achieved. For Oxen keen to advance their career or seeking work, September to early November may see interesting chances to pursue.

With many demands on his resources, the Ox would do well to watch spending at this time and check the terms of any major transaction.

More positively, his personal life can bring him considerable pleasure and there will be opportunities to go to parties and other get-togethers and catch up with relations and friends he has not seen for some while. By sharing news and seeking the opinions of others (rather than keeping his thoughts to himself), he could benefit from the advice and generosity of another person. For some Oxen, romance can also add excitement to this time. August and December are likely to see much social and domestic activity.

Overall, the Goat year will have had its awkward moments, but the Ox is a realist and by adapting and doing his best, he will still have learned and accomplished a great deal during it.

The Year of the Monkey starts on 8 February and will be an interesting one for the Ox. Although he will have reservations about the speed of certain developments, many of his plans will work out well and some good opportunities will come his way.

The Ox is always keen to develop his knowledge and skills and the Monkey year will encourage this. Whether in his work or his personal interests, if he has the chance of training or can undertake personal study and research, he will find his time well spent. Professional and personal development can be rewarding this year and this is an area all Oxen would do well to consider.

At work, the aspects are also encouraging, although the Ox should still expect some volatility. A lot can happen quickly, sometimes too quickly for the Ox's liking, but by making the most of the opportunities that open up, he can further his position and use his strengths to advantage.

This also applies to Oxen who feel unfulfilled in their present position and those seeking work. By keeping alert for openings, they could identify a new and sometimes very different position which offers the fresh challenge they desire. They do, though, need to be swift in making their application and could help their prospects by finding out more about the duties involved and so be better prepared at interview. In the Monkey year, initiative, purpose and going that one step further can make a difference. April, May, September and November could see important developments.

Also, if at any time the Ox should be offered training, or the chance to deputize for someone or become involved in a new initiative, he should seize the opportunity. This is very much a year which rewards commitment.

Progress made at work will lead to many Oxen increasing their income and as a result many will proceed with plans they have long had in mind, including updating equipment and improving their home. When considering purchases, the Ox's thoroughness can lead to some useful acquisitions. Also, if he is in a position to make provision for the future, this too can be helpful.

Being conscientious, the Ox drives himself hard, and throughout the year it is important he allows himself a respite and sets time aside for pursuits he enjoys. The Monkey year encourages trying the new, and whenever the Ox hears of something that intrigues him or is inspired by an idea, he should follow it up. If he can involve those close to him, this can often add meaning to the activity. In the Monkey year, the Ox does need to be receptive to what is available and allow time for some well-deserved leisure.

The Ox is selective in his socializing and can be reserved until he knows someone well. However, in the Monkey year some interesting social opportunities can arise and he would do well to take up any that appeal to him. The Monkey year favours participation. April, June, August and December will see the most social activity.

For Oxen enjoying romance or those who meet someone new, during the course of the year, the relationship is likely to strengthen steadily. Oxen do like to take their time in matters of love and affection.

The Monkey year is a fast-paced one, however, and in the Ox's home life some matters may arise which require swift attention. These can include decisions the Ox or another family member may have. Frank discussion will be helpful in determining the best way forward. In addition, some plans for the home could move ahead as the right opportunity suddenly arises. A lot can happen quickly this year and while this may not suit the Ox's character, improvements can often result.

Throughout the year, a great deal of pleasure can be had by sharing interests and enjoying time with loved ones. Here the thoughtfulness of many Oxen can add a special ingredient to home life. August and December could be eventful months and give rise to some surprise occasions or travel opportunities.

Although the Ox may not always feel at ease with the fast pace of the Monkey year, he can gain a lot from it. In his work, this is an excellent time to add to skills, and this can have considerable value later on. Developing personal interests can also be satisfying. Throughout the year, the Ox will value the support of those around him and his thoughtful approach will be appreciated. This will be a busy year, but personally and professionally a rewarding one. It is a time for seizing (and enjoying) the moment.

The Metal Ox

The Metal Ox possesses great resolve and is prepared to work long and hard for what he wants. However, despite his best endeavours, his progress in recent times may have been muted. While the Monkey year will bring its challenges, it is a more positive one for him and will see him enjoying some worthy successes.

For any Metal Ox who may start the year feeling discontented, now is a time to focus on the present rather than feel fettered by what has gone before. To help, these Metal Oxen should set themselves some goals to work towards. With purpose, and their considerable Metal Ox resolve, they will find a lot can become possible this year, but the initiative does rest with them.

The Metal Ox's work situation can give rise to some interesting opportunities, especially for those Metal Oxen who feel they have not been making the most of their potential recently. With the expertise the Metal Ox has built up, not only can he be influential in his workplace but, as specific situations arise or positions fall vacant, he will often have the skills needed to advance his career and reap the rewards of his loyalty and commitment. April to early June, September and November could see significant developments, although whenever the Metal Ox sees an opening, he should be quick to show interest.

For Metal Oxen who feel there is a lack of suitable opportunities where they are, as well as those seeking work, again the Monkey year can hold encouraging – and surprising – developments. By keeping alert for openings and talking to friends and contacts, these Metal Oxen could be alerted to companies looking to recruit or advised of an opening worth considering. Resolve and persistence can yield significant results this year.

Monkey years also favour enterprise and some Metal Oxen may decide to become self-employed or find ways to put an interest or skill to profitable use. The Monkey year is rich in possibility.

Progress at work can help financially and many Metal Oxen will enjoy a rise in income over the year. Some will also benefit from the receipt of an additional sum. However, the Metal Ox does need to budget well, ideally setting funds aside for specific requirements. With good planning, not only will he be pleased with his decisions but he could also benefit from some favourable purchasing opportunities. On quite a few occasions this year, he will delight in some luck.

The Monkey year will also bring encouraging developments in his personal interests. Some Metal Oxen will have ideas or projects that will particularly enthuse them, and by setting time aside for these, they will not only enjoy what they do but also the way their activities develop. With this being a year of opportunity, some may be tempted by a new pursuit or decide to join an activity group or support a cause. This is a time to be receptive to what is available and to develop ideas and skills.

Some of the Metal Ox's activities can have a good social element and over the year he will have the chance to spend time with those who are like-minded. However, there are also quite a few Metal Oxen who like to keep themselves to themselves. These Metal Oxen should be careful not to become too insular. Going out and participating in what is going on around them can do them a lot of good and the Monkey year will offer a variety of attractions. Reserved Metal Ox, do take note and look to embrace the spirit of this interesting year. For socializing, April, June, August and December could be active months.

Many Metal Oxen do enjoy the close and enduring friendship of those they have known for a great many years and over the year one of these close friends could seek advice on a delicate matter. Not only will they welcome the support and suggestions the Metal Ox may offer, but his words may be of more value than he may realize. Once again this year, there will be quite a few who value the Metal Ox's level-headed approach.

The Metal Ox's home life will see much activity. Not only will the Metal Ox himself have plans he is keen to carry out, but both he and his loved ones could face work choices which impact on established routines. At such times it is important that the Metal Ox is forthcoming and discusses his views. With good dialogue, better decisions can be made and some plans (including of a practical nature) more easily advanced. This is a year favouring joint effort.

With the Metal Ox and other family members likely to be leading busy lifestyles, it is also important that time is set aside for shared interests and taking advantage of what is available locally. In addition, many a Metal Ox home will have a special occasion to celebrate, often occurring in the late summer. The Metal Ox will also delight in the travel opportunities the year brings.

In general, the Year of the Monkey holds great promise for the Metal Ox but it is a time to be focused and involved. In both his work and personal interests, there will be the chance to further ideas and skills. The Metal Ox will be helped by the support of those close to him, although to fully benefit he needs to be forthcoming as well as watch his sometimes go-it-alone tendencies. He does, though, have much in his favour this year and his resolve, experience and initiative can deliver good results.

Tip for the Year
Decide on your objectives and work purposefully towards them. With firm intent and your skills and experience, you can accomplish a great deal. Also, preserve time for your loved ones and personal interests. If you keep your lifestyle in balance, you can make this a gratifying year.

The Water Ox

The Water Ox will have seen a great deal happen in recent years and in this one can look forward to reaping some perhaps overdue rewards. This can be a progressive year. However, to get the best from it, the Water Ox needs to set his plans in motion and believe in himself. With determination, he can make this a significant time.

One area which will see considerable activity will be the Water Ox's work situation. Water Oxen following a particular career will often have the opportunity to learn about other aspects of their work. By taking advantage of what is offered, including training, they will find their new knowledge not only helping their current role but often preparing them for promotion. This is a year favouring self-development and any Water Oxen who feel their career has stalled recently will be able to get it back on track, maybe in a new and more fulfilling position.

For Water Oxen who are hoping for a more substantial career move or seeking employment, again the Monkey year can open up important possibilities. By widening the scope of what they are prepared to consider, many of these Water Oxen could secure a position which offers the challenge they have needed. April to early June, September and November could see encouraging developments, but such is the nature of the year that events could move surprisingly swiftly at any time.

The Water Ox's personal interests are also favourably aspected and he will be keen to take his knowledge and skills further. Whether he prefers creative, practical or sporting pursuits, by looking to extend what he does, he will derive increasing pleasure from what he is able to achieve. If he can join others, this can add to the fun. This can be an inspiring year and any Water Oxen who start the year dissatisfied could find a new interest the tonic they need.

Many Water Oxen can look forward to a financial improvement this year, often from an increase in income, but perhaps also from a gift or other source. However, in view of his commitments and plans, the Water Ox will need to manage his finances with care, ideally setting aside funds for specific requirements. With discipline, though, he will be thrilled with what he is able to do.

The Monkey year will tempt many Water Oxen to travel and they will delight in some of the places they visit, especially if these are related to their interests or exciting in themselves. In addition, there could be local events to attend. By taking advantage of the opportunities that come his way, the Water Ox will enjoy his travelling over the year.

Many of his activities will also have a good social element, and while it can sometimes take the Water Ox some time to feel at ease with other people, he will enjoy a good rapport with some of those he meets during the year. For any Water Ox who is alone and perhaps nursing recent hurt, new friends and perhaps a new romance can restore the sparkle that has been missing from their life. April, June, August and December could see the most social opportunities.

The Water Ox's home life will see considerable activity over the year and some Water Ox homes will undergo quite a transformation. A few Water Oxen may take advantage of an opportunity to move to more suitable accommodation. With such a lot happening, good communication will be important. With flexibility and co-operation, though, this can be a domestically active but pleasing year.

Overall, the Monkey year is filled with possibility, but to realize his ambitions, the Water Ox has to be the driving force. With initiative and determination, however, his accomplishments can be considerable. At work, new skills and duties will aid his progress, while time spent on personal interests can be rewarding, with new ideas and knowledge often developing in an encouraging manner. In so many areas of the Water Ox's life, this is a year for moving forward. On a personal level, he will be supported by those around him, and if he is forthcoming with his thoughts, he will find that important developments can often be set in motion. This year the talents and personal qualities of the Water Ox can reward him well.

Tip for the Year

Seize any chances to add to your skills, knowledge and experience. This can help your current situation as well as increase your options for later. Also, enjoy spending time with your loved ones. Joint pursuits can bring great pleasure and lead to more support.

The Wood Ox

With wood as his element, the Wood Ox is eminently practical and also aware that he needs to allow time to reach some of his goals. In the Monkey year, events can assist in some surprising ways. This will be a fortunate year for him and almost all areas of his life will see encouraging developments.

Key among these will be his work. Being conscientious and having shown commitment for some time now, the Wood Ox may find himself being prepared for greater duties. This could be through training or the chance to take on additional responsibilities. By making the most of what arises, the Wood Ox will be excellently placed to benefit when other opportunities become available. This is a year to prove himself and look to move forward.

Many Wood Oxen will take on a greater role with their present employer, but should the Wood Ox feel that his career could benefit from a move elsewhere, he should keep alert for openings as well as talk to contacts in his industry. As a result, he could find himself head-hunted, or recommended for a position, or ideally qualified for a particular vacancy.

The aspects are also promising for Wood Oxen seeking work. When these Wood Oxen detect an opening, they will find it helpful to enquire about the particular duties involved so they can stress their suitability for the role. In this Monkey year, extra effort will count for a lot. Also, as many Wood Oxen will find, once a position is obtained, it can quickly be built upon. April to early June, September and November could see important developments, but opportunities need to be seized quickly throughout the year. Work-wise, these can be significant times for the Wood Ox.

With his sense of commitment, the Wood Ox puts a lot of energy into his activities and during the year it is important he maintains a good lifestyle balance, including allowing time for his personal interests. Those that give him the chance of additional exercise and/or take him out of doors could be of particular benefit. The practical nature of many Wood Oxen will come to the fore this year as they become intrigued by new subjects, focus on a particular project or further their knowledge in some way, and they can find their interests of great value.

Progress made at work will increase the income of many Wood Oxen and some may find additional work or an enterprising idea helping their situation too. However, the Wood Ox will need to cover his many commitments as well as set sufficient funds aside for plans and possible deposits. The more thoroughly he manages his situation, the better he will fare. Also, if entering into a new agreement, he does need to check the implications and draw on the expertise of others. The Wood Ox may like to act independently, but the advice of experienced family members or professionals can often help and reassure him.

While the Wood Ox's outgoings will be considerable, he should try to allow for a holiday at some time during the year. Some Wood Oxen may decide to arrange this at the last moment and so take advantage of some very good offers. Whatever he does, the conscientious Wood Ox can benefit from a break. June and August could see good travel possibilities, including some that arise by chance or at short notice.

The Wood Ox will also find himself in demand on a social level. Over the years he will have built up a close social circle and several times this year there could be special occasions in store. The Wood Ox's friends will often be glad of his support and his dependable nature. April, June, August and December could see much social activity. The Wood Ox's work and interests can also lead to meeting new people, and any Wood Ox who is alone or who moves to a new situation over the course of the year will find that some people he meets now could prove helpful in the near future. The unattached in particular can find this Monkey year surprising and delighting them.

Domestic life will be busy and, especially for Wood Oxen with a partner, eventful too. There will be home improvements and other plans to carry out, as well as some problems and repairs to address. Once started, projects can develop in exciting ways, with the Wood Ox's inventiveness and practical nature to the fore. Shared interests can also add to the fun of this active and lively Monkey year.

Some Wood Oxen may also start a family, while those who are already parents will delight in (and occasionally despair over) the activities of their baby or young child. Domestically, as in so many other respects, the Monkey year will bring some special times.

In general, the aspects are favourable for the Wood Ox this year. Personal development is encouraged and at work the Wood Ox may reap substantial benefits from the opportunities that open up for him. He will need to be active and ready to respond swiftly, but what he accomplishes now can prepare him for future success. The potential value of the present time should not be underestimated.

Tip for the Year

Build on your capabilities. What you undertake now can help you both in the present and the future. Also, ensure your lifestyle is balanced: set time aside to enjoy with your loved ones as well as to pursue your own interests.

The Fire Ox

The Monkey year has a certain vibrancy about it. It encourages activity, involvement and effort, and while the Fire Ox may sometimes be surprised by what happens during it, a lot can work out in his favour. However, to benefit fully, he will need to adapt. He may have thought a lot about the longer term and what he would like to see happen, but, as the saying reminds us, 'There are many routes to the top.' New routes will open up for many Fire Oxen this year.

Throughout the year the Fire Ox will enjoy the support and friendship of many of those around him. By being open with his thoughts and feelings, he will find they can often help and reassure one another and create some good bonds. In addition, he could have occasion to assist a close friend with what could be a delicate personal matter. Here his thoughtfulness and care will be much appreciated. Also, there will be much fun to be had during the year. Whether partying, playing sport, undertaking other outdoor activities or following other pursuits, the Fire Ox will have many opportunities to enjoy himself. And, as with so much this year, the greater his involvement, the more he can get from the present time.

This also applies to the many Fire Oxen who will experience change this year, whether moving to a new place of education or work or changing location entirely. By taking advantage of the opportunities that are available to them rather than remaining too inward-looking, these Fire Oxen can develop their interests, discover new activities and meet and befriend others. On a personal level, the Monkey year has great potential. Late April, June, August to mid-September and December could be particularly lively months and the second half of the year will generally be busier than the first.

For some Fire Oxen, the year will have romantic possibilities too, with a chance meeting often becoming more meaningful as the year develops.

Although the Fire Ox likes to retain a certain independence and may not always be fully in accord with certain family members, he will value their support during the year. When considering choices or experiencing change, he should talk over his views and feelings and take heed of the advice offered. That way, any anxieties he may have can also be considerably eased.

The Monkey year can also have its surprises, including travel opportunities. For some Fire Oxen there could be the chance to go on holiday with others or to visit a place of interest or a special attraction. The spontaneity and buzz of the Monkey year will lead to many Fire

Oxen enjoying occasions that just seem to happen, especially in late summer.

The Fire Ox should also make good use of local resources, as these can also help him get more out of the present time.

The majority of Fire Oxen will reach an important juncture in their education this year. There will be exams to prepare for, coursework and projects to complete and new subjects to learn. The demands will be considerable and these Fire Oxen need to remain organized. By working consistently and focusing on what needs to be done, many can make good headway and gain qualifications they can build on in the future. New study possibilities can also open up and some of the more unexpected developments of the year may benefit the Fire Ox in important ways.

For Fire Oxen in work, there are also encouraging developments in store. For those already established in a position, there could be the chance to take on different duties or transfer to another role. Although these Fire Oxen may feel daunted by what is expected of them, if they apply themselves, they can gain experience in another area and widen their prospects for the future. This is very much a year to embrace opportunities.

Fire Oxen seeking work will find that by actively pursuing vacancies and showing initiative, they can gain that all-important foothold. While some positions they are offered may not be the most inspiring, once these Fire Oxen have proved their reliability, greater responsibilities can (often quickly) follow on. April to early June, September and November could be months of possibility.

Personal interests can also develop in an encouraging manner and in many cases give rise to other possibilities. New interests could also have future value. In so many respects, the developments of this year will have longer-term benefits for the Fire Ox.

With a lively social life and many interests, he will, however, need to manage his finances carefully. His disciplined nature will help, however, and if he is able to keep control over his spending, he will be able to do a surprising amount. Any Fire Oxen who enter into sizeable agreements this year should also check the details carefully and seek professional advice if necessary. The more thorough they are, the better.

Overall, the Year of the Monkey can be a fine and interesting one for the Fire Ox. It will require effort, but what he learns now can be significant in terms of his onward development. And although the Fire Ox values his independence, liaising with others can help him get more from the year as well as enrich his life. This can be a good year for him, but it requires commitment *and* involvement.

Tip for the Year
Make the most of the opportunities that arise this year, whether in your studies, work or personal interests. Even if these are different from what you anticipated, unexpected benefits can often follow on. The year is rich in possibility.

The Earth Ox

The Earth Ox has a careful and diligent nature and when he starts something, he likes to see it through. During the Monkey year he can look forward to accomplishing a good deal.

To get the most from the year, as it starts he should consider what he would like to do over the next 12 months. Dialogue with others can be especially helpful, and in some instances, plans can quickly take shape.

One area that will be particularly satisfying is the Earth Ox's interests. As well as continuing with activities he enjoys, he could set himself some new challenges, possibly learning or improving a skill, putting an interest to particular use or starting something completely different. Some Earth Oxen may be tempted to write about their interests, either online or for possible publication. Over the year, many will delight in the way they can use their talents. Also, if there are special exhibitions or interest-related events that the Earth Ox would like to attend, he should consider going. The Monkey year can open up a world of opportunities.

For Earth Oxen who are alone and who desire more contact with others, including those who have experienced some personal upset in recent times, it would be worth investigating what local activities are available. Whether joining a local group, enrolling on a course or participating more in their community, they can find their involvement making a real difference to their lives.

In many of the Earth Ox's activities, he will be grateful for the support of others, and his social life is favourably aspected. Shared activities can be particularly enjoyable and there will also be the chance to meet new people. Although some Earth Oxen can be reserved individuals, they can gain a lot this year by opening up more and engaging with others. April, June, late July to early September and December could see the most social activity.

The Monkey year can also bring good travel opportunities. Not only should the Earth Ox keep alert for attractive offers, but if there is a particular place he is keen to visit, he should make enquiries and see what is possible. As with so much this year, once he starts to follow up his ideas, chance can play a helpful part. The Monkey year can also bring surprises in the form of some quickly arranged visits, unexpected invitations to stay with others or surprise weekends away. Monkey years are rich in possibility.

With the active nature of the year, the Earth Ox's outgoings will be considerable, however, and he would do well to keep a close watch on spending and budget ahead for plans and requirements. Here his discipline will be a great asset. He will also need to be thorough when dealing with paperwork and check anything that is unclear or unsatisfactory, otherwise he could find himself embroiled in protracted bureaucracy. With all forms of finance and paperwork, close attention is advised this year.

The Earth Ox's home life, however, can be a source of considerable pleasure. Once more he will very much enjoy the way he is able to turn his thoughts into reality, and over the course of the year notable improvements will be made and new purchases add to the comfort and energy-efficiency of many an Earth Ox home.

There will also be family occasions for the Earth Ox to enjoy. He may particularly appreciate spending time with people who live some distance away. In addition, he will follow the activities of family members with fond interest. Younger relations may often be grateful for his advice and support and may reciprocate by offering technical or other expertise. In this interesting year, the support, goodwill and affection of family members will mean a lot to the Earth Ox, as well as enable many of his plans to proceed smoothly.

The Monkey year is one of possibility for the Earth Ox and by following through his ideas (and sharing these with others), he can achieve a great deal. There will also be an element of luck to the year. Problems can, however, still arise. If affected, it is important the Earth Ox talks to others, especially those qualified to advise. This is no time to keep his concerns to himself. Overall, though, this can be a constructive year for him. His domestic and social life and personal interests can all prove rewarding. Travel, too, can be delightful – and there could be some pleasant surprises in store as well.

Tip for the Year
Spend time enjoying and developing your interests. What you do now can not only be satisfying but often lead to other possibilities. Also, value your relations with others and be sure to share your thoughts and ideas. With the support of others, you can achieve a great deal.

Famous Oxen

Lily Allen, Hans Christian Andersen, Gemma Arterton, Johann Sebastian Bach, David Blaine, Napoleon Bonaparte, Albert Camus, Jim Carrey, Charlie Chaplin, George Clooney, Harlan Coben, Bill Cosby, Diana, Princess of Wales, Marlene Dietrich, Walt Disney, Patrick Duffy, Jessica Ennis-Hill, Jane Fonda, Edward Fox, Michael J. Fox, Peter Gabriel, Gal Gadot, Elizabeth George, Richard Gere, Ricky Gervais, William Hague, Handel, King Harald V of Norway, Adolf Hitler, Dustin Hoffman, Anthony Hopkins, Billy Joel, former King Juan Carlos of Spain, Tony Keith, Anna Kendrick, John Key, B. B. King, Keira Knightley, Mark Knopfler, Burt Lancaster, Bruno Mars, Queen Mathilde of Belgium, Chloë Moretz, Kate Moss, Carey Mulligan, Eddie Murphy, Jack Nicholson, Leslie Nielsen, Bill Nighy, Barack Obama, Gwyneth Paltrow, Oscar Peterson, Lionel Richie, Wayne Rooney, Nico Rosberg, Tim Roth,

Rubens, Meg Ryan, Amanda Seyfried, Jean Sibelius, Bruce Springsteen, Meryl Streep, Lady Thatcher, Scott F. Turow, Vincent van Gogh, Sigourney Weaver, the Duke of Wellington, Arsène Wenger, Pharrell Williams, W. B. Yeats.

13 February 1926 to 1 February 1927 — *Fire Tiger*

31 January 1938 to 18 February 1939 — *Earth Tiger*

17 February 1950 to 5 February 1951 — *Metal Tiger*

5 February 1962 to 24 January 1963 — *Water Tiger*

23 January 1974 to 10 February 1975 — *Wood Tiger*

9 February 1986 to 28 January 1987 — *Fire Tiger*

28 January 1998 to 15 February 1999 — *Earth Tiger*

14 February 2010 to 2 February 2011 — *Metal Tiger*

The Tiger

The Personality of the Tiger

It's
the zest,
the enthusiasm,
the giving the little bit more,
that makes the difference.
And opens up so much.

The Tiger is born under the sign of courage. He is a charismatic figure and usually holds very firm views. He is strong-willed and determined and sets about most of his activities with tremendous energy and enthusiasm. He is very alert and quick-witted and his mind is forever active. He is a highly original thinker and is nearly always brimming with new ideas or full of enthusiasm for some new project or scheme.

The Tiger adores challenges and loves to get involved in anything that he thinks has an exciting future or that catches his imagination. He is prepared to take risks and does not like to be bound either by convention or the dictates of others. He likes to be free to act as he chooses and at least once during his life he will throw caution to the wind and go off and do the things he wants to do.

The Tiger does, however, have a somewhat restless nature. Even though he is often prepared to throw himself wholeheartedly into a project, his initial enthusiasm can soon wane if he sees something more appealing. He can also be rather impulsive and there will be occasions in his life when he acts in a manner he later regrets. If he were to think things through or be prepared to persevere in his various activities, he would almost certainly enjoy a greater degree of success.

Fortunately the Tiger is lucky in most of his enterprises, but should things not work out as he hoped, he is liable to suffer from severe bouts of depression and it will often take him a long time to recover. His life often consists of a series of ups and downs.

He is, however, very adaptable. He has an adventurous spirit and rarely stays in the same place for long. In the early stages of his life he is likely to try his hand at several different jobs and he will also change his residence fairly frequently.

The Tiger is very honest and open in his dealings with others. He hates any sort of hypocrisy or falsehood. He is also well known for being blunt and forthright and has no hesitation in speaking his mind. He can be rebellious at times, particularly against any form of petty authority, and while this can lead him into conflict with others, he is never one to shrink from an argument or avoid standing up for what he believes is right.

The Tiger is a natural leader and can rise to the top of his chosen profession. He does not, however, care for anything too bureaucratic or detailed, and he does not like to obey orders. He can be stubborn and obstinate and throughout his life he likes to retain a certain amount of independence in his actions and be responsible to no one but himself. He likes to consider that all his achievements are due to his own efforts and he will not ask for support from others if he can avoid it.

Ironically, despite his self-confidence and leadership qualities, he can be indecisive and will often delay making a major decision until the very last moment. He can also be sensitive to criticism.

Although the Tiger is capable of earning large sums of money, he is rather a spendthrift and does not always put his money to best use. He can also be most generous and will often shower lavish gifts on friends and relations.

The Tiger cares very much for his reputation and the image that he tries to project. He carries himself with an air of dignity and authority and enjoys being the centre of attention. He is very adept at attracting publicity, both for himself and the causes he supports.

The Tiger often marries young and he will find himself best suited to those born under the signs of the Pig, Dog, Horse and Goat. He can also get on well with the Rat, Rabbit and Rooster, but will find the Ox and Snake a bit too quiet and serious for his liking and will be highly irritated by the Monkey's rather mischievous and inquisitive ways. He will also find it difficult to get on with another Tiger or a Dragon – both partners will want to dominate the relationship and could find it difficult to compromise on even the smallest of matters.

The Tigress is lively, witty and a marvellous hostess at parties. She takes great care over her appearance and is usually most attractive. She can be a very doting mother and while she believes in letting her children have their freedom, she makes an excellent teacher and will ensure that her children are well brought up and want for nothing. Like her male counterpart, she has numerous interests and likes to have sufficient freedom to go off and do the things she wants to do. She has a most caring and generous nature.

The Tiger has many commendable qualities. He is honest, courageous and often a source of inspiration to others. Providing he can curb the wilder excesses of his restless nature, he is almost certain to lead a fulfilling and satisfying life.

The Five Different Types of Tiger

In addition to the 12 signs of the Chinese zodiac there are five elements and these have a strengthening or moderating influence on the signs. The effects of the elements on the Tiger are described below, together with the years in which they were exercising their influence. Therefore Tigers born in 1950 and 2010 are Metal Tigers, Tigers born in 1962 are Water Tigers, and so on.

Metal Tiger: 1950, 2010

The Metal Tiger has an assertive and outgoing personality. He is very ambitious, and while his aims may change from time to time, he will work relentlessly until he has obtained what he wants. He can, however, be impatient for results and become highly strung if things do not work out as he would like. He is distinctive in his appearance and is admired and respected by many.

Water Tiger: 1962

This Tiger has a wide variety of interests and is always eager to experiment with new ideas or satisfy his adventurous nature by going off to explore distant lands. He is versatile, shrewd and has a kindly nature. He tends to remain calm in a crisis, although he can be annoyingly indecisive at times. He communicates well with others and through his many capabilities and persuasive nature usually achieves what he wants in life. He is also highly imaginative and is often a gifted orator or writer.

Wood Tiger: 1974

The Wood Tiger has a friendly and pleasant personality. He is less independent than some of the other types of Tiger and more prepared to work with others to secure a desired objective. However, he does have a tendency to jump from one thing to another and can easily become distracted. He is usually very popular, has a large circle of friends and invariably leads a busy and enjoyable social life. He also has a good sense of humour.

Fire Tiger: 1926, 1986

The Fire Tiger sets about everything he does with great verve and enthusiasm. He loves action and is always ready to throw himself wholeheartedly into anything that catches his imagination. He has many leadership qualities and is capable of communicating his ideas and enthusiasm to others. He is very much an optimist and can be most generous. He has a likeable nature and can be a witty and persuasive speaker.

Earth Tiger: 1938, 1998

This Tiger is responsible and level-headed. He studies everything objectively and tries to be scrupulously fair in all his dealings. Unlike other Tigers, he is prepared to specialize in certain areas rather than get distracted by other matters, but he can become so involved in what he is doing that he does not always take into account the opinions of those around him. He has good business sense and is usually very successful in later life. He has a large circle of friends and pays great attention to both his appearance and his reputation.

Prospects for the Tiger in 2016

The Goat year (19 February 2015–7 February 2016) offers interesting prospects for the Tiger and the closing months will see a considerable amount happen.

One of the strengths of the Tiger is his ability to come up with ideas. He is resourceful, enterprising and likes to be involved in the action. Whether in his work or own interests, he will have ideas he is keen to explore. However, as the Goat year draws to a close he will need to be careful not to spread his attention too widely. Being distracted or attending to too many things at once could undermine him. Particularly in his work, it is putting in the effort that will bring the best results. October could be an especially busy and interesting month work-wise.

The closing months of the year will also bring many temptations to spend. While the Tiger will be pleased with some of the useful items and gifts he buys at this time, he needs to be careful about making too many impulse buys.

His domestic and social life will see much activity and the Tiger will need to manage his time well, remain organized and discuss arrangements with others. Failure to communicate adequately or plan ahead could lead to some awkward moments and add to pressures. With care, though, the closing months of the year can be a full and interesting time for the Tiger, and some good news is possible over the festive season.

The Monkey year, which starts on 8 February, has energy and verve, and while it suits the Tiger's enterprising nature, it is also a time when he will need to exercise care rather than forge ahead regardless. In 2016 it will be much more a case of making the most of situations *as they are*. Tigers, take note and do be mindful. That way you can make this year much easier and ultimately more rewarding.

At work, this is a time for consolidation and steady progress. Tigers who are relatively new in their current position will find this an excellent time to establish themselves and learn about different aspects of their industry. By being involved and seizing any chances to network, these Tigers can do themselves – and their prospects – considerable good.

For Tigers who have been in their present position for some time and are hoping to advance their career, the Monkey year can also bring important developments. Although progress may not be easy, or necessarily substantial, by drawing on their experience, many of these Tigers will have the chance to take on a greater role or move elsewhere. However, it will be a case of focusing on current duties and building a platform for future growth rather than expecting rapid progress.

For Tigers looking for a position, the job-seeking process may be wearying, with disappointments in store. Results *will* require effort, but will be all the more deserved when they come. When taking on a position, again the Tiger would do well to show commitment, take advantage of any training and build for the future. April, July, September and November could see interesting developments, although throughout the year opportunities need to be seized quickly before they slip away.

One area for particular care is the Tiger's relations with others. With colleagues in particular, he needs to liaise well and take the views of others into consideration. To act too independently or be on the periphery of developments could deny him support and good opportunities. Should a disagreement arise with a colleague, he should try not to let this distract him and do his best to defuse the problem. In awkward situations, he needs to tread carefully this year. Fortunately, due to his diligent nature, in most cases he will.

The Tiger likes to keep himself busy and there will be a lot to interest him this year. He will enjoy immersing himself in what is going on around him as well as following through his own ideas. If he has been considering taking up a new activity, this would be a good year to do so.

Travel, too, is favourably aspected. Some trips could be arranged hastily, perhaps in response to a late offer or unexpected (but welcome) invitation.

The Tiger's financial prospects are reasonably aspected, and with careful control of his budget, he will be pleased with the many plans and purchases he is able to proceed with. Where household items are concerned, his eye for style and suitability will be on excellent form, with some purchases a tad unusual but appealing.

Financial paperwork, however, does need to be dealt with carefully and on time. While this may be irksome, delays or mistakes could be to the Tiger's disadvantage. Should any matter concern him, he should seek professional guidance. Without due attention, bureaucratic matters could become protracted this year. Tigers, take note.

Domestically, life will often be conducted at a fast pace. Amid all the activity, however, there will be some personal achievements to celebrate and plans to move forward. Travel and other family events will also be much appreciated. The Tiger's suggestions can lead to some fine occasions. In this busy year, quality time and good communication *are* important, otherwise tensions and misunderstandings may arise. The Tiger needs to be aware of this and allow time for everyone to relax and catch up. For family activities, May, August and December could be busy and nicely varied months.

The Tiger has an extensive social circle, but as the year progresses, contact with certain friends may lessen as circumstances change. Also, a disagreement may arise. Friendships do not always run smoothly. Nevertheless, the Tiger will often shine in company and also have the chance to meet new people. Despite some vexations, the Monkey year does have its brighter side and April, August, September and December will see the most social activity.

Some years seem to go well, while others are troublesome. For the Tiger, the Monkey year is in the middle. There will be problems and pressures, but also some good opportunities, especially when it comes to developing his ideas, skills and interests. Fortunately there is much that the Tiger can do to negate the more awkward aspects, and by remaining aware, being mindful of the views of others and making the most of situations *as they are* (rather than as he might wish), he can fare reasonably well, extend his experience and enjoy the many activities this lively year can bring.

The Metal Tiger

This will be an interesting year for the Metal Tiger and while he will face some demanding situations, there will also be much to enjoy. Throughout the year, though, he will need to be aware of changing situations and the opinion of others. To be obtuse, go his own way or not fully consult those around him could cause problems. This is a time to tread carefully and show flexibility.

During the year many Metal Tigers will be involved in significant decision-making. This could involve retirement, relocation or going ahead with some long-held aspirations. In all cases, the Metal Tiger should take the time to talk to those close to him, as well as to professionals, about his options. Actions need to be thought through rather than rushed. For the hasty and impetuous, snags could arise. Metal Tigers, take note. As in so much this year, mindfulness and dialogue can make an important difference.

In the Metal Tiger's work, this will be a year of change. Some Metal Tigers will decide to retire completely and will welcome having the time for interests and projects they may have wanted to get underway for some time. Again, with support and advice, this transition can be made easier. Other Metal Tigers, however, will be keen to remain at work, though they may consider reducing their hours, going part time or doing some work on their own. For many, this Monkey year can be a significant one. April, July, September and November could be decisive months.

Although Metal Tigers who retire will see a reduction in income, financially the aspects are generally positive. Some Metal Tigers could benefit from an extra payment or the fruition of a policy and, by managing their resources well, be able to proceed with major purchases and plans. Here the Metal Tiger's keen eye for a good buy can serve him well and his sense of style may also result in the purchase of some splendid items which can be a source of pleasure to him and others.

Travel, too, is favourably aspected, and if possible, the Metal Tiger should aim to go away for a holiday at some time during the year. Some special events may also appeal. For outdoor enthusiasts, including those who follow sport, the Monkey year can have particularly exciting moments in store.

With his wide interests, the Metal Tiger will also enjoy the recreational possibilities that open up over the year. Not only will he continue to pursue existing interests, but could find his curiosity whetted by new activities. Metal Tigers who are newly retired will particularly appreciate the chance to take their interests further.

The Monkey year can prove a varied and illuminating one, but in virtually all the Metal Tiger sets out to do, he needs to liaise with others and seek advice where necessary. His extensive network of friends and contacts can help. Some could be in a similar situation to his own, and some decisions could be made easier by some mutual support.

The Metal Tiger can also look forward to some interesting social occasions over the year. These could include personal celebrations with friends as well as going to events and attractions. April, August, September and December could be full and lively months.

For Metal Tigers who are alone and would perhaps welcome more contact with others, the Monkey year can open up important possibilities. By taking advantage of what is available and perhaps becoming involved in local activity groups or enrolling on a course, these Metal Tigers can add some purpose to their lifestyle.

Domestically, both the Metal Tiger and his loved ones will have significant decisions to take this year. These could concern retirement, work changes or, for some, downsizing and relocating. Given the importance of such decisions, time needs to be allowed to discuss them fully and carefully consider the implications. Metal Tigers, do be thorough and careful.

Liaising with others could also be important if a matter arises which gives rise to some anxiety. This could concern a relation or close friend. Rather than keep his concerns to himself, the Metal Tiger would do well to draw on the expertise of those (including professionals) who may be able to suggest solutions or rectify problems. As with all years, this one will bring a few difficulties. There could also be niggles (especially bureaucratic ones) which exasperate the Tiger. However, with help and a sense of perspective, these can often be dealt with effectively. In tricky or complex matters, the Metal Tiger should not feel alone.

Overall, the Monkey year will be a demanding one for the Metal Tiger. Decisions will need taking and new situations will require readjustment. The aspects may be variable, but by being forthcoming and drawing on the support of those around him, the Metal Tiger can benefit. Whether pursuing interests, rediscovering talents or being fortunate in purchases, he can also enjoy himself this year. Tricky it may sometimes be, but is also one of possibility.

Tip for the Year
Explore your ideas and seize your opportunities. Also, do involve others and value the support of those around you. With input and good advice, your year can become easier.

The Water Tiger

The Water Tiger will have seen a lot happen in the last few years. This one will be a good time to take stock, give some thought to current activities and move ahead steadily. While Monkey years have their awkward aspects, they do hold hidden benefits and can have significant consequences. This may not be the easiest of years for the Water Tiger, but it can be a valuable one.

At work, many Water Tigers will have seen important developments in recent times, both in their own role and in their workplace. As a result, rather than look to make a change, many will prefer to concentrate on their current duties. Professionally, this can be a far more fulfilling year, with many Water Tigers playing a valued role where they are, including, for some, training and mentoring others.

There will, though, be some Water Tigers who are keen to develop in new ways and decide to look elsewhere. For these Water Tigers, as well as those seeking work, the Monkey year can be challenging. Openings may be limited and competition fierce. However, the Water Tiger is born under the sign of courage and is both resourceful and determined. While there may be disappointments along the way, persistence *will* pay off and quite a few Water Tigers will secure a new position. This may come with a steep learning curve, but these Water Tigers will welcome the opportunity. April, July, September and November could see encouraging developments.

A valuable aspect of the year will be the chances the Water Tiger will have to network and meet others. His personality and competence will impress many. In addition, if he is considering specific work-related ideas, he would do well to seek the opinion of those with the necessary expertise. With the aspects as they are, this is not a time for acting too independently.

In money matters, the Water Tiger can fare reasonably well and may be able to supplement his income through an interest or skill. Some Water Tigers may benefit from the receipt of extra funds as well as be fortunate in making purchases. However, with a variety of commitments and probably some costly ideas, the Water Tiger will need to budget well, including for travel plans. With good control, though, he will be pleased with what he is able to do.

The Water Tiger's personal interests can also develop in an encouraging manner. He will often be keen to make more of his knowledge and skills, and creative activities can be especially satisfying. Some Water Tigers could be attracted by new pursuits. If so, they should aim to find out more. The Monkey year offers a range of possibilities.

In view of his active lifestyle, the Water Tiger knows a great many people, and his social circle is set to grow. Throughout the year, he should seize any chances he has to run his ideas past his friends and seek their opinion over any concerns. Some will be well placed to help and advise.

However, while the Water Tiger's relations with many will be good, differences of opinion could arise or a minor issue cause concern. At such times, or should the Water Tiger find himself in a potentially awkward situation, he will need to be wary and remain his tactful self.

This warning apart, there will be much for him to enjoy. Some of the year's more spontaneous social occasions will be particularly memorable. April, late July to the end of September and December could be interesting months.

Domestically, a lot is set to happen. Loved ones could be involved in some substantial changes, often work-related, which could affect existing routines and plans. Good discussion can help. Some of what occurs may not have been envisaged but will have important consequences for all. However, despite busy and possibly changing lifestyles, the Monkey year will also have its special moments. Often these will involve celebrating the success of a younger relation and the Water Tiger will be both proud and supportive.

Travel is favourably aspected and where possible the Water Tiger should take a holiday with his loved ones over the year. A change of scene can do everyone good.

Overall, the Year of the Monkey will have its problem areas and the Water Tiger will need to be alert. Any differences of opinion should ideally be diffused before they have the chance to escalate or undermine the Water Tiger's position, and he should aim to act *with others* and *with support* rather than independently. Care is needed, but the Monkey year is not without opportunity. In particular, personal interests can develop in an encouraging way, and at work this can often be a more fulfilling year as the Water Tiger will have greater chance to develop his strengths. Progress *will* require effort, but the Water Tiger can nevertheless prepare the way for more substantial opportunities in the future.

Tip for the Year
Be aware of what is going on around you and prepared to adjust accordingly. Also, draw on the support and advice of others. Allow time for recreational pursuits and share activities with those who are special to you.

The Wood Tiger

The Wood Tiger is perceptive and alert. He is good at gauging situations, in particular whether the time is right to act or to hold back. And his judgement will serve him well this year. Monkey years can be tricky and by being aware and sometimes keeping a low profile, the Wood Tiger can avoid some of the more awkward elements while benefiting from the opportunities. His adroitness can be a real asset this year.

At work, this is a year for steady progress. Many Wood Tigers will have been involved in change in recent years and this pattern is set to continue, as new ways of working are introduced and additional objectives set. With the experience he has built up, the Wood Tiger will often find himself central to what takes place. Some of this may be challenging and require flexibility, but in the process the Wood Tiger can underline his strengths and help his reputation. Effort made now can bear fruit later, and this can be a significant stage in the Wood Tiger's career development.

In view of his role and the expectations likely to be placed on him, he will, however, need to work closely with his colleagues. This is no year to be on the sidelines or act too independently.

The majority of Wood Tigers will remain with their present employer over the year, but for those who feel their prospects can be improved by a move elsewhere or are currently seeking work, the Monkey year can have unexpected developments in store. In their quest, these Wood Monkeys could come across a position that is very different from what they have done before but really appeals to them. In some cases, this could be in another industry or location. If the Wood Tiger takes action, he could benefit. April, July, September and November could see some particularly encouraging developments.

With a change in duties, quite a few Wood Tigers will see their income rise correspondingly. Many could also benefit from a gift or bonus. The Wood Tiger's financial situation is likely to improve over the year, but he will have many commitments and substantial outgoings, especially if he is looking to replace equipment and carry out certain plans. As a result, he will need to be disciplined. The Monkey year rewards strict control over budget.

Travel is favourably aspected and even if not travelling too far in distance, the Wood Tiger could find some places he visits especially memorable. Throughout the year, he should also avail himself of the facilities available in his local area. The Monkey year can provide a good mix of things to do.

Personal interests, too, can develop in encouraging ways. Given his practical nature, the Wood Tiger will often have ideas he is keen to follow through and, whether making something for the home or tackling another project, will be pleased with the results.

With his busy lifestyle, he knows a great many people and his social circle is set to grow over the year. There will also be some lively social occasions. April, late July to the end of September and December could see a lot of social activity.

However, while the Wood Tiger's relations with others will generally be positive, Monkey years can bring problems, and should the Wood Tiger sense any difficulty arising or find himself in a dispute with another person, he should proceed with care. His diplomatic nature can help, but minor situations may escalate and the Wood Tiger needs to be on his guard. Without care, a friendship could be lost or issue cause upset. Wood Tigers, take note and do be wary in volatile situations.

Domestically, changing situations could impact on existing routines and there needs to be good co-operation between everyone in the household. Also, while certain home improvements will be carried out successfully, plans will need to be kept flexible and undertaken only when time allows. Rush could cause added pressure and possible oversights. This is a year which favours joint effort, spreading activities out and appreciating quality time. During the year, both younger and more senior relations could look to the Wood Tiger for advice over what may be far-reaching decisions and his assistance can be of considerable value. He will be at the heart of many a home this year, and his qualities much appreciated.

Overall, the Wood Tiger can fare well in the Monkey year and what he does behind the scenes will often be of future value. Whether adapting to change, adding to skills, liaising with others or concentrating on objectives, he will find that if he puts in the effort, important consequences can often follow on. For many Wood Tigers, this Monkey year will be good preparation for the successes soon to come. Should any problems arise, the Wood Tiger should try to deal with these effectively, lest they escalate. Fortunately, his astute nature will help and will allow him to make the most of the opportunities the year brings.

Tip for the Year
Proceed steadily. Do not rush. The more you devote yourself to your tasks and plans, the better the results will be. Also, value your relations with those around you. What you do for others, and they for you, can enrich your year.

The Fire Tiger

This will be a significant year for the Fire Tiger. Not only does it mark the start of a new decade in his life, but what he does now can influence the next few years. However, while much will go well, the year will not be without its challenges and the Fire Tiger will need to be alert and flexible as he sets about his various activities.

In his home life, the year can see important developments. Accommodation will feature strongly, with quite a few Fire Tigers moving to a home which better suits their needs. Over the year, dreams will, for some, come true, with a place of their own. However, those who remain where they are will also devote a lot of time to making their home as they want, and their flair for style and colour will help make certain areas distinctive and homely.

For Fire Tigers with a partner, there will be a lot to do and both partners will enjoy seeing their plans develop. Many Fire Tigers will have cause for celebration this year. Not only will they be marking their thirtieth birthday, but some could become parents. Those who already have a family will do much to encourage their children, and their ideas, enthusiasm and care can strengthen family bonds and lead to some special times.

While there will be many demands on the home budget, if possible the Fire Tiger should try to go away with his loved ones over the year. A break can be appreciated by everyone, as will visits to local attractions, some of which, such as museums, parks and beauty spots, can be free to enjoy.

Many Fire Tigers will be grateful for the support of senior relations and, when faced with major decisions, glad of their input. Over the year, their love and generosity will mean a great deal.

In view of his various commitments, the Fire Tiger may decide to cut back on his social life this year. However, it is important he does not deny himself opportunities to spend time with others or attend interesting events. His social life can bring important balance to his lifestyle. In addition, there is a risk that some friendships could, due to changed circumstances, fall away. Although friendships do evolve over time, the Fire Tiger will have to be careful not to jeopardize some important contacts. Fire Tigers, take note.

While the aspects advise care, the Monkey year can also spring surprises. For the unattached, including those who have had some recent personal difficulty, a chance introduction could bring them into contact with someone who could quickly become important. Exciting romantic possibilities could be in store. April, August to early October and December could be pleasing and interesting months.

The Fire Tiger is often blessed with creative talent and by developing his ideas and using his skills to advantage, he will often derive great satisfaction from what he is able to do over the year. Interest-wise this can be an inspiring time.

The Fire Tiger can also make steady progress in his work and may have the chance to extend his role. In addition, new technologies and systems will be introduced in many a workplace, and by familiarizing himself with these (and overcoming initial reservations), he could benefit from what arises. He does, however, need to work closely with others and be an active team player. The greater his involvement, the more chance he will have to demonstrate his strengths. Similarly, when pressures arise, the Fire Tiger's often innovative approach and willingness to adapt can impress others and be to his future advantage.

For Fire Tigers who feel the time is right for change, as well as those seeking work, the Monkey year can be tricky but potentially significant. Obtaining a new position will not be easy, especially in the face of fierce competition. However, the Fire Tiger is purposeful, and by showing prospective employers his resolve and desire to learn, he may well secure a position in a different capacity from before. This could involve considerable adjustment, but once settled, the Fire Tiger can gain the skills, experience and platform for more substantial progress in the future. April, July, September and November could see encouraging developments.

The Fire Tiger's efforts at work can bring an increase in income, and his improved situation will allow him to proceed with many of his plans. However, he will still need to budget wisely. Also, when entering into any major agreements, he needs to check the obligations and, where appropriate, obtain proper guidance. The more vigilant he is, the better.

Overall, this will be a full and potentially important year for the Fire Tiger and what he achieves now can help him as he looks to progress over the next few years. The Monkey year will require effort and discipline, but the Fire Tiger's ideas, skills and potential will be recognized. There will also be some significant personal times, and amid the year's pressures, there will be a lot to share and enjoy.

Tip for the Year
Though there may be many demands on your time, do be attentive to those around you and keep your lifestyle balanced. Also, have self-belief. What you do now can be an important factor in the success that lies ahead. Good luck.

The Earth Tiger

This will be a busy year for the Earth Tiger. It can bring personal happiness, but challenges too. However, lessons can be learned from the more demanding times.

For the many Earth Tigers in education, the pressures will be considerable. Not only will there be much material to learn, but exams to prepare for. In quite a few instances, a lot will rest on the results obtained.

To do well, these Earth Tigers will need to remain focused and organize their time. With discipline and consistent application, not only will many be pleased with the results they obtain but also inspired by certain subject areas or new skills. This can be an instructive and potentially rewarding time. In addition, what the Earth Tiger gains this year, whether in knowledge or qualifications, can often be taken further in following years.

However, while good progress can be made, the Monkey year can also bring salutary warnings. Should the Earth Tiger slack or make assumptions, there could be disappointments in store. For some Earth Tigers, mock examinations could be a wake-up call to put in more effort. Results *will* need to be worked for this year.

In addition to his studying, the Earth Tiger should avail himself of the recreational facilities available to him. Involvement in sport, music or drama can not only be fun but also allow the Earth Tiger to make more of certain strengths.

Any Earth Tigers who move to a new place of education, should also aim to participate in what is going on around them. Joining clubs and meeting like-minded people will enable them to settle down quickly and will have a positive effect on their work. Monkey years are times of great possibility, but do require effort.

For Earth Tigers in work or seeking it, the Monkey year can also bring significant developments. For those in a position, the demands and pressures are set to increase and the Earth Tiger may be concerned about the expectations placed upon him or having to deal with matters he does not feel properly trained for. Some parts of the year will push him out of his comfort zone. However, by rising to the challenge and doing his best, he will not only acquire valuable skills but also discover more about his own strengths. These can be instructive times and often indicate the type of work the Earth Tiger should consider concentrating on in the future.

Many Earth Tigers can look forward to making steady progress this year and the experience they gain will help their prospects. There will, though, be some who feel their current position is not right for them and decide to look elsewhere. For these Earth Tigers, and those seeking work, the Monkey year can bring surprises. Obtaining a position will be difficult. However, effort will be rewarded and by taking advice from employment professionals, these Earth Tigers could be alerted to companies looking to recruit and secure a position with long-term possibilities. April, July, September and November could see encouraging developments.

There will be many demands, however, on the Earth Tiger's often limited resources, and financial discipline will be required. The Earth Tiger would do well to set limits on the amount he spends on certain activities. If he takes the time to consider more major purchases rather than rush, he could also find himself benefiting from favourable buying opportunities.

His various activities will bring him into contact with many people and socially these can be interesting times. For some Earth Tigers there will be many good times with friends. However, the Monkey year can also bring more difficult moments. Without care, the exuberant high jinks of some Earth Tigers could cause problems. If at any time the Earth Tiger has reservations about situations in which he finds himself, he should be wary. Similarly, if a disagreement arises with a friend, he should try to diffuse it before it escalates. Monkey years do have a personally challenging element. Earth Tigers, take note. April, late July to early October and December can be active months for socializing and, for some, could bring meaningful romance.

During the year, the Earth Tiger should also aim to communicate well with family members. By sharing news and, when under pressure, asking for advice, he will benefit from their support. In addition, if he is forthcoming about his ideas, he could find interesting possibilities opening up.

There may be unexpected travel opportunities, too, sometimes with little warning. By making the most of what occurs, the Earth Tiger can greatly enjoy himself.

Overall, the Monkey year will be demanding and the Earth Tiger will need to put in the effort to get results. However, by developing his skills and adding to his experience, he can build an important platform for future growth. And many of the events of the year, both the good and sometimes disappointing, can be instructive. This may not be the smoothest of years, but during it the Earth Tiger will experience and gain a great deal.

Tip for the Year
Make the most of your opportunities. Whether studying or at work, put in the time and effort. What you do now can prepare the way for the successes soon to come.

Famous Tigers

Paula Abdul, Amy Adams, Kofi Annan, Sir David Attenborough, Christian Bale, Victoria Beckham, Ludwig van Beethoven, Jamie Bell, Tony Bennett, Tom Berenger, Chuck Berry, Usain Bolt, Jon Bon Jovi, Sir Richard Branson, Matthew Broderick, Emily Brontë, Garth Brooks, Mel Brooks, Isambard Kingdom Brunel, Agatha Christie, Charlotte Church, Suzanne Collins, Robbie Coltrane, Bradley Cooper, Sheryl Crow, Tom Cruise, Penelope Cruz, Charles de Gaulle, Lana Del Rey, Leonardo DiCaprio, Emily Dickinson, David Dimbleby, Drake, Dwight Eisenhower, Queen Elizabeth II, Enya, Ralph Fiennes, Roberta Flack, Frederick Forsyth, Jodie Foster, Megan Fox, Lady Gaga, Crystal Gayle, Ellie Goulding, Buddy Greco, Germaine Greer, Ed Harris, Hugh Hefner, William Hurt, Ray Kroc, Shia LaBeouf, Stan Laurel, Jay Leno, Groucho Marx, Karl Marx, Marilyn Monroe, Demi Moore, Alanis Morissette, Rafael Nadal, Robert Pattinson, Jeremy Paxman, Marco Polo, Beatrix Potter, Renoir, Nora Roberts, Kenny Rogers, the Princess Royal, Dylan Thomas, Julie Walters, H. G. Wells, Oscar Wilde, Robbie Williams, Tennessee Williams, Sir Terry Wogan, Stevie Wonder, William Wordsworth.

2 February 1927 to 22 January 1928 — *Fire Rabbit*

19 February 1939 to 7 February 1940 — *Earth Rabbit*

6 February 1951 to 26 January 1952 — *Metal Rabbit*

25 January 1963 to 12 February 1964 — *Water Rabbit*

11 February 1975 to 30 January 1976 — *Wood Rabbit*

29 January 1987 to 16 February 1988 — *Fire Rabbit*

16 February 1999 to 4 February 2000 — *Earth Rabbit*

3 February 2011 to 22 January 2012 — *Metal Rabbit*

The Rabbit

The Personality of the Rabbit

Whenever
Wherever
With whoever.
Always I try to understand.
Without this, one flounders.
But with understanding,
at least you have a chance.
A good chance.

The Rabbit is born under the signs of virtue and prudence. He is intelligent, well mannered and prefers a quiet and peaceful existence. He dislikes any sort of unpleasantness and will try to steer clear of arguments and disputes. He is very much a pacifist and tends to have a calming influence on those around him. He has wide interests and usually a good appreciation of the arts and the finer things in life. He also knows how to enjoy himself and will often gravitate to the best restaurants and nightspots in town.

The Rabbit is a witty and intelligent speaker and loves being involved in a good discussion. His views and advice are often sought by others and he can be relied upon to be discreet and diplomatic. He will rarely raise his voice in anger and will even turn a blind eye to matters that displease him just to preserve the peace. He likes to remain on good terms with everyone, but he can be rather sensitive and takes any form of criticism very badly. He will also be the first to get out of the way if he sees any form of trouble brewing.

The Rabbit is a quiet and efficient worker and has an extremely good memory. He is very astute in business and financial matters, but his degree of success often depends on the conditions that prevail. He hates being in a situation which is fraught with tension or where he has to make sudden decisions. Wherever possible, he will plan his various activities with the utmost care and a good deal of caution. He does not like to take risks and does not take kindly to change. Basically, he seeks a secure, calm and stable environment, and when conditions are right he is more than happy to leave things as they are.

The Rabbit is conscientious and because of his methodical and ever-watchful nature he can often do well in his chosen profession. He makes a good diplomat, lawyer, shopkeeper, administrator or priest, and he excels in any job where he can use his superb skills as a communicator. He tends to be loyal to his employers and is respected for his integrity and honesty, but if he ever finds himself in a position of great power he can become rather intransigent and authoritarian.

The Rabbit attaches great importance to his home and will often spend a lot of time and money maintaining and furnishing it and fitting it with all the latest comforts – the Rabbit is very much a creature of comfort! He is also something of a collector and there are many Rabbits who derive much pleasure from collecting antiques, stamps, coins, *objets d'art* or anything else which catches their eye or particularly interests them.

The female Rabbit has a friendly, caring and considerate nature, and will do all in her power to give her home a happy and loving atmosphere. She is also very sociable and enjoys holding parties and entertaining. She has a great ability to make the maximum use of her time and although she involves herself in numerous activities, she always manages to find time to sit back and enjoy a good read or a chat. She has a great sense of humour, is very artistic and is often a talented gardener.

The Rabbit takes considerable care over his appearance and is usually smart and well turned out. He also attaches great importance to his relations with others and matters of the heart are particularly important to him. He will rarely be short of admirers and will often have several serious romances before he settles down. He is not the most faithful of signs, but he will find that he is especially well suited to those born under the signs of the Goat, Snake, Pig and Ox. Due to his sociable and easy-going manner he can also get on well with the Tiger, Dragon, Horse, Monkey, Dog and another Rabbit, but he will feel ill at ease with the Rat and Rooster, as both these signs tend to speak their mind and be critical in their comments and the Rabbit just loathes any form of criticism or unpleasantness.

The Rabbit is usually lucky in life and often has the happy knack of being in the right place at the right time. He is talented and quick-witted, but he does sometimes put pleasure before work and wherever possible will opt for the easy life. He can at times be a little reserved and suspicious of the motives of others, but generally will lead a long and contented life and one which – as far as possible – will be free of strife and discord.

The Five Different Types of Rabbit

In addition to the 12 signs of the Chinese zodiac there are five elements and these have a strengthening or moderating influence on the signs. The effects of the elements on the Rabbit are described below, together with the years in which they were exercising their influence. Therefore Rabbits born in 1951 and 2011 are Metal Rabbits, Rabbits born in 1963 are Water Rabbits, and so on.

Metal Rabbit: 1951, 2011

This Rabbit is capable, ambitious and has very definite views on what he wants to achieve in life. He can occasionally appear reserved and aloof, but this is mainly because he likes to keep his thoughts to himself. He has a quick and alert mind and is particularly shrewd in business matters. He can also be very cunning in his actions. He has a good appreciation of the arts and likes to mix in the best circles. He usually has a small but very loyal group of friends.

Water Rabbit: 1963

The Water Rabbit is popular, intuitive and keenly aware of the feelings of those around him. He can, however, be rather sensitive and take things too much to heart. He is very precise and thorough in everything he does and has an exceedingly good memory. He tends to be quiet and at times rather withdrawn, but he expresses his ideas well and is highly regarded by his family, friends and colleagues.

Wood Rabbit: 1975

The Wood Rabbit is likeable, easy-going and very adaptable. He prefers to work in a group rather than on his own and likes to have the support and encouragement of others. He can, however, be rather reticent in expressing his views and it would be in his own interests to become a little more open and let others know how he feels on certain matters. He usually has many friends, enjoys an active social life and is noted for his generosity.

Fire Rabbit: 1927, 1987

The Fire Rabbit has a friendly, outgoing personality. He likes socializing and being on good terms with everyone. He is discreet and diplomatic and has a very good understanding of human nature. He is also strong-willed and provided he has the necessary backing he can go far in life. He does, not, however, suffer adversity well and can become moody and depressed when things are not working out as he would like. He has a particularly good manner with children, is very intuitive and there are some Fire Rabbits who are even noted for their psychic ability.

Earth Rabbit: 1939, 1999

The Earth Rabbit is a quiet individual, but nevertheless very astute. He is realistic in his aims and prepared to work long and hard in order to achieve his objectives. He has good business sense and is invariably lucky in financial matters. He also has a most persuasive manner and usually experiences little difficulty in getting others to fall in with his plans. He is held in high esteem by his friends and colleagues and his views are often sought and highly valued.

Prospects for the Rabbit in 2016

The Year of the Goat (19 February 2015–7 February 2016) will have been a generally encouraging one for the Rabbit and the closing months will be busy ones.

At work, new situations will often arise, giving the Rabbit the chance of increased responsibility. September could be particularly active, and for Rabbits keen to advance their career or seeking a position, some attractive opportunities may arise.

Many Rabbits can also look forward to receiving an extra payment or bonus towards the year's end. However, the closing months will see a lot of spending and the Rabbit would do well to watch his outgoings and make early provision for larger outlays.

The Rabbit's personal life is also set to become busier, with an increasing number of social opportunities, and for some who are unattached, good romantic possibilities. September and December will often be lively months.

Domestically, too, there will be much to arrange and good liaison with others will be necessary, especially if certain plans are to be carried out and last-minute rushes avoided. Amid all the activity, there could also be travel opportunities, some arising with little warning.

The Year of the Monkey starts on 8 February and will be a reasonable one for the Rabbit. During it, he will be able to build on recent developments and make steady progress, but there will also be some matters which could cause concern.

One of the Rabbit's strengths is his ability to get on well with people. This will help him this year. Whenever he is facing problems or uncertainty or is in a dilemma, it is important he talks to others, preferably those who have first-hand knowledge in the relevant area. 'A worry shared is a worry halved' will be the case for many Rabbits this year.

Domestically, several key developments will occur which will need addressing. The Rabbit or a close relation could be involved in a considerable change of routine or a commute which impacts on others. Also, there could be specific plans to see through, perhaps concerning improvements to the home, a special family event or a personal aspiration. With good co-operation and aims to work towards, a lot can take place this year.

The Monkey year can also give rise to a pleasing mix of social occasions, and time spent together can be an important aspect of family life. In addition, a holiday and change of scene can be welcome.

As always, there will, though, be problems along the way, and for a few there may be a health issue, either affecting the Rabbit himself or a relation. If a particular concern presents itself, professional advice should be obtained. Also, to help fitness levels, the Rabbit should give some thought to the quality of his diet and, if sedentary for much of the day, take advice on appropriate forms of exercise. Extra attention to his own well-being would be wise, along with perhaps a bid to improve the family diet.

Rabbits enjoying romance, perhaps started in the previous Goat year, will find this likely to become more significant as the Monkey year progresses. Engagement or marriage is possible for some, while for those currently unattached, a chance meeting or introduction made through friends could transform their situation. Affairs of the heart can bring great joy this year and even Rabbits who experience heartbreak could meet someone who is new, potentially significant and very supportive. March, June, July and October could be lively months with good opportunities to meet others.

However, while there will be a lot happening, the Rabbit cannot afford to be lax. In the Monkey year, situations can suddenly arise which need careful handling. Whether these involve a difference of opinion, the attitude of another person or a plan that runs into difficulty, they need to be kept in perspective. Here the Rabbit's judgement can be a reliable indicator of the best way to proceed.

Another area which will require care this year is finance. Although the Rabbit is generally adept in money matters, this is no time for risk or complacency. If entering into any new agreement, he needs to check the terms and implications. Forms and official correspondence also need to be dealt with promptly and with care. Uncharacteristic lapses or mistakes could be to the Rabbit's disadvantage. If he has uncertainties, he should seek advice from experts or contact an advice line. This is no year for risk.

At work the Rabbit will also find his skills tested in many ways. New schemes and initiatives may affect his workload, and as roles change, he could be given additional training or find his duties changing substantially. Some weeks will be pressured and, being conscientious, the Rabbit will be keen to master what is required. However, demanding though parts of the year will be, the changing situations will give the Rabbit the chance to impress and gain the skills necessary for future progress. It is by being tested that strengths become apparent, and no matter whether the Rabbit remains with his present employer or takes a position elsewhere, what he learns and demonstrates can lead (often quite quickly) to greater opportunity. February, May, September and October could see encouraging developments.

For Rabbits seeking work, persistence can again pay off. While these Rabbits may not necessarily get a position with the precise duties they were seeking, their new role can give them experience in a different area and develop their skills further. By making the most of what arises, the Rabbit can widen his options for later.

The Monkey year will also encourage the Rabbit to make more of his own interests. By building on his knowledge and setting himself personal challenges, he can take great satisfaction from what he does. The Monkey year is a vibrant and encouraging one, and by keeping informed of the latest developments in his areas of interest, the Rabbit will often be inspired to do more.

Overall, the Monkey year will require effort and some situations will be challenging. There could be change to contend with and matters which may concern the Rabbit. However, by seeking support and approaching difficult situations in his usual competent way, he can derive much value from the year. There will be excellent opportunities to extend skills and enhance future prospects. In money matters, the Rabbit will need to be careful and he should also pay some attention to his well-being and lifestyle. However, his home life will be busy and his social life and interests will add richness to the year.

The Metal Rabbit

The Metal Rabbit likes to plan and be well-prepared. This way he can not only make the best of situations but also use his time more effectively. However, while he may have some ideas for the year ahead, he must not regard these as set in stone. Monkey years can bring surprises and while a lot can be achieved this year, it requires flexibility.

One area which will be central to many Metal Rabbits' thinking will be their work situation. Quite a few will retire or decide to reduce their hours this year. However, when they set about their plans, it could be they are asked to reconsider their leaving date, or find that, despite a reduction in hours, unexpected developments cause them to work longer than intended. Plans will be liable to alteration this year.

There will also be some Metal Rabbits who, while leaving their present position, will be keen to use their experience in another capacity. Friends could be especially helpful in making suggestions and introductions. For Metal Rabbits who do decide on another position, this could again be different than originally envisaged but could present an interesting new challenge.

Work matters may not always proceed as envisaged, but February, May, September and October are likely to be important months.

With many Metal Rabbits retiring or altering their working commitments, some adjustments will be needed financially. Here the Metal Rabbit's careful nature will be an asset, and by looking at his budget and making modifications, he will still be able to proceed with many of his plans. Where more major outlay is concerned, advance provision will allow more to go ahead as well as help reduce financial pressures later. The more thorough and disciplined the Metal Rabbit is, the better he will fare. However, Monkey years do have their awkward elements and should the Metal Rabbit be tempted to take risks or make assumptions (without checking facts), he may find himself at a disadvantage. Money matters require care and scrutiny this year.

The Monkey year will, though, offer up some good opportunities for recreation. For Metal Rabbits who follow sport, drama or music, there could be specific events to follow and the Metal Rabbit would also do well to keep alert to what is happening in his area. In addition, many Metal Rabbits will decide to travel this year. By making early enquiries, not only could they sometimes benefit from a special offer but also find their trips broadening out to include other attractions. Monkey years can bring good if unanticipated opportunities.

The Metal Rabbit could also have interest-related ideas he is keen to pursue. By setting them in motion, not only will he be satisfied with what he does but he could find certain activities giving rise to other possibilities. Actions taken this year tend to have a knock-on effect.

During the year the Metal Rabbit should also give some thought to his well-being, including the quality of his diet and level of exercise. If he feels either could be improved, or he has any specific concerns, he should seek advice. Extra attention to his own well-being can make a difference this year.

The Metal Rabbit can look forward to a variety of interesting social occasions and will often find his network of acquaintances growing. However, while he will enjoy excellent relations with most people, he will need to be careful. An uncharacteristic *faux pas*, lapse or difference of opinion may cause upset. Metal Rabbits, do take note; the Monkey year can spring traps for the unwary and indiscreet.

For Metal Rabbits keen to become involved in a new activity this year, there may be the chance to help in their community or join a local organization. March, June to early August and October could see the most social activity.

Domestically, this will be a year of interesting developments. Not only will many Metal Rabbits experience changes in their working routine, but for those who retire, there will be adjustments to be made. To help at this time of transition, it is important that the Metal Rabbit is open and shares matters that are on his mind. This can lead to greater under-standing and plans being more easily advanced.

Travel and shared interests are favourably aspected and some travel opportunities or spur of the moment activities can add surprise and delight to the year. This is a time to adapt and make the most of the chances that arise. The Metal Rabbit will also often play an important part in arranging some key family occasions, especially in the spring and early summer.

However, while there will be much to enjoy, as with all years, problems can sometimes raise their head, and if the Metal Rabbit becomes concerned about a particular matter, or a decision he or another person is about to take, it is important he checks the facts and implications and, if necessary, seeks additional advice.

By the end of the year, many Metal Rabbits will look back and be surprised at all the changes that have occurred. The year will have bought some unforeseen opportunities and by seizing these, the Metal Rabbit will have benefited in several ways. The Monkey year is a time of great possibility.

Tip for the Year

Give time to your personal interests. These can not only bring you pleasure but also lead on to other possibilities. Also consider implementing some positive lifestyle changes. This can be an active and beneficial year for you.

The Water Rabbit

The Water Rabbit has a talent for reading situations well and during a year when situations may be unclear or the way ahead uncertain, he will benefit from holding back and waiting for clarity. The Monkey year will contain some awkward moments, but with patience and his customary skill, the Water Rabbit will successfully steer his way round these and emerge with some important gains to his credit.

Rather than regard this as a year for major progress, he would do well to focus on what is possible now. This especially applies to his own interests. By setting time aside for these, he can derive much satisfaction from what he undertakes over the year. For Water Rabbits who enjoy creative pursuits in particular, this can be an inspiring time. Water Rabbits who have let their interests lapse or would welcome something different to do should consider starting something new. This can add a fresh ingredient to their lifestyle and unanticipated benefits will often follow on. In addition, some may decide to exercise more or follow a keep-fit programme. Whatever he does, the Water Rabbit should aim to give some time to himself this year.

Travel will also bring pleasure and if possible the Water Rabbit should try to take a holiday over the year. With advanced planning, some exciting possibilities can open up. In addition, some short breaks or weekends away can be very enjoyable.

The Water Rabbit is very family-oriented and over the year there will be quite a few domestic matters requiring his attention. Both he and his loved ones could face important choices, and some could be complex, but if time is spent considering the options, unforeseen benefits can be gained.

Throughout the year, openness and discussion will often help. With accommodation matters, including home maintenance issues, the more involved everyone is, the better. With recreational activities favourably aspected, shared interests and family trips can also bring some agreeable times.

Many Water Rabbits will be part of a close social circle and this can be of great value to them during the year. Trusted friends can provide a listening ear as the Water Rabbit mulls over possibilities. He will also be glad to reciprocate and assist friends when needed. His personal interests will often have a good social element, and for the unattached, the year has exciting romantic possibilities in store. March, June to early August and October could be active and lively months socially.

At work, the Water Rabbit's ability to gauge situations will be especially useful. In some organizations, office politics will be in play and there will be moments which will concern the Water Rabbit, particularly as his objectives may be affected. Although his work situation may at times be challenging, this year it is very much of a case of focusing on his role and, when appropriate, keeping a low profile. Situations *will* settle and good opportunities arise after what can be uncertain moments. In the meantime the Water Rabbit needs to keep alert, be patient and do his best.

Some Water Rabbits could find themselves attracted by positions elsewhere and welcoming the new possibilities a change will bring.

For Water Rabbits seeking work, finding a position will require time, but if they remain persistent, interesting doors can open for many. In quite a few instances, what is offered will require considerable readjustment but give these Water Rabbits an important base to build upon. February, May and September to early November could see significant developments.

Financial matters, however, will require care. Although the Water Rabbit usually manages his budget well, the Monkey year can bring some unexpected household or family expenses and there could also be activities that he is keen to spend money on. Throughout the year he should keep tabs on his situation, making advance provision for forthcoming expenses and checking the terms of any new obligations. The more thorough he is, the better.

Overall, the Year of the Monkey will be a fair one for the Water Rabbit. In his work, situations outside his control could impact on his role, but interesting opportunities can eventually emerge and the experience he gains can be of present and future value. In money matters, care is advised. The Water Rabbit will, though, particularly enjoy the way his personal interests develop, and socially and domestically there will be good times to be had. With significant decisions, good dialogue and co-operation are, however, essential. This may not be the easiest of years for the Water Rabbit, but benefits can follow on from it.

Tip for the Year
Keep your lifestyle in balance and situations in perspective. Concentrate on the present and be persistent. Your qualities and strengths will serve you well and lead on to reward. Time given to personal interests can be of especial benefit.

The Wood Rabbit

The last few years will have been eventful for the Wood Rabbit. There will have been some personal achievements and hard-won successes, but there will have been disappointments too. As the Monkey year begins, many Wood Rabbits will have a strong desire to move ahead and make more of their strengths. They *can* make headway this year, but it may not prove as straightforward as they would like. Monkey years can throw up their challenges, but by adapting and making the most of situations, the Wood Rabbit can often turn events to his advantage.

At work, this can be a busy and significant year. During it many Wood Rabbits will experience change, possibly with the introduction of new directives and systems as well as new personnel. For the Wood Rabbit, who likes stability and just to get on, certain developments can be unsettling. However, he has skills which can serve him well, and by keeping up to date with developments and adapting accordingly, he may well find that the changes taking place bring opportunities to advance his career. In addition, the new responsibilities that many Wood Rabbits take on will not only give them experience in a new capacity but also increase their options for later.

The majority of Wood Rabbits will remain with their present employer over the year, but there will be some who feel their longer-term prospects may be helped by a move elsewhere. For these Wood Rabbits, and those seeking work, the Monkey year can open up interesting possibilities. By keeping alert for vacancies and talking to people they know, many could discover an opening which represents a significant change from previous positions but offers the potential for development. Monkey years can bring surprises and this one may well bring the opportunities and incentive that have been lacking in the Wood Rabbit's work in recent times. February, May, September and October could see interesting developments.

The Wood Rabbit's income may well increase during the year, but with home repairs and new equipment likely to be needed, together with other plans, his outgoings will be considerable and he should keep tabs on spending, as this could easily become greater than anticipated. Financial matters require extra care this year. Also, he needs to be thorough with paperwork. A delay, oversight or risk could be to his disadvantage.

Although the Wood Rabbit will be kept busy this year, he should set time aside for personal interests and make sure this important part of his lifestyle is not neglected due to other demands. If sedentary for much of the day, he may consider pursuits that involve additional exercise. By putting some of his free time to good use, he will often feel energized by what he does.

In addition, should he feel below par or have concerns about his well-being at any time, he should seek advice.

Travel will once again feature on the agenda of many Wood Rabbits this year. Opportunities may arise quickly and should be seized quickly too.

The Wood Rabbit will also appreciate the social opportunities of the year. Shared interests can give rise to some lively occasions and his social circle is set to widen. For the unattached, the year is not without romantic possibility, with some Wood Rabbits meeting someone in a curious way which seems as if it was meant to be. March, June to early August and October could see the most social opportunities.

In the Wood Rabbit's home life, some important decisions will be called for, possibly concerning changes in work routine and home maintenance issues. Here full and frank discussion will be to the advantage of all. Should any disagreement arise during the year, often as a result of tiredness, pressure or uncertainty, again talking matters through, showing understanding and reaching consensus will help. All years have their trickier moments and this will be no exception.

Amid the considerable domestic activity, there will, however, be family highlights to enjoy, especially as personal milestones or special birthdays or anniversaries are marked. Time spent together will also be of benefit, rather than everyone being continually busy with individual concerns. Here the Wood Rabbit's inclusive ideas can benefit all. April and July could be interesting months in many a Wood Rabbit household.

In general, the Year of the Monkey will be busy, with the Wood Rabbit needing to be flexible as situations change. There will times of pressure, but the Wood Rabbit's measured approach and ability to relate well to others will often enable him to turn situations to his advantage. Setting time aside for personal interests and attending to his own well-being will help. He will also value shared times in the company of family and friends in this interesting and frequently surprising year.

Tip for the Year
Seize any chances to add to your skills and to meet other people. With involvement, support and a willingness to adapt, you can do your situation and prospects considerable good.

The Fire Rabbit

The Fire Rabbit is ambitious and is also aware that in order to achieve certain aims he needs to build on his experience. And this is what many Fire Rabbits will do this year. The Monkey year is one for steady progress.

Throughout the year the Fire Rabbit will be helped by the support of those around him. By being prepared to talk over his situation and aims, he can benefit greatly from the assistance offered. As he strives to move forward, he can also be reassured by the knowledge that he is not alone and that many believe in him.

At work, many Fire Rabbits will have established themselves in a certain role and over the year will have the opportunity to further their experience. Internal vacancies may arise or, as the workload increases, these Fire Rabbits may be offered extra responsibilities. Over the year there will be good chances for them to prove themselves in new ways as well as extend their knowledge of their workplace and industry.

For those who feel opportunities are lacking where they are and would welcome a change, as well as those seeking work, the Monkey year can hold important developments. The job-seeking process will be challenging, but by keeping alert and informed (contacts and connections may again be useful), many of these Fire Rabbits can secure a new position which uses their skills in a different way and has prospects for the future. To benefit, the Fire Rabbit should not be too restrictive in his search. February, May, September and October could see encouraging developments.

The Fire Rabbit's income may increase during the year, but money matters will require careful management. With many demands on his resources, and deposits sometimes required, the Fire Rabbit will need to be disciplined and control spending. Saving for what he wants will not only make him appreciate his purchases all the more but often give him the chance to obtain better value too.

The Monkey year can bring good travel possibilities and some Fire Rabbits will take advantage of special offers as well as travel to a destination they have long wanted to see. In addition, shorter trips, including special events held locally, can be a source of much fun, and the Fire Rabbit should keep himself informed of what is happening.

Many Fire Rabbits have specific interests and have built up considerable expertise in these. During the year the Fire Rabbit should enjoy his knowledge and consider ways of extending what he does. No matter whether he prefers practical, physical or creative pursuits, time set aside for activities he enjoys can be a source of much pleasure as well as open up other possibilities. Fire Rabbits who have let their interests lapse would do well to consider taking up an activity again. This can often restore some balance to their busy lifestyle.

The Fire Rabbit would also do well to give some consideration to his well-being, including his diet and general level of exercise. Should he feel modifications are needed or have any concerns, he should seek guidance.

The Fire Rabbit attaches much importance to his relations with others and over the year can look forward to the chance to extend his social circle. Some of the people he meets could be helpful in providing knowledge and encouragement, whether with his work or personal interests. For the unattached, including those who have experienced recent heartache, someone new could offer the support and love they very much need. March, June, July and October could see good social opportunities and some particularly enjoyable occasions.

The Fire Rabbit's domestic life will also see considerable activity. Celebrations could be in order as some Fire Rabbits get engaged or married or become parents. These can be busy and exciting months and good dialogue and flexibility over arrangements are advised. The summer and the closing weeks of the year will be especially active.

However, while many plans and hopes will come to fruition, there will also be pressures, especially as routines change or uncertainties loom. Here patience and support can be of considerable value. In addition, more senior relations (or professionals the Fire Rabbit may know) may be able to advise. All years have their tricky moments and often concerns can be successfully addressed and not detract from the domestic achievements and happiness of the year.

Overall, the Monkey year will be an interesting and constructive one for the Fire Rabbit. Many Fire Rabbits will make steady and potentially important progress in their work, gaining the skills and experience needed for the fulfilment of some ambitions. Personal interests can also develop well, and socially and domestically, there will be good times to enjoy, with the Fire Rabbit benefiting from the support of others and sharing special times with loved ones. A satisfying year.

Tip for the Year
Build on your position and skills. Experience gained now can be an important factor in your subsequent progress. Also, set time aside for interests and for those who are close to you. With a good lifestyle balance, you will be able to take real pleasure in what this year offers.

The Earth Rabbit

This will be a demanding year for the Earth Rabbit. Much will be expected of him and while many activities will go well, the year does call for effort.

For Earth Rabbits born in 1999, this year can mark an important stage in their education. Many will not only find themselves having to study a wide range of topics but will also have the additional pressure of exams to prepare for. Some weeks could be particularly frenetic and it will be a case of remaining organized and using study time well. With the advanced nature of some subjects, some Earth Rabbits may find themselves struggling and having doubts. However, with persistence, and asking for help when necessary, important progress can be made and many complexities mastered. In addition, the Earth Rabbit would do well to keep in mind the benefits particular qualifications can bring.

Despite the pressure and uncertainty he may feel this year, deep down the Earth Rabbit knows he has the talent to accomplish a great deal and what he learns this year (including about himself) can be an important stage in his development.

There will also be some Earth Rabbits who are in work or who seek work this year. The positions these Earth Rabbits hold, or are offered, may not always inspire them, and their duties may sometimes be routine. However, such positions can still provide useful experience and be a platform from which to progress. And once in work, if the Earth Rabbit shows commitment, other responsibilities can soon be offered. The Earth Rabbit is at the start of his working life and this is the first rung on what can be a long and promising career ladder. February, May and September to mid-November could see interesting work developments.

While parts of the year can be demanding, it will also have many pleasing aspects. Hobbies and personal interests can develop well and, particularly with activities that can be enjoyed with friends, a great deal of fun can be had. For some activities, extra support and instruction will be available, and by taking advantage of this, the Earth Rabbit will often be pleased with how he is able to improve his skills. The Monkey year is an encouraging one and will offer him the chance to progress.

There will also be opportunities for the Earth Rabbit to travel this year. These could include chances to visit places that are relevant to his studying or interests. Many Earth Rabbits can also look forward to enjoying a holiday as well as visiting some fun attractions. The Monkey year has vitality and can enthuse the young Earth Rabbit.

Another aspect he will enjoy will be the social opportunities the year brings. He will find his social circle increasing and, with his lively and alert manner, will find himself popular company. Over the year there will certainly be parties and other special events to look forward to, with March, June to mid-August and the closing weeks of the year particularly busy.

However, while there will be much to enjoy, the Earth Rabbit does need to pay attention to his well-being. To overindulge, be reckless or ignore guidelines could leave him regretting his folly. In 2016, some self-care is advised.

For some Earth Rabbits, the Monkey year can have romantic possibilities and this will add to the enjoyment. However, it should be noted that Monkey years have their more awkward elements and sometimes romance or a particular friendship may cause anguish and need to be kept in perspective. As the Earth Rabbit will find, the path of true love – and friendship – can sometimes be rocky.

Also, if the Earth Rabbit feels under pressure at any time, whether as a result of his studies or another worry he may have, it is important he does not bear this alone. His family and those close to him are keen to support, and if he is forthcoming, they can do much to allay his concerns as well as assist in other ways.

With the various activities the Earth Rabbit will be keen to pursue and the items he will doubtless be wanting to buy, he will need to be disciplined in money matters. While there may be many temptations, this is a year to keep control over the purse-strings and avoid risk. And if he has doubts or problems over any money issue, he should seek advice.

For the Earth Rabbit born in 1939, the Monkey year can contain some very special occasions, including some notable personal or family milestones. In addition, the more senior Earth Rabbit will value the affection and support of family members and the assistance and advice they may offer.

He will also be pleased with the way certain hopes are realized. Whether obtaining equipment for his home or visiting particular places, when he decides upon something, interesting results can often ensue.

The Earth Rabbit will, though, need to be attentive in financial matters and deal promptly with correspondence. This is no year for risk and if he has any doubts, he should seek advice. Similarly, if he has any other financial concerns during the year, he should not forget that there are professionals who will often be able to assist.

The Earth Rabbit is blessed with a creative mind and can derive much pleasure from his interests. Those encouraging an element of self-expression can be especially rewarding this year.

Whether born in 1939 or 1999, the Earth Rabbit will find that the Monkey year will have its pleasures but results will have to be worked for and some challenges overcome. However, the Earth Rabbit has great strength of character and if he keeps in mind the results he wants and makes the effort, he can reap some fine and deserved rewards. For the Earth Rabbit born in 1999, skills and qualifications gained now can prove very significant in the long term.

Tip for the Year
Use your time well. Focus on your objectives and be determined. Your efforts can yield some fine results. Also, enjoy your good relations with those around you and do seek support at times of uncertainty.

Famous Rabbits

Margaret Atwood, Drew Barrymore, David Beckham, Harry Belafonte, Ingrid Bergman, St Bernadette, Jeff Bezos, Kathryn Bigelow, Michael Bublé, Nicolas Cage, Lewis Carroll, Fidel Castro, John Cleese, Confucius, Marie Curie, Johnny Depp, Novak Djokovic, Albert Einstein, George Eliot, W. C. Fields, James Fox, Cary Grant, Ashley Greene, Edvard Grieg, Oliver Hardy, Seamus Heaney, Tommy Hilfiger, Bob Hope, Whitney Houston, Helen Hunt, John Hurt, Anjelica Huston, Enrique Inglesias, E. L. James, Henry James, Sir David Jason, Angelina Jolie, Michael B. Jordan, Michael Keaton, John Keats, Enda Kenny, Lisa Kudrow, Gina Lollobrigida, George Michael, Sir Roger Moore, Andy Murray, F. Murray Abraham, Mike Myers, Brigitte Nielsen, Graham Norton, Michelle Obama, Jamie Oliver, George Orwell, Edith Piaf, Brad Pitt, Emeli Sandé, Elisabeth Schwarzkopf, Neil Sedaka, Jane Seymour, Maria Sharapova, Neil Simon, Frank Sinatra, Sting, Quentin Tarantino, Charlize Theron, J. R. R. Tolkien, KT Tunstall, Tina Turner, Luther Vandross, Sebastian Vettel, Queen Victoria, Muddy Waters, Orson Welles, Hayley Westenra, Walt Whitman, Will-i-Am, Kate Winslet, Tiger Woods.

3 February 1916 to 22 January 1917 — *Fire Dragon*

23 January 1928 to 9 February 1929 — *Earth Dragon*

8 February 1940 to 26 January 1941 — *Metal Dragon*

27 January 1952 to 13 February 1953 — *Water Dragon*

13 February 1964 to 1 February 1965 — *Wood Dragon*

31 January 1976 to 17 February 1977 — *Fire Dragon*

17 February 1988 to 5 February 1989 — *Earth Dragon*

5 February 2000 to 23 January 2001 — *Metal Dragon*

23 January 2012 to 9 February 2013 — *Water Dragon*

The Dragon

The Personality of the Dragon

I like giving things a go.
Sometimes I succeed,
sometimes I fail.
Sometimes the unexpected happens.
But it is the giving things a go
and the stepping forward
that make life so interesting.

The Dragon is born under the sign of luck. He is a proud and lively character and has a tremendous amount of self-confidence. He is also highly intelligent and very quick to take advantage of any opportunity. He is ambitious and determined and will do well in practically anything he attempts. He is also something of a perfectionist and will always try to maintain the high standards he sets himself.

The Dragon does not suffer fools gladly and will be quick to criticize anyone or anything that displeases him. He can be blunt and forthright in his views and is certainly not renowned for being either tactful or diplomatic. He does, however, often take people at their word and can occasionally be rather gullible. If he ever feels that his trust has been abused or his dignity wounded, he can sometimes become very bitter and it will take him a long time to forgive and forget.

The Dragon is usually very outgoing and is particularly adept at attracting attention and publicity. He enjoys being in the limelight and is often at his best when he is confronted by a difficult problem or tense situation. In some respects he is a showman and he rarely lacks an audience. His views are highly valued and he invariably has something interesting – and sometimes controversial – to say.

He also has considerable energy and is often prepared to work long and unsocial hours in order to achieve what he wants. He can, however, be rather impulsive and does not always consider the consequences of his actions. He also has a tendency to live for the moment and there is nothing that riles him more than to be kept waiting. The Dragon hates delay and can get extremely impatient and irritable over even the smallest of hold-ups.

The Dragon has an enormous faith in his abilities, but he does run the risk of becoming over-confident and unless he is careful he can sometimes make grave errors of judgement. While this may prove disastrous at the time, he does have the tenacity and ability to bounce back and pick up the pieces again.

The Dragon has such an assertive personality, so much willpower and such a desire to succeed that he will often reach the top of his chosen profession. He has considerable leadership qualities and will do well in positions where he can put his own ideas and policies into practice. He is usually successful in politics, show business, as the manager of his own department or business, and in any job that brings him into contact with the media.

The Dragon relies a tremendous amount on his own judgement and can be scornful of other people's advice. He likes to feel self-sufficient and there are many Dragons who cherish their independence to such a degree that they prefer to remain single throughout their lives. However, the Dragon will often have numerous admirers and many will be attracted by his flamboyant personality and striking looks. If he does marry, he will usually marry young, and will find himself particularly well suited to those born under the signs of the Snake, Rat, Monkey and Rooster. He will also find that the Rabbit, Pig, Horse and Goat make ideal companions and will readily join in with many of his escapades. Two Dragons will also get on well together, as they will understand each other, but the Dragon may not find things so easy with the Ox and Dog, as both will be critical of his impulsive and somewhat extrovert manner. He will also find it difficult to form an alliance with the Tiger, for the Tiger, like the Dragon, tends to speak his mind, is very strong-willed and likes to take the lead.

The female Dragon knows what she wants in life and sets about everything she does in a determined and positive manner. No job is too small for her and she is often prepared to work extremely hard to secure her objectives. She is immensely practical and somewhat liberated. She hates being bound by routine and petty restrictions and likes to have sufficient freedom to go off and do what she wants to do. She will keep her house tidy, but is not one for spending hours on housework – there are far too many other things that she prefers to do. Like her male counterpart, she has a tendency to speak her mind.

The Dragon usually has many interests and enjoys sport and other outdoor activities. He also likes to travel and often prefers to visit places that are off the beaten track rather than head for popular tourist destinations. He has a very adventurous streak in him and providing his financial circumstances permit – and the Dragon is usually sensible with his money – he will travel considerable distances during his lifetime.

The Dragon is a very flamboyant character and while he can be demanding of others and in his early years rather precocious, he will have many friends and will nearly always be the centre of attention. He has charisma and so much confidence that he can often become a source of inspiration to others. In China he is the leader of the carnival and he is also blessed with an inordinate share of luck.

The Five Different Types of Dragon

In addition to the 12 signs of the Chinese zodiac there are five elements and these have a strengthening or moderating influence on the signs. The effects of the elements on the Dragon are described below, together with the years in which they were exercising their influence. Therefore Dragons born in 1940 and 2000 are Metal Dragons, Dragons born in 1952 and 2012 are Water Dragons, and so on.

Metal Dragon: 1940, 2000

This Dragon is very strong-willed and has a particularly forceful personality. He is energetic, ambitious and tries to be scrupulous in his dealings with others. He can also be blunt and to the point and usually has no hesitation in speaking his mind. If people disagree with him or are not prepared to co-operate, he is more than happy to go his own way. He usually has very high moral values and is held in great esteem by his friends and colleagues.

Water Dragon: 1952, 2012

This Dragon is friendly, easy-going and intelligent. He is quick-witted and rarely lets an opportunity slip by. However, he is not as impatient as some of the other types of Dragon and is prepared to wait for results rather than expect everything to happen at once. He has an understanding nature and is willing to share his ideas and co-operate with others. His main failing is a tendency to jump from one thing to another rather than concentrate on the job in hand. He has a good sense of humour and is an effective speaker.

Wood Dragon: 1964

The Wood Dragon is practical, imaginative and inquisitive. He loves delving into all manner of subjects and can quite often come up with some highly original ideas. He is a thinker and a doer and has the drive and commitment to put many of his ideas into practice. He is more diplomatic than some of the other types of Dragon and has a good sense of humour. He is very astute in business matters and can also be most generous.

Fire Dragon: 1916, 1976

This Dragon is ambitious, articulate and has a tremendous desire to succeed. He is a hard and conscientious worker and is often admired for his integrity and forthright nature. He is very strong-willed and has considerable leadership qualities. He can, however, rely a bit too much on his own judgement and fail to take into account the views and feelings of others. He can also be rather aloof and it would certainly be in his own interests to let others join in more with his various activities. He usually enjoys music, literature and the arts.

Earth Dragon: 1928, 1988

The Earth Dragon tends to be quieter and more reflective than some of the other types of Dragon. He has a wide variety of interests and is keenly aware of what is going on around him. He also has clear objectives and usually no problems in obtaining support and backing for any of his ventures. He is very astute in financial matters and often able to accumulate considerable wealth. He is a good organizer, although he can at times be rather bureaucratic and fussy. He mixes well with others and has a large circle of friends.

Prospects for the Dragon in 2016

The Dragon likes to live life at a fast pace, but as even he accepts, sometimes it is necessary to slow down a little and take stock. And this is what the Goat year (19 February 2015–7 February 2016) will have allowed many Dragons to do. Goat years are not times for spectacular progress but for reappraisal and aiming for a better lifestyle balance.

As the Goat year draws to a close, the Dragon will find this a satisfying time. At work there will be the chance for many Dragons to put their strengths to greater use, and for those in a creative environment in particular, there can be some encouraging outcomes. September and November could see considerable activity, including for those Dragons looking for a change or for work.

There will also be good social opportunities in the closing months of the year, with an interesting mix of occasions to enjoy. December could be especially busy, and for the unattached and those newly in love, affairs of the heart could be promising.

The Dragon's domestic life will also see a lot happening, possibly including travel, and the earlier arrangements can be decided upon, the better and less frenetic some activities will turn out to be. Quality time in the company of loved ones can lead to some special occasions in the closing weeks of the year.

Although the Dragon may have had to temper his ambitions in the Goat year, on a personal level he will have gained much over the last 12 months, including insights into himself as well as ideas about the future. In 2016 he will be able to develop these further – a lot further.

The Dragon is famed for his energy and drive, and as the Monkey year starts, he will sense the winds of change starting to blow and will resolve to set important wheels in motion. However, while the aspects are generally favourable, he should be careful not to overreach himself. This Monkey year, which starts on 8 February, can trip up the unwary, with haste possibly leading to oversights and mistakes. This can be a successful year, but plans do need to be carefully considered.

At work, the aspects are, however, particularly encouraging for the Dragon. Monkey years favour enterprise and a plethora of new ideas, systems and products will be introduced in this one. The Dragon, with his keen and alert nature, will often latch onto developments and be well placed to benefit. Whether he decides to stay in his existing place of work or to look elsewhere, his strengths can lead to promotion. Many Dragons will also feel more motivated, with ideas to explore, objectives to work towards and skills to develop. There will be a lot happening this year, which appeals to the Dragon's mentality, and he will enjoy the challenges presented.

Some Dragons will be looking to take their career in a new direction, and for these Dragons, as well as those seeking work, the Monkey year can be one of interesting possibilities. By considering different ways in which they can use their skills and keeping alert for vacancies, many will find a position offering the change they desire. This may come with a steep learning curve and change of routine, but what many Dragons are offered now will be the chance they have been wanting for some time. April, May, August and November could see good opportunities arising.

However, while the aspects are favourable, when setting about his activities, the Dragon does need to be thorough. To take risks or proceed without adequate preparation could undermine his chances. In 2016 he must not take situations for granted, but be attentive and well-prepared.

In particular, Dragons seeking work or to make a career change will find the extra effort they can put into their applications can make an appreciable difference.

Progress at work will often lead to the Dragon increasing his income, although, with his busy lifestyle, his outgoings will be considerable and he will need to keep a close watch on spending. Also, if entering into any new agreements, he should check the implications. This is no year for risk or rush. Early provision for specific purchases or big plans will lead to more being realized. Monkey years favour preparation and attention to detail.

Over the year, new interests, recreational pursuits and innovative products will capture the imagination of many Dragons and they will be keen to find out more. Many a Dragon will have an interesting mix of things to do this year and several outlets for his talents.

With his engaging nature, the Dragon enjoys company and both his home and social life will see considerable activity this year. However, in both it is important he remains mindful of the views of others and consults those around him when he has ideas in mind. That way, he can not only benefit from the advice and support offered but sometimes be alerted to other considerations or snags he may have overlooked. The more feedback the Dragon has this year, the better he will fare. In addition, he should also seize any chances to extend his work and social circle. This is a year for reaching out and being involved.

Travel and shared interests could bring good social opportunities and May, August, September and December could be particularly lively months.

For the unattached, this can be a significant year. Many Dragons will find love and some will decide to marry or settle down. Monkey years favour a coming together.

Dragons who are more independent-minded (of which there are quite a few), do embrace the spirit of the time and involve yourself more in things that are going on. It will be well worth while.

In the Dragon's domestic life, a lot is set to happen, and good co-operation will be needed. While keen, the Dragon cannot expect to hold sway all the time, but should show some flexibility over arrangements.

With some ambitious practical activities in particular, timescales need to be kept fluid. Monkey years can throw up their quandaries as well as create additional options, and these need to be addressed before actions are finalized. As with so much this year, the Dragon needs to keep alert and be responsive to what arises.

In addition to the practical activities of the year, shared interests will be particularly appreciated, with the summer months seeing special occasions in many a Dragon household. Some unexpected travel opportunities could also arise and many Dragons will enjoy the chance to see some impressive sights.

In general, the Monkey year holds interesting prospects for the Dragon. Active and enterprising, he can do well. However, he must not aim to do it all by himself. This is a year for seeking support and building contacts. The Dragon has much to offer and his prospects are encouraging, but he needs to be mindful and, at times, flexible. This is no time for rush or risk, and in many matters, including finance, he needs to be thorough and consider his options carefully. However, there is much to be gained this year and with his consummate skill, the Dragon will seize his opportunities and enjoy his positive relations with those around him.

The Metal Dragon

The element of metal helps to make a sign more resolute and this certainly applies to the Metal Dragon. Purpose, resourcefulness and determination – these are all hallmarks of his character, and they will continue to serve him well this year.

For the Metal Dragon born in 2000, this will be a year of great possibility. New opportunities will open up and allow him to make greater use of his strengths. In his education, he could select subjects for more specialist study as well as enjoy the chance to try new activities. Throughout the year the emphasis will be on development and many Metal Dragons will be satisfied with the progress they feel they are making.

A further feature of the year is that situations will often allow the Metal Dragon to engage more fully in what is going on around him, and this may help his level of confidence and highlight personal strengths. In so many ways the young Metal Dragon can get a lot from the year, even though it may sometimes require stepping out of his comfort zone.

Throughout the year the young Metal Dragon should also draw on the support available to him. If he has concerns over a subject area or particular decision, rather than hold back, he should seek guidance. Metal Dragons have a mind of their own, and with that can come a stubborn streak. This is something they should watch. To close their mind to certain opportunities or subject areas could be counter-productive and affect their performance. Monkey years favour an open-minded approach and, as the Metal Dragon may find, surprising discoveries may result.

The Metal Dragon can have great fun this year in seeing how his interests and recreational pursuits develop. Not only can many of these involve close friends but sometimes lead to the Metal Dragon attending particular occasions or meeting like-minded people. If there are interest-related skills the Metal Dragon would like to make more of, he should set time aside for practice as well as using the resources available.

There will also be chances to travel and the Metal Dragon will be glad of the opportunity to visit new areas and experience some lively events, especially during the summer.

With a wide range of activities to do, however, as well as items he will want to buy, he will need to be disciplined in his spending and avoid too many impulse purchases. Without care, he could come to regret his haste.

In his home life there will be occasions he will enjoy, and by being a part and contributing, he will find his input often appreciated. Here again, to get the most value from the year, participation is key.

For Metal Dragons born in 1940, the Monkey year can also contain interesting developments. These Metal Dragons will once again have particular ideas in mind, possibly related to their accommodation, the purchase of equipment, activities they are keen to do or places they would like to go. However, to realize their plans, they do need to liaise with others. It is joint effort that will bring results this year.

Also, where financial outlay is involved, the Metal Dragon will need to be thorough, taking the time to check terms and costs and keeping paperwork in order. Money and bureaucratic matters could be problematic this year and require careful attention.

The Metal Dragon will, however, delight in some of the family occasions taking place this year, and some good news concerning a younger relation. He will be glad to offer assistance to close relations and his thoughtfulness will be appreciated. July and August could be active months in many a Metal Dragon household.

During the year the Metal Dragon will also be keen to pursue his interests. Certain projects will occupy his time in satisfying ways and in some cases new equipment can open up interesting new possibilities. In addition, he will appreciate going out, whether to local events or attractions or to enjoy outdoor amenities. The Monkey year can offer many and varied pleasures.

For all Metal Dragons, whether born in 1940 or 2000, this can be an interesting year, but to make the most of it, they need to curb their independent tendencies and speak openly about their ideas, hopes and plans. The Metal Dragon should also remain open-minded and explore the possibilities this Monkey year offers, including developing personal interests. Money matters require care, but generally, with support and the traditional game Metal Dragon attitude, the Metal Dragon can make this a rewarding year.

Tip for the Year
Seek advice and support. With encouragement and assistance, you can set many of your ideas in motion. Also, take advantage of the opportunities that can so suddenly and often fortuitously arise this year.

The Water Dragon

This will be a busy year for the Water Dragon, but while he may have plans for the year ahead, they may not always take the course he envisaged. This can be an eventful and significant year, but also a sometimes surprising one.

At work, many Water Dragons will face decisions. Some may retire or be offered retirement. For these Water Dragons, there will be personal adjustments to make and lifestyle changes to consider. Those who do retire or reduce their working commitments should not only draw on the advice available to them but also give some thought to projects they would now like to pursue. The Monkey year can open up some good possibilities.

For those who continue in work, changes are also afoot. In many a workplace there will be new procedures, technologies and products for the Water Dragon to familiarize himself with. Steeped in tradition, he may not find change easy. However, despite some reservations, he will often have the chance to make greater use of his strengths. Also, when the inevitable teething problems occur or pressures arise, due to his experience, he will often have valuable suggestions to make. The work situation of some Water Dragons will be demanding during parts of the year, but there will be opportunities to make strengths count.

There will also be some Water Dragons who are keen to change their position, perhaps to one involving less of a commute or a different type of work. In both cases, the Monkey year may bring surprises. Very often, friends or contacts could alert the Water Dragon to an interesting new possibility. Many a Water Dragon will welcome the opportunities that open up in this Monkey year.

Quite a few Water Dragons have an enterprising streak and some may also decide to put a skill or interest to profitable use. Some could be attracted by new interests too. By being receptive to what the Monkey year can bring, the Water Dragon can derive considerable satisfaction from what he is able to do.

He will also appreciate the social opportunities that arise. In addition to meeting friends (and often valuing their thoughts), he could be attracted by several special events. His interests will also bring him into contact with others. May, August to early October and December could be particularly busy months, and for any Water Dragons who have had recent difficulty or sadness to contend with, there will be the chance to involve themselves in activities and get to know some like-minded people.

The Water Dragon has an adventurous nature and will welcome the travel opportunities this Monkey year will bring, including the chance to visit some awe-inspiring attractions. There can be an element of surprise connected with some trips, possibly with further invitations or other travel opportunities arising or the chance to visit additional places while away.

In money matters, the Water Dragon will, though, need to exercise care. He is likely to want to make some expensive purchases for his home as well as carry out other plans, and should keep a close watch on spending. This is a year for good financial management. He should also be vigilant when entering into agreements or attending to important paperwork. This is not a time for risk.

In his home life, this will be a busy and interesting year. In view of his changing work situation, there will be decisions to take, and good discussion will help. Major purchases for the home also need to be talked through. Initial plans may change, but the more that can be undertaken jointly, the better the outcome will be.

Shared interests, travel possibilities and the progress of younger family members can also delight the Water Dragon. In addition, a family member may surprise him with personal news. Monkey years have their memorable moments and July and August are likely to be especially active months.

In general, the Water Dragon will be kept busy throughout the Monkey year. For many, there will be important work decisions to take. This is an encouraging year for personal interests, and activities pursued or taken up now can prove satisfying and have potential future benefit. Money matters will need careful attention, but with the goodwill the Water Dragon enjoys, he will have the support of those around him. To benefit fully, he does need to be forthcoming and watch his sometimes independent tendencies, and a more flexible approach would not come amiss either. But overall this is an interesting and personally rewarding year for the Water Dragon.

Tip for the Year

Consult others and be mindful of their views. Their support can make an important difference to how you fare. The Monkey year can bring unexpected chances and choices. To benefit, be flexible. Time spent on interests and recreational pursuits can also be rewarding.

The Wood Dragon

One of the talents of the Wood Dragon is that he is alert and aware. He reads situations and people well and his abilities will stand him in good stead this year. There will be quite a few encouraging developments, and by being aware of things in the offing, the Wood Dragon will often be well positioned to act.

In his work the year can see substantial change. Colleagues he has worked with for many years could move on and in the process create promotion opportunities. In these instances, the Wood Dragon should be quick to signify interest. Some Wood Dragons will now secure responsibilities they have been working towards for some time. Also, other changes can occur. Sometimes developments within the Wood Dragon's industry or reviews conducted by his employer will lead to changes being introduced. Again, the Wood Dragon will often be able to benefit, perhaps by being offered a substantial change in responsibility or becoming involved in new initiatives. The emphasis this year is on moving forward.

Throughout the year the Wood Dragon's prospects will also be helped by the good working relations he has with his colleagues and the reputation he has built up. He should make the most of any networking opportunities, as the contact he has with others can be an important factor in the headway he makes.

Although the majority of Wood Dragons will make good progress with their present employer, some will feel the time is right for a fresh challenge. These Wood Dragons, and those seeking work, should keep themselves informed of employment developments in their area. This way, they may be alerted to positions that have just become available and, by responding quickly, could secure an opening that offers the chance to develop their skills in other ways.

Many Wood Dragons can look forward to an increase in income over the year, but they will need to manage their finances with care. With ongoing domestic commitments and probably some expensive purchases, the Wood Dragon's outgoings will be considerable. Where possible, he should budget in advance for forthcoming expenses. This is a year for discipline and good management. Also, paperwork will require care and attention. Lapses or rush could lead to problems. Wood Dragons, take note.

One of the Wood Dragon's strengths is his curious nature and over the year he could be intrigued by a new recreational pursuit or subject he hears about. By setting time aside to follow it up, he could find himself enjoying the chance to learn something new. In addition, he could have several ideas he is keen to take further. This can be an often stimulating and rewarding time.

There will be a good social element to some activities, and for Wood Dragons interested in music or sport, there could be several events they will particularly appreciate. Those who are keen to meet others could find a local group worth joining. May, late July to early October and December could see many social opportunities.

The Wood Dragon's domestic life will also see much activity and there may be major occasions to look forward to – perhaps an engagement, wedding, birth, work success or personal milestone. At such times the Wood Dragon will not only feel proud but also play an important part in organizing the celebrations. The Monkey year will, for many, contain special times, with the spring and late summer often busy and lively.

With all the commitments the Wood Dragon and other family members have, it is, though, important that there is good co-operation throughout the year and that quality time together does not suffer. Shared projects and interests can be particularly appreciated, and if possible, a holiday or other break together can also do everyone good.

Overall, this can be a successful year for the Wood Dragon, particularly as there will be chances to develop his work situation and personal interests. By keeping alert and making the most of his ideas and opportunities, he will be pleased with the often interesting challenges that open up. He will be helped by the good relations he enjoys with those around him and the support they offer. Money matters will require careful attention and, with many demands on his time, it is important he strives for a good lifestyle balance, but he can make this a full and personally rewarding year.

Tip for the Year

Be alert and if an idea or tempting opportunity arises, be quick to follow it up. Time is of the essence this year. Liaise well with others and value time with those who are special to you. Your relations with others can be important and meaningful. Treasure them.

The Fire Dragon

As the Fire Dragon enters his fortieth year he will be keen to make it a special one. And it can be. Resolute, determined and with a desire to move forward, the Fire Dragon will regard this as a year for action and he will often be helped by circumstances. There will be instances this year when he will find himself in the right place at the right time and benefiting from moments of good fortune. He will have much on his side – but there is a 'but'. While he will enjoy his successes, he must not push his luck too far. Monkey years are encouraging, but can trip up the unwary. The Fire Dragon also needs to be mindful of the views of others. As a Dragon, he may like to set his own course and keep his thoughts close to his chest, but this is a year to work with others and pay attention to those all-important relationships.

In his work, events can occur suddenly. Staff movements or absences could create vacancies to be filled, responsibilities to be taken on and promotion to be gained. By responding quickly, the Fire Dragon could find his in-house knowledge placing him in a strong position to benefit. Even if he has not been in his present position for too long, there will often be scope this year to take his career to a new level.

Colleagues, especially those more senior to him, may also help his career along. In some cases they may arrange training and/or make it possible for him to broaden his role, and by making the most of his opportunities, he will be preparing himself for more substantial progress in the near future. A lot will happen for a reason this year and the Fire Dragon's commitment can see him reaping some important and timely rewards.

With the aspects as they are, he should also work closely with others as well as seize any chances to network. His skills and personable nature will impress many, and for Fire Dragons contemplating change, their reputation and contacts can be important factors in their progress.

There will also be some Fire Dragons who will feel ready for a more substantial career challenge and will be looking for positions which offer greater scope. For these Fire Dragons, and those seeking work, the Monkey year can open up interesting possibilities. By keeping alert for vacancies and considering what they would now like to do (here employment advisers can be helpful), quite a few will find an opening offering the very chance they desire. For some, there could be a lot of learning involved and the early weeks could be challenging, but the Monkey year will allow many Fire Dragons to prove themselves in a different capacity. Such are the aspects that those who take on new duties early on in the year could be offered additional responsibilities later on. April, May, September and November could see encouraging work developments.

The progress enjoyed by many Fire Dragons at work will lead to an increase in income, but this is nevertheless a year for care and vigilance. With some ambitious plans, including travel, the Fire Dragon's outgoings will be considerable and he will need to budget ahead for future requirements. Also, when attending to forms or any kind of financial paperwork, he should check the facts and be thorough. Risks or oversights could work to his disadvantage. Fire Monkeys, take note.

The Fire Dragon has a curious nature and with this being his fortieth year, he may well feel like starting something new. Whether taking up a different interest, starting a fitness discipline or setting himself a new personal aim, he will often feel energized and inspired by what he decides on. For any Fire Dragons who have let their interests lapse or do not have a particularly balanced lifestyle, now is the time to address this and set time aside for themselves.

The Fire Dragon will also value the support of his friends, especially as some will have first-hand experience that may help him with his activities and decisions. The input of others can be important this year.

In addition, the Fire Dragon will enjoy the social opportunities of the year, including some celebrations that may be held in his honour. For the unattached, romantic possibilities could also await. On a personal level, this Monkey year can be a special one, with May, late July to early October and December seeing much social activity.

The Fire Dragon's domestic life will also see a great deal happen this year. Loved ones will often be keen to mark his fortieth year and some surprises will be particularly delightful. There could also be the chance to enjoy a special holiday.

Amid the activity, there will also be plans to see through and decisions to take. The more these can be agreed jointly, the better. With good co-operation, some ambitious household projects can be advanced.

Overall, the Fire Dragon's fortieth year will be an important one and encourage him not only to develop his career but also to enjoy and make more of his skills. Personal interests can be fulfilling and the Fire Dragon will also delight in the special occasions that take place, including some surprises that have been lined up for him. Travel, too, is favourably aspected. The Fire Dragon's domestic life will be busy and frequently gratifying, although he will need to control his budget and avoid risk. The Fire Dragon is ambitious and likes to make the most of his opportunities, and this year his efforts can not only bring rewards now but, significantly, pave the way for the success that awaits in his new decade.

Tip for the Year
Seek support and share activities. With backing and goodwill, so much more can be achieved. Also, give time to yourself, pursue your interests and explore your ideas. Monkey years encourage personal and professional development.

The Earth Dragon

The Earth Dragon has a keen and enquiring nature. He is also open-minded, and when he sees something of potential interest, he is prepared to find out more. His ability to adapt and embrace change will serve him particularly well this year.

At work, many an Earth Dragon will be facing important new developments. Not only could staff movements and new initiatives lead to openings arising, but for those in large organizations, tempting vacancies could arise in other sections and locations. As a result, the Monkey year can bring some excellent opportunities, and with the experience many Earth Dragons have behind them, they will be strong and often successful candidates. To help their progress, these Earth Dragons should take advantage of any training that may be offered and use any chances to network. Extra effort can reap dividends, both now and in the near future. In addition, new duties can highlight particular strengths and help influence the Earth Dragon's future career direction.

There will also be some Earth Dragons who feel their situation will be helped by moving to another employer. Again, their contacts can be helpful, either in alerting them to possible openings, putting in a good word on their behalf or offering timely advice.

The aspects are also encouraging for Earth Dragons seeking work. By widening the nature of their search, many could secure an opening offering the chance to use their skills in new ways. What happens this year can have future significance and April, May, September and November could see encouraging developments.

Financially, although his income may well increase, the Earth Dragon will have many commitments as well as be involved in some large transactions over the year, especially regarding equipment. At all times he will need to be thorough, checking facts, seeking advice when appropriate and being aware of any obligations he may be taking on. This is no time for risk.

With his bright and alert nature, the Earth Dragon is, however, likely to enjoy a good mix of different activities over the year. New ideas could capture his imagination and for those who are sedentary for much of the day, physical activities, including those with a keep-fit element, may be worth considering.

In many of his activities, the Earth Dragon will enjoy the support of those around him. With friends often in similar situations to his own, he will value his chances to meet up with them and exchange thoughts. A close friend could be especially helpful if he has an important personal decision to make. New activities and situations can also introduce the Earth Dragon to others, and for the unattached, the year may see a transformation in their situation with what could be a very special romance. For those currently in love, marriage may beckon. On a personal and social level, this can be a pleasing year, with May, late July to early October and December seeing the most activity.

For Earth Dragons with a partner, the Monkey year will also see important developments. With hopes and plans for themselves and their home, these Earth Dragons will explore many ideas and carry out many plans, although where large outlay is concerned, these need to be carefully considered and budgeted for. In addition, while enthusiastic, the Earth Dragon should avoid involving himself in too many projects all at once. To overcommit himself could add pressure and sometimes lead to less satisfactory results.

It is also important that the Earth Dragon shares any matters that are on his mind. Monkey years favour joint approaches. He may also find it helpful to draw on the expertise of senior relations. Throughout the year, it is important he involves others rather than keeps matters (and anxieties) to himself.

The Monkey year has an element of spontaneity about it and the Earth Dragon may have unexpected opportunities to travel or attend social occasions. Again, he should be alert and prepared to take advantage of what becomes possible.

In general, the Monkey year will offer the Earth Dragon the chance to develop himself and his situation. His prospects are good, but he needs to seize the moment and make the most of the opportunities that arise. Throughout the year he also needs to liaise well with others and be involved in what is going on around him. This is no year to be too independent in approach. However, the Earth Dragon's ideas can develop well and his enthusiastic nature will help many of his activities. Although he will need to exercise care in money matters, on a personal level, the strong relationships many Earth Dragons enjoy will help make this a fulfilling and potentially successful year.

Tip for the Year
Be open to possibility. As ideas occur and situations open up, there is scope for growth. Make the most of it, for important benefits can follow on, both now and in the near future.

Famous Dragons

Adele, Maya Angelou, Jeffrey Archer, Joan Armatrading, Joan Baez, Count Basie, Maeve Binchy, Sandra Bullock, Michael Cera, Courteney Cox, Bing Crosby, Russell Crowe, Benedict Cumberbatch, Roald Dahl, Salvador Dali, Charles Darwin, Neil Diamond, Bo Diddley, Matt Dillon, Christian Dior, Placido Domingo, Fats Domino, Dan Fogler, Sir Bruce Forsyth, Sigmund Freud, Rupert Grint, Che Guevara, James Herriot, Paul Hogan, Joan of Arc, Boris Johnson, Sir Tom Jones, Immanuel Kant, Martin Luther King, John Lennon, Abraham Lincoln, Elle MacPherson, Michael McIntyre, Hilary Mantel, Queen Margrethe II of Denmark, Liam Neeson, Florence Nightingale, Nick Nolte, Sharon Osbourne, Al Pacino, Pelé, Edgar Allan Poe, Vladimir Putin, Nikki Reed, Keanu Reeves, Ryan Reynolds, Sir Cliff Richard, Rihanna, Shakira, George Bernard Shaw, Martin Sheen, Blake Shelton, Alicia Silverstone, Ringo Starr, Karlheinz Stockhausen, Emma Stone, George Strait, Shirley Temple, Maria von Trapp, Louis Walsh, Andy Warhol, Mark Webber, the Earl of Wessex, Mae West, Sam Worthington.

23 January 1917 to 10 February 1918 — *Fire Snake*

10 February 1929 to 29 January 1930 — *Earth Snake*

27 January 1941 to 14 February 1942 — *Metal Snake*

14 February 1953 to 2 February 1954 — *Water Snake*

2 February 1965 to 20 January 1966 — *Wood Snake*

18 February 1977 to 6 February 1978 — *Fire Snake*

6 February 1989 to 26 January 1990 — *Earth Snake*

24 January 2001 to 11 February 2002 — *Metal Snake*

10 February 2013 to 30 January 2014 — *Water Snake*

The Snake

The Personality of the Snake

I think
And think some more.
About what is,
About what can be,
About what may be.
And when I am ready,
Then I act.

The Snake is born under the sign of wisdom. He is highly intelligent and his mind is forever active. He is always planning and always looking for ways in which he can use his considerable skills. He is a deep thinker and likes to meditate and reflect.

Many times during his life he will shed one of his famous Snake skins and take up new interests or start a completely different job. The Snake enjoys a challenge and he rarely makes mistakes. He is a skilful organizer, has considerable business acumen and is usually lucky in money matters. Most Snakes are financially secure in their later years, provided they do not gamble – the Snake has the distinction of being the worst gambler in the whole of the Chinese zodiac!

The Snake generally has a calm and placid nature and prefers the quieter things in life. He does not like to be in a frenzied atmosphere and hates being hurried into making a quick decision. He also does not like interference in his affairs and tends to rely on his own judgement rather than listen to advice.

At times the Snake can appear solitary. He is quiet, reserved and sometimes has difficulty in communicating with others. He has little time for idle gossip and will certainly not suffer fools gladly. He does, however, have a good sense of humour and this is particularly appreciated in times of crisis.

The Snake is certainly not afraid of hard work and is thorough in all that he does. He is very determined and can occasionally be ruthless in order to achieve his aims. His confidence, willpower and quick thinking usually ensure his success, but should he fail it will often take a long time for him to recover. He cannot bear failure and is a very bad loser.

The Snake can also be evasive and does not willingly let people into his confidence. This secrecy and distrust can sometimes work against him and these are traits that all Snakes should try to overcome.

Another characteristic of the Snake is his tendency to rest after any sudden or prolonged bout of activity. He burns up so much nervous energy that he can, if he is not careful, be susceptible to high blood pressure and nervous disorders.

It has sometimes been said that the Snake is a late starter in life and this is mainly because it often takes him a while to find a job in which he is genuinely happy. However, he will usually do well in any position that involves research and writing and where he is given sufficient freedom to develop his own ideas and plans. He makes a good teacher, politician, personnel manager and social adviser.

The Snake chooses his friends carefully and while he keeps a tight control over his finances, he can be particularly generous to those he likes. He will think nothing of buying expensive gifts or treating his friends or loved ones to the best theatre seats in town. In return, he demands loyalty. The Snake is very possessive and can become extremely jealous and hurt if he finds his trust has been abused.

The Snake is also renowned for his good looks and is never short of admirers. The female Snake in particular is most alluring. She has style, grace and excellent (and usually expensive) taste in clothes. A keen socializer, she is likely to have a wide range of friends and the happy knack of impressing those who matter. She has numerous interests and her opinions are often highly valued. She is generally a calm person and while she involves herself in many activities, she likes to retain a certain amount of privacy in her undertakings.

Affairs of the heart are very important to the Snake and he will often have many romances before he finally settles down. He will find that he is particularly well suited to those born under the signs of the Ox, Dragon, Rabbit and Rooster. Provided he is allowed sufficient freedom to pursue his own interests, he can also build up a very satisfactory relationship with the Rat, Horse, Goat, Monkey and Dog, but he should try to steer clear of another Snake as they could very easily become jealous of each other. The Snake will also have difficulty in getting on with the honest and down-to-earth Pig and will find the Tiger far too much of a disruptive influence on his quiet and peace-loving ways.

The Snake certainly appreciates the finer things in life. He enjoys good food and often takes a keen interest in the arts. He also enjoys reading and is invariably drawn to subjects such as philosophy, political thought, religion or the occult. He is fascinated by the unknown and his enquiring mind is always looking for answers. Some of the world's most original thinkers have been Snakes, and although he may not readily admit it, the Snake relies a lot on intuition and is often psychic.

The Snake is certainly not the most energetic member of the Chinese zodiac. He prefers to proceed at his own pace and to do what he wants. He is very much his own master and throughout his life he will try his hand at many things. He is something of a dabbler, but at some time – usually when he least expects it – his efforts and hard work will be recognized and he will invariably meet with the success and the financial security he so desires.

The Five Different Types of Snake

In addition to the 12 signs of the Chinese zodiac there are five elements and these have a strengthening or moderating influence on the signs. The effects of the elements on the Snake are described below, together with the years in which they were exercising their influence. Therefore Snakes born in 1941 and 2001 are Metal Snakes, Snakes born in 1953 and 2013 are Water Snakes, and so on.

Metal Snake: 1941, 2001

This Snake is quiet, confident and fiercely independent. He often prefers to work on his own and will only let a privileged few into his confidence. He is quick to spot opportunities and will set about achieving his objectives with an awesome determination. He is astute in financial matters and will often invest his money well. He has a liking for the finer things in life and a good appreciation of the arts, literature, music and food. He usually has a small group of extremely good friends and can be generous to his loved ones.

Water Snake: 1953, 2013

This Snake has a wide variety of interests. He enjoys studying all manner of subjects and is capable of undertaking quite detailed research and becoming a specialist in his chosen area. He is highly intelligent, has a good memory and is particularly astute when dealing with business and financial matters. He tends to be quietly spoken and a little reserved, but he does have sufficient strength of character to make his views known and attain his ambitions. He is very loyal to his family and friends.

Wood Snake: 1965

The Wood Snake has a friendly temperament and a good understanding of human nature. He is able to communicate well and often has many friends and admirers. He is witty, intelligent and ambitious. He has numerous interests and prefers to live in a quiet, stable environment where he can work without too much interference. He enjoys the arts and usually derives much pleasure from collecting paintings and antiques. His advice is often highly valued, particularly on social and domestic matters.

Fire Snake: 1917, 1977

The Fire Snake tends to be more forceful, outgoing and energetic than some of the other types of Snake. He is ambitious, confident and never slow in voicing his opinions, and he can be very abrasive to those he does not like. He does, however, have many leadership qualities and can win the respect and support of many with his firm and resolute manner. He usually has a good sense of humour, a wide circle of friends and a very active social life. He is also a keen traveller.

Earth Snake 1929, 1989

The Earth Snake is charming, amusing and has a very amiable manner. He is conscientious and reliable in his work and approaches everything he does in a level-headed and sensible way. He can, however, tend to err on the cautious side and never likes to be hassled into making a decision. He is adept in dealing with financial matters and is a shrewd investor. He has many friends and is very supportive towards the members of his family.

Prospects for the Snake in 2016

The Year of the Goat (19 February 2015–7 February 2016) will have been an interesting one for the Snake, and while it will have contained some frustrating times, he will still have been able to accomplish a great deal. His fortunes will continue fair for the remaining months.

One characteristic of the Goat year is that it is no respecter of plans. Changes can suddenly occur, activities get interrupted or new possibilities come into the equation. And so it will be for the Snake. While there will be activities he would like to get on with, actually doing them could be more difficult. In the remaining months of the year, he will need to be flexible and adapt as required.

At work, new pressures could arise and there could be an increased workload. Some reprioritizing may be needed, but busy though the Snake may be, he can still achieve some notable results. September and November could be two particularly busy months.

Goat years encourage creative activity and Snakes who work in a creative environment or enjoy creative pursuits should make the most of their talents at this time. Many could receive an encouraging response. The Snake could also be fortunate in some purchases he makes towards the end of the year.

Domestically and socially, a lot is set to happen. There will be an element of spontaneity, too, and the Snake needs to be flexible over arrangements. Again, it is a case of making the most of what occurs.

However, this can be a full and interesting time. September and the end of the year could be particularly lively.

The Year of the Monkey begins on 8 February and will be a reasonable one for the Snake. Pleasing progress will be possible, but it is also a year for care. Risks and oversights could cause difficulty and the Snake should keep alert for problematic areas.

At work, the Monkey year will bring change. Although the thorough and careful Snake may be concerned with the speed of some developments, he also recognizes that change can mean opportunity. As a result, when openings arise which he feels could benefit him, he should not delay in putting himself forward. Time is of the essence in Monkey years.

The majority of Snakes will stay with their current employer over the year, though often with substantially different duties. Although this may be challenging, Monkey years can offer an incentive that can benefit many Snakes.

For those who feel their situation could be helped by a move elsewhere, as well as those seeking work, the year can often have fortuitous developments in store. By keeping alert, many Snakes could secure a position which offers the change they want as well as prospects for growth. Sometimes success could come on the back of a series of disappointments. Work-wise, the Monkey year is encouraging and will bring the chance for many Snakes to move their career forward. March, April, September and October could be significant months.

When taking on a new role, the Snake could also benefit from the training offered and the way his new duties allow him to extend his skills. To help his prospects, he should also consider other ways of furthering his knowledge. If there is a subject that appeals to him or a qualification he feels may be useful, he should set time aside to follow it up. What he does now can be an investment in his future.

Where personal interests are concerned, this can also be an inspiring time, with the Snake often being tempted to try something different.

However, while the year has its rewarding elements, it also has its more cautionary aspects. When setting about more demanding activities, the Snake does need to follow guidelines and not compromise personal safety. It is better to be safe than sorry. Ambitious travel plans could also be problematic, and if planning long journeys, the Snake needs to check the times and connections and go prepared.

More positively, the Snake's financial prospects indicate improvement. Progress made at work will increase the income of many Snakes and some will supplement their means through an enterprising idea or benefit from a gift. By managing his resources carefully, the Snake will be pleased with what he is able to do this year.

The Snake likes to keep his circle of friends relatively small and it takes him some time before he lowers his reserve in company. This year he will again appreciate the support offered by his good friends, but a disagreement or awkward situation could arise which could test a certain friendship. Care and diplomacy will be needed.

Tricky though some moments may be, the Monkey year will bring many pleasures. The Snake could particularly enjoy the variety of activities the year offers, and many who are unattached will also enjoy its romantic prospects. April, May, August and September will be busy and lively months.

Home life, too, will be busy, and with the Snake and those close to him often involved in a myriad of activities, it is important there is good communication. Preoccupation, pressure or tiredness could cause awkward moments. If the Snake has concerns at any time, these need to be acknowledged and talked through. Extra care and attention can make a considerable difference this year.

The Snake's domestic life will, however, also hold many rewards. Personal and family successes will be especially appreciated, as will shared interests and some of the year's more spontaneous occasions and treats. Projects on the home can go well, though these should not be rushed and should be carried out as time allows.

Overall, the Year of the Monkey will see a bewildering amount happen in the Snake's life. This is an excellent year for career and personal development, and skills acquired or developed now can help future prospects. Personal interests will also be satisfying, and finances are likely to improve, but extra care is advised in potentially hazardous activities. Where relations with others are concerned, this is a year for mindfulness, but fortunately the Snake is usually alert and will often be able to steer his way around the year's more awkward aspects. This will be a constructive time, but the Snake needs to be careful and prepared to act promptly and as situations demand.

The Metal Snake

This will be a satisfying year for the Metal Snake, although to get the best from it he will need to be flexible. This is no time for intransigence or being wedded to just one approach.

For the Metal Snake born in 1941, the Monkey year can see interesting developments, but he does need to be forthcoming and draw on the advice and assistance of others. Their input can not only set his plans in motion but often give a fillip to them as well.

Many Metal Snakes will be particularly grateful for assistance when making purchasing decisions, especially those of a more technical nature. By talking over requirements and getting advice, the Metal Snake will be able to make more appropriate choices. He could also derive great pleasure from more aesthetic items bought for his home. Over the year he could make some particularly delightful acquisitions, and Metal Snakes who collect specific items could find something that has eluded them for some time. The Metal Snake could be very fortunate in his purchases this year.

With his wide interests, he will also enjoy going out as well as appreciate what is available more locally, including amenities, places of interest or special events. Some Metal Snakes may also enjoy participating in their community, but whatever they choose to do, by keeping informed about what is happening, they can look forward to some agreeable times.

Travel, too, will be tempting, and while actual travelling may be tricky (delays could be a problem), the Metal Snake will enjoy his times away.

In his home life, good communication will again be important. If the Metal Snake talks over ideas he may be considering, projects he may like to get underway or concerns he may have, he can receive some good advice. Also, should he have a potentially hazardous or demanding task to carry out, he does need to exercise care, and ideally call on the services of a professional. This is no year to risk personal safety. Metal Snakes, take note.

Once again this year the Metal Snake will value ways he can reciprocate the kindness shown him by his loved ones. Whether giving time and support to family members or sharing in some of the year's special occasions (of which there can be several), he will find family bonds both important and meaningful. And the affection others have for him can often be underlined as he celebrates his seventy-fifth birthday.

The Metal Snake will also appreciate the year's social opportunities, but the Monkey year does have its trickier aspects and some Metal Snakes may be troubled by a difference of opinion or an awkward situation. Ideally, this should be addressed before it has a chance to escalate. Monkey years can spring traps for the unwary. Metal Snakes, again take note.

For Metal Snakes born in 2001, this will be a year of great possibility. With his eager nature, the young Metal Snake will be keen to try out a great many things. New and existing interests can develop well and the skills (and sometimes new equipment) gained can enable the Metal Snake to do more. He can also be inspired by the instruction available to him or the encouragement of family and friends. Personal interests can provide much pleasure this year and also perhaps some confidence-building.

However, while there is much fun can be had, where physical or potentially hazardous activities are involved, the Metal Snake does need to follow the recommended procedures. This is no year to be foolhardy or compromise his safety.

Also, throughout the year, he should take careful note of the views and advice of others. To be too self-willed could lead to problems. Should a friendship issue be of concern to him at any time, he should keep it in perspective and try to defuse any ill-feeling, lest it spoil an otherwise good year. Again, he should be prepared to consult others if necessary. Help and good advice are available.

In his education, the Metal Snake's commitment will be reflected in his progress. Particular strengths will be encouraged and some Metal Snakes will become particularly inspired by certain topics. Monkey years are encouraging, but to get the best results, the Metal Snake will need to apply himself.

Whether born in 1941 and 2001, the Metal Snake can make this a constructive year. However, it is not a time to act alone. Throughout, the Metal Snake should consult others and if any problems concern him, he should try to address these rather than ignore them and hope they go away. He should also take particular care when engaging in potentially hazardous activities. However, he will welcome the opportunities this Monkey year will bring.

Tip for the Year

Look to develop your interests, ideas and skills. This can be an inspiring time. However, do be aware of the views of others and participate in what is going on around you rather than remain independent.

The Water Snake

The Water Snake is creative in his thinking but he is also careful. He likes to proceed in his own way (and time), but in the Monkey year he could find himself buffeted by events and out of his comfort zone. Challenging though some parts of the year may be, he should take heart, for the winds of change will ultimately blow in his favour.

Almost all areas of the Water Snake's life will feel the effects of change this year, but his work position will be one of the most significant. Some Water Snakes will feel they have reached the stage where they want to do something different, either altering (or possibly reducing) their work commitments or taking on a fresh challenge. The Water Snake does not like to feel staid or restricted and will find that events can often work to his advantage this year. As personnel change and new initiatives are introduced, these fluid situations can provide the opening he wants. For some Water Snakes there could be option to retire or reduce their hours, while others will have opportunity to move to a more specialist role.

What occurs, and the speed with which some decisions have to be made, may not sit comfortably with the Water Snake, but Monkey years *are* fast-moving and he will have to respond accordingly. Such is the nature of Monkey years that decisions could be foisted on the Water Snake at almost any time, but March to early May, September and October could be particularly important months.

For Water Snakes who decide to leave their present employer, perhaps hoping for a position with more convenient hours or an easier commute, as well as those seeking work, the Monkey year may again bring surprises. Securing another position will not be easy, but by chance many could learn of a suitable opening, often in a different capacity.

With the decisions the Water Snake is likely to face, he will find it helpful to draw on the views of those around him. Not only will his loved ones encourage him and provide good advice, but some friends and colleagues (both present and former) could offer useful opinions as well as help him clarify his own preferences.

Decisions taken now can have financial implications, particularly for Water Snakes who retire or reduce their hours. However, many Water Snakes are adept in financial matters, and by managing their situation with care, they will often be satisfied with how they fare. For some, the Monkey year can bring unexpected extra funds, perhaps in the form of a gift, a profitable idea or, for a lucky few, a competition win.

Another area which can see encouraging developments this year is the Water Snake's interests. Monkey years are full of possibility and some Water Snakes will become enthused by a new project or idea. They can take this further by meeting up with others who share their interest and if there is a course, class or group in their area, it would be worth getting in contact. Many Water Snakes enjoy having an element of research in what they do (so satisfying their curiosity) and some may decide to delve into family or local history or visit places of interest this year. The Monkey year can open up an array of possibilities.

Travel will often be on the agenda too. Not only will the Water Snake be keen to arrange a holiday but, when time allows, will also enjoy shorter trips. The unexpectedness of some of these will add to their appeal. However, while the Water Snake will enjoy his time away, some of his journeys may be problematic. Water Snakes, take note and be prepared.

The Water Snake may know a lot of people, but he generally prefers to keep his social circle small. This year, while he will yet again value his close friends, a delicate situation could arise which concerns him. At such times, he will need to be cautious and think through the most appropriate response. The diplomacy of quite a few Water Snakes will be tested this year, and their sincerity and way with words will be valued.

Although the Monkey year may have its awkward moments, it will also contain many chances for the Water Snake to go out and enjoy himself. April, May and August to early October could be interesting times socially.

For Water Snakes who are enjoying newfound love or who would welcome the chance to meet someone special, the Monkey year could see exciting developments. For the unattached, affairs of the heart can play a big part in the year.

The Water Snake's home life will also see much activity. Again, while he likes to plan, situations can alter, requirements change and new possibilities arise, often at short notice, and he will need to adjust accordingly. Also, if a particular matter is worrying him, rather than keep his concerns to himself (and perhaps not be fully aware of the facts), he should consult others. The more open he is, the more easily the best outcomes can be agreed upon.

While there will be some busy and perhaps tricky times, there will also be a lot for the Water Snake to delight in. Shared interests will be particularly valued, as will some surprise occasions. Celebrations could be in order, with a special family birthday or anniversary to mark. The Monkey year will certainly have highlights that will make many Water Snakes proud.

Careful, thorough and thoughtful, the Water Snake may not always feel comfortable with the pace of the Monkey year. But by proceeding in the way he feels is right for him (the Water Snake relies a lot on instinct), he will often benefit from the changes it brings. Personal interests can be especially satisfying. There may also be matters of concern, and diplomacy, good advice and extra information may be required. But while the Monkey year will bring its challenges, many of the Water Snake's plans and activities will work out well. Overall, a year to be alert, adaptable and open to possibility.

Tip for the Year
Do not act alone. Be forthcoming about your plans and seek support. With assistance, you will be better able to benefit from the changes taking place. Also, allow time to develop your personal interests. These can be both satisfying and beneficial in other ways.

The Wood Snake

This will be a constructive year for the Wood Snake and will bring some moments of good fortune. However, it will not be without its difficulties. This year it is a case of proceeding steadily but carefully.

At work, many Wood Snakes will have experienced considerable change in recent years, and those who are relatively new to their present position should concentrate on familiarizing themselves with the different aspects of their work and getting themselves known. Effort and commitment can reap important benefits in the Monkey year. Some Wood Snakes, including those who change their duties early on in 2016, could have the chance to take on further responsibilities later on, such are the encouraging aspects.

Wood Snakes who are well established where they are will also often have the opportunity to take on a greater role. Admittedly, some of these Wood Snakes may not like the speed of the developments, but Monkey years are not ones for delay.

For Wood Snakes who are unfulfilled in their current position, as well as those seeking work, the Monkey year can also open up interesting possibilities. To benefit, these Wood Snakes should widen the scope of their search and look at different ways in which they could use their skills. If eligible, some may find refresher courses of value. By being active in their quest and swift in following up openings, many will secure the chance they have been hoping for. March to early May, September and October could be important months.

Progress at work may also assist financially, but to benefit fully, the Wood Snake should control spending and, where possible, set sums aside for his plans and projects. Good management can make a noticeable difference this year. Also, the Monkey year can have salutary reminders for the risk-taker and the careless. Official forms, in particular, require close attention, otherwise the Wood Snake may find himself involved in protracted correspondence. Vigilance is advised.

The Wood Snake has an inquisitive mind and with this being a time of new ideas and exciting product launches, he may well become fascinated by innovations taking place or products becoming available. The more inventive Wood Snake could also be inspired by his own ideas in this stimulating year.

There will also be good opportunities for the Wood Snake to travel this year, and sometimes his work and key interests can also lead to additional trips. But while he can look forward to seeing some impressive sights, some journeys may be problematic. To help, the Wood Snake should go well-prepared and thoroughly check his connections, travel times and itinerary.

Another awkward aspect of the year could concern relations with a friend. Sometimes a comment may be misconstrued or an uncomfortable matter surface. At such times the Wood Snake should try to deal with the situation before it has the chance to escalate. Often a willingness to talk will help, although should he feel in need of more information or advice, he should ask someone who is competent to advise. There could be challenging moments this year, but with good judgement and support, most difficulties can be satisfactorily settled.

While the aspects do call for mindfulness and care, the Monkey year can also give rise to many interesting social occasions. Special events, parties and other get-togethers can all bring lively times for the Wood Snake. Late March to the end of May and August to early October could be busy months and, for the unattached, a current or new romance (sometimes started in bizarre circumstances) could add special joy to this already full year.

The Wood Snake's domestic life will also see much activity. Some weeks will be pressured, particularly when news is awaited concerning certain decisions and applications, and amid the activity, it is important that quality time is not neglected. Here the Wood Snake's ability to suggest joint activities can add pleasure and variety to family life. July and September could see considerable domestic activity, with good news or a celebration possible.

Overall, the Year of the Monkey will be a satisfying one for the Wood Snake, although he will need to be active, flexible and involved. If he responds swiftly to changes, he can not only gain a lot from what opens up but also develop his knowledge and skills. Current and new interests can also bring pleasure. Throughout, the Wood Snake will need to be mindful of others and an uncharacteristic indiscretion or niggling concern may cause difficulty. With awareness and his usual good judgement, however, he may steer his way round the year's trickier aspects and find greater fulfilment in what he does.

Tip for the Year
Be thorough and put in the effort. With commitment, you can make useful progress. Also, embrace the spirit of the time and the changes it brings. Benefits can often follow on.

The Fire Snake

As the Monkey year begins, if not shortly before, the Fire Snake will sense this is a time for action. And in almost all areas of his life, he will enjoy positive developments. Throughout the year, however, he must not push his luck too far. To overreach himself or become too preoccupied with one area of his life at the expense of another could lead to difficulty. Good balance will be key.

At work, in particular, this is no year to stand still. Although many Fire Snakes will be established in a particular role, they should consider how they would like their career to develop. To help this process, they should make the most of any training available to them. Similarly, if there is the chance to cover for an absent colleague, take an attachment in another section or contribute to a particular initiative, by expressing interest, they can not only add to their experience but also increase their options for later. If they are quick to act, many can make important headway and take their work to new levels. Some Fire Snakes will also substantially change the nature of what they do over the year. The Monkey year will, for many, provide the opportunities they have been working towards for some time.

For Fire Snakes who are feeling unfulfilled where they are, as well as those seeking work, the Monkey year can be a time of reappraisal. These Fire Snakes should consider the direction they would now like their career to take. By keeping alert for openings, many will obtain a position which offers the chance (and incentive) they need. Positions taken on this year can often be a springboard to greater responsibilities later on, and March to early May, September and October could see encouraging developments, but whenever the Fire Snake sees an opportunity he should act swiftly.

The progress many Fire Snakes make at work will help financially and some could also benefit from a profitable idea or interest. Anything extra can help with current commitments as well as enable some important plans to go ahead. In some instances, the Fire Snake could obtain items on very favourable terms, and by keeping alert for offers and investigating options, he will fare well. With important paperwork, though, he will need to be thorough and organized. If he is lax or careless, problems may ensue. Monkey years do require vigilance.

They also promote the development of both work skills and personal interests. Although the Fire Snake will have many commitments, over the year he should set time aside for interests he enjoys. Many Fire Snakes could be attracted by new recreational pursuits, some with a keep-fit element, while for the creative-minded, some ideas could develop in exciting fashion.

The Fire Snake also enjoys travel and during the year his spirit of adventure could be satisfied by visiting places new. However, there may be problems along the way and he should go prepared.

This need for care also applies to social situations. While the Fire Snake enjoys a variety of pursuits and gets on well with many people, he could find a friendship coming under strain this year. It may be that commitments prevent regular contact or interests clash. Something that may seem minor could escalate and be folly to ignore. Fire Snakes, take note, and do not take friendships for granted.

However, while care is needed, the Fire Snake will enjoy numerous social occasions. His interests can often have a good social element and work changes too can lead to him making important new friends and connections. April, May and August to early October could be favourable months socially and for some Fire Snakes who start the year unattached, romance is capable of transforming their situation, with some marrying or settling down over the year.

The Fire Snake's domestic life will see considerable activity and again his ambitious nature can come to the fore. Whether installing new equipment, redecorating and refurbishing certain rooms or, for a few, moving to more suitable accommodation, the Fire Snake will be keen to get his plans underway. Circumstances and the support of others will often help, but with ambitious undertakings the Fire Snake does need to be thorough, consult others and avoid rush.

In addition, he should ensure there is a respite from all the activity now and again. Quality time with his loved ones can be of particular value. Also, as certain hopes are realized, there will be some well-deserved achievements to celebrate. Domestically, April and October could be special months.

Overall, the Monkey year offers great scope for the Fire Snake. By being determined to make things happen and putting in the effort, he will find results quickly following on. This is also an excellent time for furthering his skills. As he recognizes, a lot of his success depends on him, and this year he can invest in himself and his future.

Tip for the Year
Be thorough and use your time well. Avoid over-committing yourself or taking unnecessary risks. With care, this can be a successful and rewarding year. Also, give time to others. With encouragement and support, you can accomplish much more.

The Earth Snake

Monkey years are times of great activity. They are also times of innovation and opportunity. The Earth Snake can profit greatly from much that happens in this one. As he will find, once plans are set in motion, circumstances will often assist. However, as with all Snakes, the Earth Snake must be careful not to make assumptions or push his luck too far. This can be a positive year, but it is also one for care.

At work, the Earth Snake is likely to see much change. Personnel may suddenly move on and new ways of working be introduced. There may be uncertainty and increased pressure, but by concentrating on his duties, the Earth Snake will be able to move ahead. By liaising well with others and showing initiative, he could find himself being encouraged by influential colleagues and trained for a greater role. With commitment and support, significant headway can be made now, and as one door opens, it will often lead on to others.

For Earth Snakes who consider their prospects could be bettered by moving elsewhere, as well as those seeking work, the Monkey year can bring some interesting opportunities. In their quest, these Earth Snakes should talk to employment advisers and may also find it helpful to get information from professional bodies. Initiative and support can be important factors this year. Once in a new position, these Earth Snakes will often revel in the chance to put their skills to more effective use. March to early May, September and October could see encouraging developments.

The headway made at work can lead to an increase in income and some Earth Snakes will also benefit from a bonus, extra payment or gift. However, while this may be an improved year financially, with many commitments and some major purchases lined up, the Earth Snake will need to keep good control over his budget. That way, he will find many of his plans and purchases can go ahead and special times can be enjoyed.

The Monkey year is an excellent one for enjoying personal interests and for the creative Earth Snake, this can be an inspiring time. Any Earth Snakes who have aspirations to make more of a particular talent or interest could find that by experimenting and doing more, new possibilities could open up for them.

Affairs of the heart are also encouragingly aspected. For some Earth Snakes, engagement, marriage and settling down will beckon, while for the unattached, a new person may fortuitously enter their life. For personal relationships, this can be a special and potentially exciting year.

For Earth Snakes with a partner, a lot is set to happen. Some ambitious accommodation ideas can – with effort – be realized, and mutual support and encouragement can be significant. This is a year for being receptive to what others may suggest or offer to do, including more senior relations.

The Earth Snake will also welcome the social opportunities of the year and will have the chance to get to know new people. Many will respond well to his sincere and genial manner and some can, in time, become good friends. Late March to the end of April and August to early October could see a lot of social activity. However, while much will go well, should the Earth Snake find a difference of opinion or awkward matter arising, he needs to check the facts and think his responses through. The personal skills of quite a few Earth Snakes will be tested this year and some situations (though often short-lived) will be troubling.

Another area which could be problematic is travel. Some journeys could be subject to delays and other disruption. However, despite these possible irritations, many Earth Snakes will enjoy their trips and holidays and benefit from the change of scene.

Overall, the Year of the Monkey will be a busy and interesting one for the Earth Snake. There will be ideas to build upon and chances to pursue. The year will require effort and some situations will be demanding, but with good use of skills and willingness to act, progress can be made and success enjoyed, and on a personal level, the Monkey year can be special. Though it requires commitment and initiative, this is a year of possibility.

Tip for the Year

Be mindful. Much is possible this year, but take note of the views of others. With care and your usual good sense, however, you can take your work, skills and interests to new levels. Also, value your relations with those who are close to you. Their support and belief can help you make more of your potential.

Famous Snakes

Jason Aldean, Muhammad Ali, Ann-Margret, Avicii, Kim Basinger, Ben Bernanke, Björk, Tony Blair, Michael Bloomberg, Michael Bolton, Brahms, Pierce Brosnan, Mark Carney, Casanova, Jackie Collins, Tom Conti, Cecil B. de Mille, Robert Downey Jr, Bob Dylan, Elgar, Michael Fassbender, Sir Alexander Fleming, Mahatma Gandhi, Greta Garbo, Art Garfunkel, J. Paul Getty, W. E. Gladstone, Johann Wolfgang von Goethe, Princess Grace of Monaco, Tom Hardy, Stephen Hawking, Audrey Hepburn, Jack Higgins, Elizabeth Hurley, Dakota Johnson, James Joyce, Stacy Keach, Ronan Keating, J. F. Kennedy, Chaka Khan, Carole King, Rory McIlroy, Mao Tse-tung, Chris Martin, Henri Matisse, John Mayer, Piers Morgan, Alfred Nobel, Mike Oldfield, Jacqueline Onassis, Hayden Panettiere, Sarah Jessica Parker, Pablo Picasso, Daniel Radcliffe, Franklin D. Roosevelt, J. K. Rowling, Jean-Paul Sartre, Franz Schubert, Charlie Sheen, Paul Simon, Delia Smith, Ben Stiller, Taylor Swift, Juno Temple, Madame Tussaud, Shania Twain, Dionne Warwick, Mia Wasikowska, Charlie Watts, Kanye West, Oprah Winfrey.

11 February 1918 to 31 January 1919 — *Earth Horse*

30 January 1930 to 16 February 1931 — *Metal Horse*

15 February 1942 to 4 February 1943 — *Water Horse*

3 February 1954 to 23 January 1955 — *Wood Horse*

21 January 1966 to 8 February 1967 — *Fire Horse*

7 February 1978 to 27 January 1979 — *Earth Horse*

27 January 1990 to 14 February 1991 — *Metal Horse*

12 February 2002 to 31 January 2003 — *Water Horse*

31 January 2014 to 18 February 2015 — *Wood Horse*

The Horse

The Personality of the Horse

There are many worn paths,
but the most rewarding
is the one you decide on and forge yourself.

The Horse is born under the signs of elegance and ardour. He has a most engaging and charming manner and is usually very popular. He loves meeting people and likes attending parties and other large social gatherings.

The Horse is a lively character and enjoys being the centre of attention. He has many leadership qualities and is much admired for his honest and straightforward manner. He is an eloquent and persuasive speaker and has a great love of discussion and debate. He also has a particularly agile mind and can assimilate facts remarkably quickly.

He does, however, have a fiery temper and although his outbursts are usually short-lived, he can often say things that he will later regret. He is also not particularly good at keeping secrets.

The Horse has many interests and involves himself in a wide variety of activities. He can, however, get involved in so much that he can often waste his energies on projects that he never has time to complete. He also has a tendency to change his interests rather frequently and will often get caught up in the latest craze or 'in thing' until something more exciting turns up.

The Horse also likes to have a certain amount of freedom and independence. He hates being bound by petty rules and regulations and as far as possible likes to feel that he is answerable to no one but himself. But despite this spirit of freedom, he still likes to have the support and encouragement of others in his various enterprises.

Due to his many talents and likeable nature, the Horse will often go far in life. He enjoys challenges and is a methodical and tireless worker. However, should things go against him and he fail in any of his enterprises, it will take a long time for him to recover and pick up the pieces again. Success to the Horse means everything. To fail is a disaster and a humiliation.

The Horse likes to have variety in life and will try his hand at many different things before he settles down to one particular job. Even then, he will probably remain alert to see whether there are any better opportunities for him to take up. He has a restless nature and can easily get bored. He does, however, excel in any position that allows him sufficient freedom to act on his own initiative or brings him into contact with a lot of people.

Although the Horse is not particularly bothered about accumulating great wealth, he handles his finances with care and will rarely experience any serious financial problems.

The Horse also enjoys travel and loves visiting new and faraway places. At some stage during his life he will be tempted to live abroad for a short period of time and due to his adaptable nature will find that he will fit in well wherever he goes.

The Horse pays a great deal of attention to his appearance and usually likes to wear smart, colourful and rather distinctive clothes. He is very attractive to others and will often have many romances before he settles down. He is loyal and protective to his partner, but despite his family commitments he still likes to retain a certain measure of independence and have the freedom to carry on with his own interests and hobbies. He will find that he is especially suited to those born under the signs of the Tiger, Goat, Rooster and Dog. He can also get on well with the Rabbit, Dragon, Snake, Pig and another Horse, but he will find the Ox too serious and intolerant for his liking. He will also have difficulty in getting on with the Monkey and the Rat – the Monkey is very inquisitive and the Rat seeks security, and both will resent the Horse's rather independent ways.

The female Horse is usually most attractive and has a friendly, outgoing personality. She is highly intelligent, has many interests and is alert to everything that is going on around her. She particularly enjoys outdoor pursuits and often likes to take part in sport and keep-fit activities. She also enjoys travel, literature and the arts, and is a very good conversationalist.

Although the Horse can be stubborn and rather self-centred, he does have a considerate nature and is often willing to help others. He has a good sense of humour and will usually make a favourable impression wherever he goes. Provided he can curb his slightly restless nature and keep tight control over his temper, he will go through life making friends, taking part in a multitude of different activities and generally achieving many of his objectives. His life will rarely be dull.

The Five Different Types of Horse

In addition to the 12 signs of the Chinese zodiac there are five elements and these have a strengthening or moderating influence on the signs. The effects of the elements on the Horse are described below, together with the years in which they were exercising their influence. Therefore Horses born in 1930 and 1990 are Metal Horses, Horses born in 1942 and 2002 are Water Horses, and so on.

Metal Horse: 1930, 1990

This Horse is bold, confident and forthright. He is ambitious and a great innovator. He loves challenges and takes great delight in sorting out complicated problems. He likes to have a certain amount of independence and resents any outside interference in his affairs. He has charm and a certain charisma, but he can also be very stubborn and rather impulsive. He usually has many friends and enjoys an active social life.

Water Horse: 1942, 2002

The Water Horse has a friendly nature and a good sense of humour and is able to talk intelligently on a wide range of topics. He is astute in business matters and quick to take advantage of any opportunities that arise. He does, however, have a tendency to get easily distracted and can change his interests – and indeed his mind – rather frequently, and this can often work to his detriment. He is nevertheless very talented and can often go far in life. He pays a great deal of attention to his appearance and is usually smart and well turned out. He loves to travel and also enjoys sport and other outdoor activities.

Wood Horse: 1954, 2014

The Wood Horse has a most agreeable and amiable nature. He communicates well with others and is able to talk intelligently on many different subjects. He is a hard and conscientious worker and is held in high esteem by his friends and colleagues. His opinions are often sought and, given his imaginative nature, he can often come up with some very original and practical ideas. He is usually widely read and likes to lead a busy social life. He can also be most generous and often holds high moral views.

Fire Horse: 1966

The element of Fire combined with the temperament of the Horse creates one of the most powerful forces in the Chinese zodiac. The Fire Horse is destined to lead an exciting and eventful life and to make his mark on his chosen profession. He has a forceful personality and his intelligence and resolute manner bring him the support and admiration of many. He loves action and excitement and his life will rarely be quiet. He can, however, be rather blunt and forthright in his views and does not take kindly to interference in his own affairs or to obeying orders. He is a flamboyant character, has a good sense of humour and will lead a very active social life.

Earth Horse: 1918, 1978

This Horse is considerate and caring. He is more cautious than some of the other types of Horse, but is wise, perceptive and extremely capable. Although he can be rather indecisive at times, he has considerable business acumen and is very astute in financial matters. He has a quiet, friendly nature and is well thought of by his family and friends.

Prospects for the Horse in 2016

The Horse has a talent for using his time well and in the Goat year (19 February 2015–7 February 2016) he will have had the opportunity to do a considerable amount. This will have been a constructive year for many Horses and what remains of it will also be busy.

At work, pressures could increase and there will be scope for many Horses to do (and earn) more and to use their skills to telling effect. Ideas they have could also be developed, and by contributing to their workplace, they can do their prospects a lot of good. September and the end of the year could see encouraging developments, including for some of the Horses who are seeking a position.

Financially, many Horses could benefit from a bonus or receive a generous gift at this time. Many will also be keen to buy specific items, and by comparing outlets and ranges, they could make some shrewd purchases.

Socially and domestically, the Horse will find himself in demand. If he can spread out his various commitments this can ease pressures later on as well as allow him to enjoy himself more. Many Horses will relish the chance to spend time with family and friends, including some they do not often see.

Overall, the Goat year will have been an active one for the Horse and while its pressures can be considerable, with focus and good use of his time, he will have done an impressive amount and enjoyed himself in the process.

Monkey years have pace and possibility and suit the Horse well. Never one for idling, he will look forward to the opportunities that await in this one. The Monkey year starts on 8 February and can be a full and interesting one for the Horse.

However, while the aspects are encouraging, the Horse will need to be disciplined. Horses can be restless, continually thinking of things to do and possibilities to explore. In the Monkey year the Horse should be careful not to spread his energies too widely and so undermine his effectiveness. It would be better to concentrate on priorities and subjects that have particular appeal rather than jump from one activity to another. Horses, take note and try to curb the more restless side of your nature.

One area which can see considerable activity is the Horse's work. Many Horses will actively look for a greater role this year. And this is a year which encourages progress. In some workplaces, as more senior personnel move on, the Horse could find his in-house knowledge makes him an ideal candidate for promotion, and if he is employed in a large organization, there could be the opportunity to transfer (and sometimes relocate) elsewhere. Whatever his situation, by keeping alert and indicating his desire to do more, he can move his career forward.

For Horses who feel their prospects can be improved by changing employer, as well as those seeking work, the Monkey year has scope and possibility. Enquiries made may alert the Horse to other ways in which he could develop his skills, and by not being too restrictive in what he considers, he may well succeed in taking on a different role, and often one with good potential for the future. March, May, June and October could see encouraging developments, but whenever the Horse sees – or thinks – of a possibility, he should pursue it.

With his outgoing nature, he will also be helped by the good working relations he enjoys with his colleagues. If in a new working environment, his early efforts to get to know others and immerse himself in what is happening will be noticed and impress. This is an excellent time to network, as the Monkey year rewards initiative.

Progress made at work can also help financially. However, to benefit fully, the Horse will need to remain disciplined, otherwise anything extra could quickly be spent, and not always in the best way. Also, should he enter into any new agreement, he does need to check the details and, if necessary, take professional advice. This is not a year to give scant attention to matters which can have important implications. Horses, take note, be thorough and do manage your finances well.

The Horse will welcome the possibilities the Monkey year offers, especially with recreational activities. New activities could appeal and the year could see many Horses enjoying the opportunity to try something different, including, for fitness enthusiasts, a new discipline. Horses who start the year feeling lacklustre or dissatisfied will find that taking action can transform their outlook.

The Horse will be on good personal form this year, with his charm and eloquence to the fore. For the unattached and those newly in love, affairs of the heart are well aspected and quite a few Horses will settle down or marry over the year. For Horses who have had disappointment in recent times, the Monkey year can mark a turning point. Quite a few will see someone significant entering their life. March, May, July and October could be the busiest months for social activity.

The Horse's domestic life will also see a great deal happen this year. Some Horses will decide to tackle major improvement projects, including altering living areas and installing new equipment, and, despite the disruption, will be delighted with benefits. There will also be some Horses who decide to move to somewhere more suitable. No matter what his plans and hopes, in all cases the Horse will need to focus on his goals and resist the temptation to engage in too many activities at the same time. If he does, a great deal can be accomplished this year.

The Horse will enjoy sharing his activities with his loved ones, including any new recreational interests. However, while this is a promising year for domestic life, a worry or upset could concern the Horse. Should he feel another person is in need of support, his care and thoughtfulness will be greatly valued. Similarly, if he himself becomes anxious over a certain matter, he should seek advice. He may be strong, but this is no year for bottling emotions inside. Monkey years favour openness and joint activities.

The Horse can fare well this year and, with his enquiring nature, will often delight in the new ideas and opportunities it brings. This is time for going ahead with his plans (some quite ambitious), as well as looking to move his situation forward. In both his work and personal interests, there will be new possibilities to consider. The Horse will need to be disciplined in money matters and be careful about spreading his energies too widely. But overall, this is an encouraging year with exciting possibilities.

The Metal Horse

The Metal Horse is very perceptive and good at reading situations. This year his talents can be put to good use. It will be an eventful 12 months and the Metal Horse can realize some special personal hopes.

Affairs of the heart can make this a significant time. For Metal Horses enjoying romance, engagement, marriage or settling down together can beckon, while for those who are alone and have perhaps been nursing some disappointment, the Monkey year can herald a transformation in their situation, with many meeting someone who is destined to become significant. Often such meetings will come about by chance and seem as if they were meant to be.

For Metal Horses who have a partner, this can be a busy and exciting year, with ambitious ideas and hopes to share. Some will be related to accommodation, with some Metal Horses moving to somewhere new (quite a few will relocate this year) and others continuing to stamp their existing home with their personality. However, while the Metal Horse may set about his plans with great enthusiasm, he needs to be realistic about what is achievable and avoid starting too many projects at the same time. This is a year which rewards planning, prioritizing and solid effort.

In addition to the considerable activity, there will be special occasions and news to celebrate. Some Metal Horses may start a family. Monkey years can be personally exciting.

They also favour a joint approach and throughout the year the Metal Horse should not hold back from asking for the opinions of others. Some, including more senior relations, will have the knowledge, skills and sometimes equipment to help. In addition, the suggestions of others may advance his plans in some way. Synergy, joint effort and an element of luck can all play a part this year. In turn, the time and help the Metal Horse gives to others will often be more welcome than he may realize. Once again his responsiveness and empathy will be much appreciated this year.

With a lot to occupy his time, he may not go out as regularly as in previous years, but will still enjoy his socializing. Shared interests, in particular, can give rise to both inspiration and fun. March, May, July and October could see some particularly pleasurable occasions.

Although the Metal Horse usually keeps himself active, he should also give some thought to his well-being, including his diet and level of exercise. To be on good form, extra attention to his well-being would not go amiss.

As far as his work is concerned, the Monkey year is encouraging. In view of the experience they have built up, many Metal Horses will now be keen to build on their position. Again the Metal Horse's ability to sense opportunity will be on excellent form, and should he have an inkling of an impending vacancy (perhaps caused by a senior colleague moving on) or of an employer about to recruit, he should be quick to express interest. Ambitious and keen, many Metal Horses will make what can be significant advances this year.

Another important factor will be the opportunities the Metal Horse has to develop his knowledge and skills, and whether familiarizing himself with different aspects of his work or concentrating on objectives, by making the most of his situation he can not only prove his worth but also help his future prospects.

For Metal Horses currently seeking work or deciding to take their career in a new direction, again the Monkey year can be one of interesting opportunity. By keeping alert for openings and considering other ways in which they could use their strengths, many will gain the chance they have been seeking. March, May, June and October could see encouraging developments, but throughout the year the Metal Horse should be prepared to move forward.

Success at work can also increase his income, but with many plans and outgoings and possible deposits, he will need to keep strict control over the purse-strings. This is a year for good financial management. Also, when entering into any agreement, the Metal Horse should check the details and seek advice if necessary. However, while care is needed, he will enjoy some moments of good fortune and benefit from some last-minute offers, sometimes related to travel or purchases for his home. Here, as with so much this year, his alert nature can serve him well.

Overall, the Year of the Monkey will be an eventful one for the Metal Horse, especially on a personal level. Love, romance and personal successes can make this a special time. It is also a year for going ahead with plans. At work there can be excellent opportunities to pursue, while personal interests can benefit from new ideas. The Metal Horse will be on inspired form and his enthusiasm, abilities and drive will enable him to reap some well-deserved rewards.

Tip for the Year
You have a lot in your favour this year: make the most of it. Put in the effort and look to progress. Also, value your relations with those around you. The support you both give and receive will be important.

The Water Horse

One of the strengths of the Water Horse is his enquiring nature. He has wide interests and will enjoy the many possibilities that can open up in this Monkey year.

For Water Horses born in 1942, this can be a particularly satisfying year. As always, the more senior Water Horse will take a keen interest in what is happening around him and involve himself in many undertakings.

In his home life he will have ambitious plans, including in some cases moving to more suitable accommodation. Water Horses who do move will have considerable sorting out to do and many decisions to make. It will not be easy, but with support and good advice, these Water Horses will feel satisfied they are making the right decision and enjoy the benefits that will ultimately be gained.

For those who remain where they are, again there will be ideas to follow through. Whether installing new equipment, having a purge on accumulated items or carrying out other improvements, they will be involved in much practical activity. However, while the Water Horse may set about some tasks with considerable enthusiasm, he does need to be realistic about what is achievable. To be over-ambitious or commit to too many undertakings at the same time could lead to confusion as well as be exhausting. He may be keen, but throughout the year he needs to prioritize and tackle specific tasks rather than spread his energies too widely. Also, with complex or physical tasks, he would do well to draw on the help of professionals.

In addition to all the practical undertakings seen over the year, the Water Horse will take a keen interest in the activities of family members. Not only will he be proud of some achievements but also dispense some timely advice. Here his eloquence and thoughtfulness will be appreciated and often influential.

The Water Horse will also enjoy sharing activities with those around him and the Monkey year will provide a good mix of things to do. Again the Water Horse's wide interests and desire to participate can be a driving factor.

He will also welcome the travel opportunities that arise and may well visit attractions related to his interests. By planning his trips carefully, he can look forward to doing a great deal, especially during late summer.

However, while a lot will go well this year, as always, problems can occur. If the Water Horse has a worry, he may find it helpful to seek professional advice. In addition, he may provide support to another person. Here his understanding can make a real difference. The Monkey year may bring its darker moments, but these will pass, and the year is predominantly an active and encouraging one.

Whether moving, buying items for his home or travelling, the Water Horse will find the year an expensive one. With care, however, and drawing on advice as necessary, he will be pleased with what he is able to do. He does, though, need to check the terms of any new agreements he enters into and be thorough when dealing with paperwork. To make assumptions or hurry unnecessarily could be to his disadvantage. This is a year for good financial management.

During the year the Water Horse will welcome the contact he has with his friends, and if alone, joining a community or interest group could be of benefit. Personal interests can also lead to good social opportunities and the Water Horse will be encouraged by the helpfulness of others. March, May, late June to the end of July and October could be active months both domestically and socially.

For the Water Horse born in 2002, the Monkey year is rich in possibility. The young Water Horse's enquiring nature will lead to him being inspired by certain aspects of his education, and this is a year to be active and engaged. It is, however, also a year for effort. Important examinations may be looming and the Water Horse will need to organize his time well. His commitment may not only be reflected in his results but also helpful as he moves on to study particular subjects in greater depth.

With this a good year for self-development, he should also make the most of chances to further his skills and strengths. Whether his interests are sporting, musical, dramatic or in another area, there will be opportunities which can inspire him. A lot of his activities can have a good social element too, and this can add to the fun. Some new friendships can also be made this year.

Although much can go well there will, though, be times of pressure and matters which may concern the young Water Horse. Rather than keeping these hidden, he will find it helpful to talk to others, whether family members, tutors or someone who has information to help. Openness can lead to worries being addressed and solutions often found.

Also, while the Water Horse will be busy with his studies and other pursuits, contributing to home life will not only help his relationships with family members but also enable more to happen, including visits to interesting attractions. Late summer could be particularly active.

Overall, the Year of the Monkey is an encouraging one for both the senior and younger Water Horse. However, to make the most of it, he will need to use his time well. The more disciplined and focused he is, the better he will fare. He will be encouraged by the support of those around him and frequently inspired by ideas and opportunities. A fulfilling year.

Tip for the Year
Consult others. By sharing your thoughts, you can open up possibilities. Enjoy what the year offers and set your plans and hopes in motion.

The Wood Horse

There is a Chinese proverb which reminds us, 'Well begun is half done,' and this very much fits in with the Wood Horse's character. He is careful, practical and likes to think things through. And giving careful thought to his next objectives will not only give him something to work towards but also make him more aware of the actions he needs to take. With focus, ideas and good backing, he can make this a successful year.

One area which will occupy the thoughts of many Wood Horses will be their work situation. Quite a few will have been affected by change in recent years, and while progress will have been made, the Wood Horse will often feel he could be doing more. In the Monkey year, unexpected opportunities can arise. A more senior colleague may suddenly leave, creating an opening, or a suggestion may give the Wood Horse an idea to follow through. Whatever occurs, by responding swiftly, he can often profit.

Some Wood Horses, perhaps wanting to alter their working commitments, reduce their commute or take on a fresh challenge, will feel the time is right for more radical change. For these Wood Horses, as well as those currently looking for a position, the Monkey year can have interesting possibilities in store. In their quest, they may find it helpful to talk to contacts and employment advisers. In many cases, their reputation will also help. And chance, too, can play a part. It may be that enquiries or an application made on the off-chance lead to the offer of a position. Such is the nature of the year that openings can occur at almost any time, but March, April, June and October could see significant developments.

Personal growth is also favourably aspected and in both his work and his personal interests the Wood Horse will have the chance to extend his capabilities. With interests and recreational pursuits, this is a good year to follow up ideas and also to try something new. Some Wood Horses may even give more attention to their lifestyle and start a suitable fitness discipline.

Travel will also feature on the agenda of many Wood Horses, with some opportunities arising by chance. The spontaneous feel of these trips will result in them being appreciated all the more.

The Wood Horse likes to be thorough and this will be an advantage when dealing with money matters this year. With commitments, purchases and possible family expenses, his outgoings will be considerable, and throughout the year he needs to keep track of spending and check the terms of any agreements he may enter into. If in doubt, he should seek clarification. This is no year to take risks or make assumptions.

Throughout the year, the Wood Horse will be appreciative of the support of others. Some close friends will not only be interested in certain activities he is engaged in but may have first-hand knowledge that could help. By talking over his ideas, the Wood Horse can also benefit from the synergy and ideas created. Through new activities and possible work changes, he will also have the chance to meet new people and his approachable manner will impress many.

For the unattached, the Monkey year can have romantic possibilities too. March, May, late June to the end of July and October can be both active and socially interesting times.

The Wood Horse's home life will also see considerable activity. There will be plans to get underway, including purchasing more efficient equipment. By talking over his thoughts and considering possibilities, the Wood Horse will be pleased with the improvements made and the time (and money) often saved. Again the Wood Horse's practical nature will be very evident, although sometimes he should keep his enthusiasm in check and avoid having too many potentially disruptive projects happening at the same time.

The Monkey year will also bring some family successes, with the achievements of younger relations likely to be a source of considerable pride to the Wood Horse. However, there could also be a few darker moments when another person may need support. Here the Wood Horse's thoughts and kindness can be of especial value.

The Monkey year is a fast-moving one with important possibilities. At work, many Wood Horses will have the opportunity to take on new and often more satisfying duties. Opportunities do need to be seized quickly, however. The Wood Horse's personal interests can also develop well. Throughout the year he will be helped by the encouragement of others and, by sharing thoughts and activities, will find a great deal can happen. This is a year for planning, action and seizing the good opportunities the year will bring.

Tip for the Year
Decide on your objectives and focus on them. With resolve and good support, you can see results this year. Also, look to develop your skills and interests. This is a progressive year filled with possibility.

The Fire Horse

This year marks the start of a new decade in the Fire Horse's life and it will be a significant one for him. Monkey years are fast-moving and bring change and opportunity. This will suit the action-orientated Fire Horse. For any Fire Horses who have felt held back in recent years or are nursing personal hurt, their fiftieth year can mark the start of a new chapter. This is very much a time to seize the initiative and move ahead.

However, while the aspects are encouraging, the Fire Horse will need to use his time well and concentrate on priorities. To try to do too much too soon or spread his attention too widely could limit his effectiveness. He may be enthusiastic, but the more focused he is, the better. In addition, he should seek support. With the help of others, more will be accomplished. His fiftieth year can be important, but it does require focus, effort and good co-operation.

In his home life, a lot is set to happen. Both he and his loved ones will be affected by change, and with a possible new commute and/or working schedules, routines may need to change. However, what occurs can have unexpected benefits, including more time to spend together.

The Fire Horse will also have plans he is keen to carry out on his home. With this an already busy year, these could take longer and be more disruptive than envisaged, and the Fire Horse needs to be realistic in what is doable at any one time. This is very much a year to tackle practical activities jointly and if a problem arises at any time, this needs to be talked through and further advice sought if necessary.

Domestically, this will certainly be a busy year, but amid all the activity, the Fire Horse's loved ones could be particularly keen to celebrate his birthday in style and line up some surprises for him.

Travel, too, will feature strongly over the year, with many Fire Horses deciding to mark their fiftieth birthday with a special holiday. By planning ahead, they could find their trip surpassing expectations. In addition there could be the chance to visit friends and relations living some distance away or to take advantage of a special offer. The Fire Horse's adventurous spirit can be well satisfied this year.

The Fire Horse will also enjoy sharing many of his activities with his close circle of friends. His interests, too, both old and new, will often have a good social element to them. Some Fire Horses may join a class, society or gym, or involve themselves more in the community, but whatever they choose to do, by being active and following up their ideas, they can get much personal value from the year. Fire Horses who are feeling lonely and/or have had some personal difficulty will benefit from going out more, including to local facilities. For some, a chance meeting could become especially meaningful. Monkey years are capable of surprises. March, May, July and October to early November could see the most social activity, but at most times of the year there will be things to do, places to go and ideas to follow through.

With his ambitious nature, the Fire Horse will often be keen to make headway at work, feeling that this is a year to make more of his potential. Many Fire Horses will be well placed to apply for openings in their present place of work and can look forward to making important advances.

Others will feel the time is right for a more major move and look to change employer. For these Fire Horses, and those looking for a position, the Monkey year can open up interesting possibilities. By keeping themselves informed of vacancies and companies recruiting in their area, many could secure a new position with potential for the future. Determined and adaptable, many Fire Horses will welcome the chance to prove themselves in another capacity. March, May to early July and October could see encouraging developments, but this is very much a year to keep alert and act swiftly when opportunities arise.

Progress at work may also help financially, but with considerable expenses likely, including exciting personal plans and travel possibilities, the Fire Horse will need to control his budget. He also needs to be thorough with paperwork. This is a year for good financial management and planning ahead.

Overall, the Monkey year is rich in possibility and the Fire Horse's drive and enthusiasm will allow him to benefit from it. However, he does need to concentrate on his priorities and draw on the support of others. Throughout the year he will be grateful for that support as well as look forward to special times with family and close friends. There will also be the opportunity for many Fire Horses to make important advances in their work and find greater fulfilment in what they do. In this year of opportunity, the ambitious and determined Fire Horse can set this new decade in his life off to a rewarding and potentially significant start.

Tip for the Year

Decide on your objectives and then act. With purpose, drive and the support of others, you can achieve a great deal this year. Also, value those around you. They can assist in important ways.

The Earth Horse

The Earth Horse is a thinker. He likes to look ahead and plan. And the Monkey year will offer him a variety of opportunities. As the saying reminds us, 'There are many routes to the top,' and by being flexible and determined, the Earth Horse can move forward on that journey this year.

This is especially the case in his work. In view of the projects and activities many Earth Horses have been engaged in recently, there will often be the chance to take on greater responsibilities. Considerable adjustment may be required, especially with the introduction of new procedures and objectives, but many Earth Horses will welcome the opportunity to build on what they do and advance their career. This can mark an important stage in their ongoing development.

Throughout the year the Earth Horse should work closely with his colleagues and, if applicable, meet others connected with his industry.

By actively participating in what is going on around him, he can not only help his present situation but also make potentially useful connections. The benefits of what he can do this year should not be underestimated.

The majority of Earth Horses will remain with their present employer, although in a considerably greater role, but for those who feel their prospects could be improved by a move elsewhere, as well as those seeking work and those who are keen to take their career in a completely different direction, the Monkey year can hold interesting possibilities. Developments can sometimes take a surprising course, but by keeping alert and following up ideas, many of these Earth Horses will secure the opportunity they have been wanting. Sometimes contacts and friends will be able to advise of companies recruiting and chances worth considering. March, May to early July and October could see important work developments.

Progress made at work may also lead to an increase in income. However, with many demands on his resources, the Earth Horse will need to keep a close watch on spending and ideally set amounts aside for requirements and plans. Also, if entering into any new agreements, he should check the obligations and question anything that is unclear. This is no year to be lax or take risks. Earth Horses, take note and manage your resources well.

One of the strengths of the Earth Horse is that he has an enquiring mind and during the Monkey year he could be enthused by a new idea, interest or activity. By setting time aside to follow this up (and it is important he allows himself some 'me time' in this busy year), he can delight in the possibilities opening up before him. If he would welcome additional company, it would be well worth considering joining a group connected with his interests or attending special events. Developing his personal interests can do the Earth Horse a lot of good this year. In addition, he should take note of the recreational facilities available locally. The Monkey year can offer a variety of things to do.

Many of the Earth Horse's activities can have a pleasing social element and he will enjoy the chance to meet others and extend his social network. Some of the people he meets this year could have expertise that is relevant to some of the plans he may be considering and he will be grateful for the advice offered. March, May, July and October could see the most social opportunities.

The Earth Horse's home life will also see considerable activity and there will need to be flexibility over some arrangements. With so much happening, it is important that there are moments of respite in the domestic whirl. Shared interests and trips out can be especially gratifying.

Both the Earth Horse and his loved ones will also have practical ideas to implement and purchases to make. Joint action will bring the best results, and while the Earth Horse may be eager to get certain undertakings completed and decisions finalized, ample time does need to be allowed, lest mistakes are made.

There could also be a matter which causes the Earth Horse some anxiety over the year. Time and patience will be needed, but the Earth Horse's thoughtfulness and assistance can be of considerable value.

For Earth Horses who are parents, the support they can give to children can also be important. Whether helping with studying or interests or assisting with decision-making, the Earth Horse's ability to advise and enthuse can make an appreciable difference.

In general, the Year of the Monkey will be a busy and often pleasurable one for the Earth Horse. In his work there will be opportunities to move ahead and develop his skills, often in new ways. Personal interests can also be satisfying, with new ideas and activities opening up rewarding possibilities. The Earth Horse will also be helped by the positive relations he has with those around him. The Monkey year is one of possibility and the Earth Horse's efforts during it will have both present and future value. A favourable and interesting year.

Tip for the Year
Be alert for opportunities to develop your skills. What arises this year can benefit you, sometimes in unexpected ways. Also, value your good relations with others, for their encouragement and assistance can be significant.

Famous Horses

Roman Abramovich, Neil Armstrong, Rowan Atkinson, Samuel Beckett, Ingmar Bergman, Leonard Bernstein, Joe Biden, Helena Bonham Carter, David Cameron, James Cameron, Jackie Chan, Chopin, Nick Clegg, Sir Sean Connery, Billy Connolly, Catherine Cookson, Kevin Costner, Clint Eastwood, Thomas Alva Edison, Harrison Ford, Aretha Franklin, Bob Geldof, Samuel Goldwyn, Rita Hayworth, Jimi Hendrix, François Hollande, Janet Jackson, Jean-Claude Juncker, R. Kelly, Calvin Klein, Ashton Kutcher, Petra Kvitová, Jennifer Lawrence, Lenin, Annie Lennox, Pixie Lott, Sir Paul McCartney, Nelson Mandela, Angela Merkel, Ben Murphy, Sir Isaac Newton, Louis Pasteur, Jodi Picoult, Gordon Ramsay, Rembrandt, Ruth Rendell, Jean Renoir, Theodore Roosevelt, Helena Rubenstein, Adam Sandler, David Schwimmer, Martin Scorsese, Kristen Stewart, Barbra Streisand, Kiefer Sutherland, Patrick Swayze, John Travolta, Usher, Vivaldi, Emma Watson, Billy Wilder, Brian Wilson, the Duke of Windsor, Caroline Wozniacki, Jacob Zuma.

1 February 1919 to 19 February 1920 — *Earth Goat*

17 February 1931 to 5 February 1932 — *Metal Goat*

5 February 1943 to 24 January 1944 — *Water Goat*

24 January 1955 to 11 February 1956 — *Wood Goat*

9 February 1967 to 29 January 1968 — *Fire Goat*

28 January 1979 to 15 February 1980 — *Earth Goat*

15 February 1991 to 3 February 1992 — *Metal Goat*

1 February 2003 to 21 January 2004 — *Water Goat*

19 February 2015 to 7 February 2016 — *Wood Goat*

The Goat

The Personality of the Goat

Amid the complexities of life,
it is the ability to appreciate that is so special.

The Goat is born under the sign of art. He is imaginative, creative and has a good appreciation of the finer things in life. He has an easy-going nature and prefers to live in a relaxed and pressure-free environment. He hates any sort of discord or unpleasantness and does not like to be bound by a strict routine or rigid timetable. He is not one to be hurried against his will, but despite his seemingly relaxed approach to life, he is something of a perfectionist and when he starts work on a project he is certain to give his best.

The Goat usually prefers to work in a team rather than on his own. He likes to have the support and encouragement of others and if left to deal with matters on his own he can get very worried and tend to view things rather pessimistically. Wherever possible, he will leave major decision-making to others while he concentrates on his own pursuits. If, however, he feels particularly strongly about a certain matter or has to defend his position in any way, he will act with great fortitude and precision.

The Goat has a very persuasive nature and often uses his considerable charm to get his own way. He can, however, be rather hesitant about letting his true feelings be known and if he were prepared to be more forthright he would do much better as a result.

The Goat tends to have a quiet, somewhat reserved nature, but when he is in company he likes he can often become the centre of attention. He can be highly amusing, a marvellous host at parties and a superb entertainer. Whenever the spotlight falls on him, his adrenaline starts to flow and he can be assured of giving a sparkling performance, particularly if he is allowed to use his creative skills in any way.

Of all the signs in the Chinese zodiac, the Goat is probably the most gifted artistically. Whether it is in the theatre, literature, music or art, he is certain to make a lasting impression. He is a born creator and is rarely happier than when occupied in some artistic pursuit. But even in this he does well to work with others rather than on his own. He needs inspiration and a guiding influence, but when he has found his true *métier*, he can often receive widespread acclaim.

In addition to his liking for the arts, the Goat is usually quite religious and often has a deep interest in nature, animals and the countryside. He is also fairly athletic and there are many Goats who have excelled in some form of sporting activity or who have a great interest in sport.

Although the Goat is not particularly materialistic or concerned about finance, he will find that he will usually be lucky in financial matters and will rarely be short of the necessary funds to tide himself over. He is, however, rather self-indulgent and tends to spend his money as soon as he receives it rather than make provision for the future.

The Goat usually leaves home when he is young but he will always maintain strong links with his parents and the other members of his family. He is also rather nostalgic and is well known for keeping mementoes of his childhood and souvenirs of places that he has visited. His home will not be particularly tidy, but he knows where everything is and it will be scrupulously clean.

Affairs of the heart are particularly important to the Goat and he will often have many romances before he finally settles down. Although he is fairly adaptable, he prefers to live in a secure and stable environment and he will find that he is best suited to those born under the signs of the Tiger, Horse, Monkey, Pig and Rabbit. He can also establish a good relationship with the Dragon, Snake, Rooster and another Goat, but he may find the Ox and Dog a little too serious for his liking. Neither will he care particularly for the Rat's rather thrifty ways.

The female Goat devotes all her time and energy to the needs of her family. She has excellent taste in home furnishings and often uses her considerable artistic skills to make clothes for herself and her children. She takes great care over her appearance and can be most attractive to others. Although she is not the most organized of people, her engaging manner and delightful sense of humour create a favourable impression wherever she goes. She is also a good cook and usually derives much pleasure from gardening and outdoor pursuits.

The Goat can win friends easily and people generally feel relaxed in his company. He has a kind and understanding nature and although he can occasionally be stubborn, he can, with the right support and encouragement, live a very satisfying life. And the more he can use his creative skills, the happier he will be.

The Five Different Types of Goat

In addition to the 12 signs of the Chinese zodiac there are five elements and these have a strengthening or moderating influence on the signs. The effects of the elements on the Goat are described below, together with the years in which they were exercising their influence. Therefore Goats born in 1931 and 1991 are Metal Goats, Goats born in 1943 and 2003 are Water Goats, and so on.

Metal Goat: 1931, 1991

This Goat is thorough and conscientious in all that he does and is capable of doing very well in his chosen profession. Despite his confident manner, he can be a great worrier and he would find it helpful to discuss his concerns with others rather than keep them to himself. He is loyal to his family and employers and will have a small group of particularly close friends. He has good taste and is usually highly skilled in some aspect of the arts. He is often a collector of antiques and his home will be very tastefully furnished.

Water Goat: 1943, 2003

The Water Goat is very popular and makes friends with remarkable ease. He is good at spotting opportunities but does not always have the necessary confidence to follow them through. He likes to have security both in his home life and work and does not take kindly to change. He is articulate, has a good sense of humour and is usually very good with children.

Wood Goat: 1955, 2015

This Goat is generous, kind-hearted and always eager to please. He usually has a large circle of friends and involves himself in a wide variety of activities. He has a very trusting nature but can sometimes give in to the demands of others a little too easily and it would be in his interests if he were to stand his ground more often. He is usually lucky in financial matters and, like the Water Goat, is very good with children.

Fire Goat: 1967

This Goat usually knows what he wants in life and often uses his considerable charm and persuasive personality to achieve his aims. He can sometimes let his imagination run away with him and has a tendency to ignore matters that are not to his liking. He is rather extravagant in his spending and would do well to exercise a little more care when dealing with financial matters. He has a lively personality, many friends, and loves attending parties and social occasions.

Earth Goat: 1919, 1979

This Goat has a considerate and caring nature. He is particularly loyal to his family and friends and invariably creates a favourable impression wherever he goes. He is reliable and conscientious in his work but sometimes finds it difficult to save and never likes to deprive himself of any little luxury he might fancy. He has numerous interests and is often very well read. He usually derives much pleasure from following the activities of the various members of his family.

Prospects for the Goat in 2016

The Goat's own year (19 February 2015–7 February 2016) can be a busy and eventful one for him, and to get the most from it he will need to be focused. He has wide interests and many ideas, but to spread his attention in too many directions could reduce his effectiveness. In what remains of his own year, he should decide on priorities and concentrate on these.

The many Goats who have experienced change in their work during their own year should aim to familiarize themselves with their duties during the closing months and establish themselves in their new role. For those seeking a position or keen for a change, some good possibilities can open up, with November and early January often significant. Goat years encourage Goats to make more of their talents, but they do need to promote themselves rather than hold back. At this time, fortune favours the bold and enterprising.

The Goat's home and social life will also see a lot happen in the closing months of the year, and again the Goat should try to plan ahead and spread arrangements out. Several weeks towards the end of the year could be especially busy. For unattached Goats and those newly in love, the end of their own year can be exciting and eventful.

With so much happening, the Goat's spending will be considerable, and possibly greater than envisaged. He would do well to watch his outgoings. With such a busy lifestyle, he should also pay some attention to his own well-being, including allowing time to rest after busy periods. As with so much in his own year, extra attention will make a difference.

The Year of the Monkey begins on 8 February and will be a good one for the Goat. However, while the aspects are on his side, Monkey years can have traps for the unwary. This is no time for the Goat to push his luck, or the goodwill he enjoys, too far. Monkey years require care and mindfulness but, in return, offer special opportunities.

One area in which the Goat will need to be particularly attentive is his relations with others. Throughout the year, he should be forthcoming and communicate well. To assume others are aware of his thoughts and feelings may lead to confusion and disappointment. Also, if, at busy times, he appears distracted or gives scant attention to what is going on, this could be resented and undermine the rapport he shares with those around him. Goats need to be particularly aware of this, for misunderstandings or inadequate communication could be problematic this year. Goats, take heed.

The Goat would also do well to consider paying some attention to his lifestyle. Although he will have many demands on his time, he should not be so busy that he misses out on the pleasure recreational activities can bring. For Goats who are keen to meet others, this is an excellent year for joining groups, enrolling on courses and taking part in shared activities. Monkey years encourage participation.

In the Goat's home life, good liaison will again be important. With several changes taking place (including to routines), implications will need to be discussed and flexibility shown. While the Goat may have specific hopes for the year, including home improvements and purchases he is keen to make, sometimes requirements will change or alternatives be suggested, and he needs to be mindful of this. Monkey years are not necessarily clear cut and several times during this one the Goat will need to revise his plans.

However, while there will be a certain fluidity to the year, a lot will go well, and time set aside for shared interests can be of real value. April, July, August and December could be favourable and busy months with enticing travel possibilities.

These will also be good months for socializing, but throughout the year the Goat will have people to meet and places to go. When in company, however, he does need to be forthcoming rather than assume others are aware of his views. Without care, misunderstandings could occur. Goats, take note.

At work, many Goats will benefit from encouraging developments. As a result of organizational decisions, staff movements and other changes, opportunities can suddenly open up and the Goat find himself excellently placed to benefit. Sometimes positions taken on now will involve a considerable shift in duties (and relocation for a few), but these Goats will welcome the chance to prove themselves in new ways.

The majority of Goats will have the chance to make important headway with their present employer this year, but some may be attracted by positions elsewhere. The emphasis of the Monkey year is on career development, and by keeping alert, the Goat can make impressive progress. This also applies to Goats seeking work. By making enquiries, keeping themselves informed of local recruitment drives and, if applicable, taking advantage of refresher or training courses, many of these Goats will be offered the opening they are hoping for. This may be a considerable change from what they have previously been doing, but can introduce them to a line of work which suits them well and in which they can ultimately be very successful. The significance of the Monkey year should not be underestimated. April, May and July to early September will see potentially important developments.

The Goat will, however, need to be thorough in money matters. His busy lifestyle, existing commitments and new ideas will make this an expensive year and he needs to keep a close watch on spending. If taking on new commitments, he should check the terms carefully, and keep paperwork, including guarantees and policies, in order. Risks, haste or assumptions (always a danger for Goats in Monkey years) can be to his disadvantage. Goats, take note.

By the end of the year, the Goat could look back and be astonished at all the changes that have taken place. By making the most of his opportunities, he can gain a great deal this year. He will need to adapt, but what he undertakes now can have important long-term value. This is also a year for being alert and mindful in his relations with others. It is a time for sharing, participating and, most importantly, communicating. By being aware of the year's trickier aspects, though, the Goat can benefit from its opportunities and often fortuitous developments.

The Metal Goat

This will be an active and interesting year for the Metal Goat, allowing him to make important headway and secure some personal goals. However, while the aspects are encouraging, he *will* need to be adaptable. Monkey years require flexibility. Also, for any Metal Goat who may start the year dissatisfied with his present position, this is a time to draw a line under what has gone before and concentrate on the *now*. The opportunities of this year should not be underestimated.

The Metal Goat's work situation can see some particularly encouraging developments. Metal Goats who are following a particular career or have been in the same position for some time could be encouraged by more senior colleagues to broaden their skills and increase their area of responsibility. Sometimes training may be offered, or the chance to deputize for someone, or, if an opening arises, the Metal Goat may be encouraged to apply. The skills and commitment of many Metal Goats can be rewarded this year. Monkey years can bring surprises too, and for those who take on more responsibility early on in the year, further opportunities may arise later on in 2016. Sometimes what is offered may (temporarily) put the Metal Goat outside his comfort zone, but it will also give him the chance to learn and prove himself in his new role.

The majority of Metal Goats will make important progress in their current place of work, but for those who feel unfulfilled and would welcome a fresh challenge, as well as those seeking work, the Monkey year can offer considerable possibility. By talking to employment officials and considering various options, many will secure an opening which will give them a foothold with a new employer. It may be slightly different from what they were intending, but Monkey years can move in curious but fortuitous ways and many Metal Goats will find their new position an ideal base on which to build. April to early June and July to early September could see important chances.

Throughout the year the Metal Goat should work closely with his colleagues and be active within any team. Some Metal Goats may be quiet, and at times uncertain, but by being visible, contributing and meeting others, they can do their prospects great good. Also, many have creative flair, and if they have ideas that could help in their place of work, they should put them forward. Monkey years favour innovation and the Metal Goat's talents could be rewarded.

Progress at work will often lead to an increase in income, but with numerous outgoings and plans, the Metal Goat will need to watch his spending and avoid too many impulse buys. Also, he should check the terms of any large transactions and keep important paperwork safely. Lapses and losses could inconvenience him. Metal Goats, take note.

Personal interests, however, could be satisfying. If there are particular skills the Metal Goat wishes to develop or a new interest that appeals to him, it would be well worth considering talking to experts or seeking instruction.

Metal Goats who are sedentary for much of the day would also find it helpful to incorporate some exercise into their routine, as well as pay attention to the quality of their diet. Attention to their well-being and lifestyle balance can make a noticeable difference this year.

With his extensive social circle, there will be many opportunities for the Metal Goat to go out, and late March, April, mid-June to August and December could be particularly lively months. Work changes and interests can also lead to the Metal Goat meeting some new people who could become potentially important. However, while he will find himself in demand, he does need to be alert. Communication problems and misunderstandings can be a feature of Monkey years. Metal Goats, do take note.

This advice also extends to close relationships. With so much happening, sometimes the Metal Goat may be preoccupied or make assumptions. Both could lead to awkward moments, and if the Metal Goat should feel stressed, tired or unsure at any time, it is better that he talks openly rather than keeps his thoughts to himself.

This is also important in view of the hopes and plans he will have for the year. This can be an exciting time, but good communication is necessary.

Monkey years are constructive, and with effort and flexibility, the Metal Goat can enjoy this one. It is a time for going ahead with plans and building on strengths. The Metal Goat will have to adapt as situations require, but a lot can follow on from what he does this year. He will value the good relations he enjoys with many of those around him and can carry out some often significant plans with his loved ones. Overall, an encouraging year that can be of far-reaching value.

Tip for the Year
Make the most of your skills and look to move forward. Positive effort can yield positive results. Also, give some attention to your lifestyle and

enjoy your recreational pursuits. Importantly, communicate well with others.

The Water Goat

With his many ideas, keen approach and inventive outlook, the Water Goat will enjoy the scope offered by this Monkey year. However, to benefit fully, he will need to be active and involved. This is no year to sit on the sidelines or delay. Instead, the Water Goat should take the initiative. As the Chinese proverb reminds us, there is 'No reward without good deeds' and the Water Goat's good deeds this year can bring considerable rewards.

For the Water Goat born in 1943, this can be a particularly interesting year. He will often have a variety of ideas and plans he would like to get underway, perhaps relating to his home, garden (if he has one) or personal interests. He will feel in inspired form, but he needs to channel his energies wisely. To be over-ambitious and start too many activities at the same time will not only bring increased pressure but may lead to less satisfactory outcomes. In this encouraging year the Water Goat needs to focus, prioritize and use his time effectively.

He would also do well to seek the opinion of others. This way, he may not only gain from the support they offer but also find discussion giving some hopes and activities useful impetus. Ideally, he should not act alone this year.

Monkey years are also capable of surprises and sometimes, once plans are underway, helpful developments can assist. Serendipity may be much in evidence this year. Also, new options can arise, especially when purchasing is involved, and the Water Goat will need to be aware and adapt accordingly. There may be some curious twists and turns this year, but they will often work to the Water Goat's advantage.

In his home, carefully planned projects can be especially satisfying, with new equipment often bringing welcome improvements. The Water Goat could also delight in buying some simple yet aesthetically pleasing items which add style and colour to the main rooms. His deft touch can often make an appreciable difference.

Personal interests, too, can bring him considerable pleasure and he may be inspired to do more. For the creative, there will be ideas to explore and talents to use and often a variety of occasions to attend. Where possible, the Water Goat should join others, and if not already a member of an interest or community group, would do well to consider joining one. Monkey years favour participation and a lot can be gained as a result. For Water Goats who are lonely, the meetings of a group they join now can become something they look forward to and, in time, value.

April, July, August and December could see pleasing social occasions and throughout the year the Water Goat will welcome meeting up with his friends and having the chance to talk through recent developments. A lot can follow on from these discussions, but where arrangements are involved, these do need to be clearly agreed upon. Misunderstandings can all too frequently occur in Monkey years and it is better to be sure than make assumptions.

This need for good communication also applies to the Water Goat's home life. Water Goats sometimes think others know what they are thinking or are conversant with their plans, but this is not always the case. Water Goats, do take careful note and be open and communicative.

The Water Goat can look forward to some pleasing family occasions this year, with the achievements of younger relations often being a source of considerable pride. Many will also enjoy visiting and perhaps staying with relations living some distance away. July and December could be busy months in many Water Goat households.

There will also be good chances for the Water Goat to travel this year, perhaps at short notice. By taking advantage of the opportunities that come his way, he will often visit (and sometimes revisit) some impressive attractions.

With some expensive purchases this year and his many activities, he does need to monitor spending, however, and thoroughly check his paperwork, including the terms of any important transactions. This is a year for vigilance.

For the Water Goat born in 2003, the Monkey year also offers great scope. With his enquiring mind, the young Water Goat could find new activities and recreational pursuits especially appealing and will often gain in confidence as he gets to do more. If he is particularly keen to do, try or acquire something, he should tell others. If he is open, more can become possible.

The adventurous nature of many young Water Goats will also be satisfied this year. There will be travel opportunities and, for those who enjoy the outdoors, exciting pursuits to enjoy.

In the Water Goat's schoolwork, this is a year for application and learning. By putting in the effort (including in subjects which may not have so much appeal), he can make important headway. This is no year to waste. The more the Water Goat engages with what is going on around him, the more he will ultimately gain. In addition, with communication important this year, he should talk to those at home about his current activities as well as any areas of difficulty. Input, assistance and advice *will* make a difference. Young Water Goats, take note.

The Year of the Monkey can be a satisfying one for the Water Goat, whether born in 1943 or 2003. It is a year for taking action and making the most of opportunities. With a positive 'can do' approach, much can be accomplished. Throughout the year the Water Goat does, though, need to involve others and get feedback and support. Lack of communication or too much independence can lead to difficulty. Water Goats, take note. Overall, however, the Monkey year is encouraging. It can be a fortunate one, although it does require effort, action and good use of time.

Tip for the Year
Develop your ideas and enjoy your interests and special talents. Monkey years encourage and inspire and can bring pleasing (and sometimes surprising) results. Also, be forthcoming with your ideas and plans. Support and advice can make a difference.

The Wood Goat

The Monkey year moves at a fast pace and brings change and opportunity. And while many Wood Goats may feel settled in their present situation, few will remain untouched by the events of the year. This will be an interesting but busy time.

At work, many Wood Goats will face new and often unanticipated developments. Long-time colleagues may suddenly depart and/or the Wood Goat's responsibilities change as new objectives are set. Some weeks could be unsettling, but by being prepared to adapt and make the most of arising situations, many Wood Goats will have the opportunity to take on new (and often more remunerative) duties.

The Wood Goat will also be helped by the good working relations he has with many of those around him. There may be a lot going on behind the scenes too and some influential colleagues may be championing the Wood Goat without his knowledge.

Many Wood Goats will benefit from openings in their present place of work, but there will be some who are keen to make a change. For these Wood Goats and those currently looking for work, the Monkey year can open up interesting possibilities. By widening the scope of what they are prepared to consider and keeping alert for vacancies, many could find a position which will be an interesting change and allow them to use their skills in new ways. Talking to colleagues and friends could be helpful and opportunities can arise in sometimes surprising ways, so the Wood Goat needs to keep alert and act swiftly. April, May and July to early September could see interesting possibilities.

In this busy year the Wood Goat's outgoings can be considerable, however, and he will need to keep a close watch on spending and, when making large purchases, compare options and terms. The more control he has, the better. He also needs to be thorough with important paperwork and seek clarification if he has questions or doubts. Monkey years are not ones to be lax or make assumptions.

Personal interests can, however, develop well, with the Wood Goat's imagination generating a variety of new possibilities. Special events being held in his area, courses or activity groups could also appeal. By being alert and receptive and participating in what is going on around him, the Wood Goat can inject an interesting new element into his lifestyle. Wood Goats whose interests and recreational pursuits have been put to one side in recent years should look to address this and preserve some 'me time'. It can be beneficial in many ways.

Travel – often at short notice – can also be pleasing this year. The Wood Goat will often be inspired by the places he visits.

Over the year he will also welcome the contact he has with his friends and the opportunity this gives to talk over recent events. The experience of some of his friends could be particularly relevant to his own situation.

In addition the Monkey year can give rise to some lively social occasions, some celebratory, which the Wood Goat will not only enjoy but also benefit from, as he can make some potentially important acquaintances this year. April, July, August and December could be fine and agreeable months socially.

The Wood Goat's domestic life will also see a lot happen this year. The Wood Goat and those close to him will often be affected by sudden changes, especially work-wise. As a consequence, this will be a time of readjustment. With good co-operation, much can be gained, however, and some well-deserved successes enjoyed. Amid the activity, the Wood Goat should encourage shared interests and be forthcoming with his own thoughts and any concerns. Good communication and openness are particularly necessary this year to avoid misunderstandings or moments of confusion. Wood Goats, take careful note.

The Year of the Monkey offers considerable scope for the Wood Goat, but he does need to seize his opportunities. Should he delay or hold back too long, chances may be missed. This is a time for him to use his talents, pursue his ideas and make the most of situations. He will be helped by the support of those around him but must remember that openness and good communication are vitally important this year. Sharing, discussion and involvement will be key to so much as well as enable the Wood Goat to get more from this most interesting of years.

Tip for the Year

Be receptive. Follow up possibilities and be prepared to adapt accordingly. Also, look to make more of your interests and special talents. This is an encouraging time. Enjoy it and use it well.

The Fire Goat

The element of fire increases a sign's drive and sense of purpose, and this is very true of the Fire Goat. Ambitious, keen and with ideas aplenty, he likes to make the most of what is going on around him. And while there will be inevitable peaks and troughs in his life, he has qualities that can take him a long way. The Monkey year offers good prospects.

At work, many Fire Goats will have seen considerable change in recent years, some of which will have happened at a bewildering pace. While some developments will have greatly concerned the Fire Goat, what he has been through will have given him considerable experience. In 2016 he will be able to draw on this. In many cases, his experience will make him an ideal candidate for the openings that will arise over the year and, in the process, he will be able to develop his often specialist skills.

The majority of Fire Goats will make progress with their present employer, but for those who are unfulfilled or currently seeking work, this can be a year of interesting possibility. By keeping informed of openings in their area, these Fire Goats may learn of a vacancy in a different type of work which offers the potential for development. Some learning and adjustment of routine may be involved, but Monkey years encourage professional growth and what is accomplished in this one can determine the direction of many a Fire Goat's future. April, May and late June to early September could see interesting developments, but throughout the year the Fire Goat should act swiftly when he sees an opening that appeals to him.

The background, reputation and versatility of the Fire Goat will often enable him to progress and impress this year, but he does need to work closely with his colleagues. Good communication and establishing an active presence in any new role are very important. Fortunately, the Fire Goat's commitment will help.

The emphasis on progress and development also applies to the Fire Goat's interests. By embracing the innovative spirit of the year, he can derive great pleasure from what he does. For the creative Fire Goat in particular, Monkey years can be inspiring times. Sometimes new recreational pursuits or a fitness discipline may appeal and if the Fire Goat can meet up with other enthusiasts, this can give certain activities greater impetus. Any Fire Goats who have let certain interests slip of late because of their busy lifestyle should look to remedy this if possible.

There is also an element of good fortune to this Monkey year and the Fire Goat will often be well placed to benefit. This can apply to travel opportunities (some arising at short notice) and the Fire Goat may also be invited to special occasions or attracted by local events. There is a spontaneity to the Monkey year which will add interest and meaning.

In view of the Fire Goat's often busy lifestyle, this will be an expensive year, though, and he will need to watch his outgoings and, when possible, remain within his budget. Too many unplanned purchases could curtail some plans later on. Also, when dealing with paperwork, the Fire Goat needs to be thorough. This is not a year for risks or being lax.

With his wide interests, the Fire Goat gets on well with many people and the Monkey year can give rise to a good mix of social occasions. As a result of friends introducing him to others, the Fire Goat could find his social circle widening and some of the people he meets now will be very in tune with his thinking and outlook. For the unattached, the Monkey year can have significant romantic possibilities. April, July, August, December and January 2017 could be lively and interesting months. However, while many occasions will go well, the Fire Goat does need to be clear when making arrangements or expressing his views. Communication problems could occur this year and could be embarrassing. Fire Goats, take note.

The Fire Goat's home life will also see considerable activity, and in view of the commitments of family members, there will need to be good co-operation between all. The Fire Goat (and others) will often be in inspired form and keen to go ahead with certain plans and acquisitions. These do, though, need to be fully discussed and costed, and ample time allowed. If too much is tackled at any one time, pressure, haste or confusion could mar certain activities.

Amid the plans and projects, the Fire Goat will also enjoy some fun times with family members. The Monkey year will contain a pleasing mix of things to do and the Fire Goat's input and thoughtfulness will yet again be much appreciated. The summer will be an especially active time.

A lot can happen this year and there will be chances for the Fire Goat to make more of his skills and interests. He does need to seize the initiative and act with determination, but what he does now can benefit him now *and* prepare him for subsequent opportunities. He will be encouraged by the support of those around him, and domestically and socially, the year will be active and meaningful. However, while this is an encouraging time, it does require commitment, openness and communication. Fire Goats, take note and enjoy this rewarding year.

Tip for the Year
Be prepared to take advantage of opportunities, even though they may require adjustment and learning. What arises now will happen for a reason and will often be to your benefit. Also, value your relations with those around you and enjoy what this Monkey year makes possible. You have much to offer.

The Earth Goat

There is a Chinese proverb which reminds us to 'Throw a long line to catch a big fish.' It means: 'Adopt a long-term plan to secure something big.' The Earth Goat would do well to remember these words in this important year. By making the most of it and looking to develop his knowledge and skills, he can benefit both now *and* in the longer term.

An interesting feature of this Monkey year will be the unexpected opportunities that arise. Sometimes it will seem as if an unseen influence is working behind the scenes, for whenever the Earth Goat sets his ideas in motion, circumstances will somehow assist. However, to make the most of his situation, he *will* need to put in the effort, even if this sometimes means venturing outside his comfort zone.

In his work, the Monkey year can see fast-moving developments. Sometimes, as staff change or new systems are introduced, more responsibilities will be given to the Earth Goat. Some weeks will be especially demanding, but by focusing on what needs to be done and being willing to learn (and adjust), he can do his reputation and prospects a lot of good. In difficulty lies opportunity, as has often been said.

The developments of the Monkey year can also highlight the Earth Goat's strengths and show where his forte lies. Monkey years are illuminating and can influence the career paths of many Earth Goats.

For Earth Goats who are dissatisfied where they are and would welcome a new challenge, as well as those seeking work, the Monkey year can be an important juncture. By considering different ways in which they could develop their skills and obtaining the appropriate advice, many of these Earth Goats could be alerted to an opening which offers good prospects for career development. It will require persistence to make the breakthrough, but Monkey years can bring significant opportunities. April, May and late June to early September could see important developments.

Progress made at work will improve the income of many Earth Goats, but spending still requires discipline. Without care, outgoings could all too easily creep up and rushed purchases be regretted later. The Earth Goat also needs to be vigilant with financial paperwork, checking details and keeping documents safely. Lapses could work to his disadvantage. Earth Goats, take note.

Although the Earth Goat will have many demands on his time, it is also important that interests and recreational activities do not get sidelined. Not only do these help keep his lifestyle in good balance but some interests give him the chance of additional exercise and social opportunities as well as encourage him to explore certain ideas. Interesting opportunities can arise this year and if the Earth Goat is tempted by a special event, course or new activity, he should follow it up. Monkey years encourage participation as well as highlight some of the Earth Goat's talents.

This Monkey year can also bring surprises, including chances to travel and/or attend events at short notice. A lot of the Earth Goat's activities will also have a good social element and the Monkey year can give rise to some lively occasions. The Earth Goat's amiable nature will make him popular company, and for Earth Goats who are feeling lonely or have had a recent personal upset, the Monkey year could put some sparkle (and romance) back into their lives. Late March, April, July, August and December could be interesting months socially and good for meeting others.

The Earth Goat's home life will also see considerable activity, especially as commitments and routines are liable to change. Also, as practical projects are started, developments can occur which can alter perspectives and lead to other ideas and approaches being considered. As with much this year, the Earth Goat will need to be prepared to adapt and make the most of situations and resources as they are.

There will also, however, be family successes to enjoy. Not only will the Earth Goat's own progress please loved ones, but close family members will have their own successes and milestones to mark. Times spent together as a unit will also be appreciated and do everyone good.

As with all years, problems can sometimes raise their head, however, and when they do, they will often stem from a lack of communication or jumping to conclusions. The Earth Goat should avoid making assumptions or think others are *au fait* with his arrangements and views. He does need to be forthcoming and clear if he is to avoid possible misunderstandings. Earth Goats, take note.

Overall, the Monkey year is a promising one for the Earth Goat but it does require commitment and looking to build on skills and strengths. What is accomplished now can be instrumental in the often considerable successes that await. There will also be many enjoyable occasions in this busy year. It is a time that encourages personal and professional growth and offers long-term gains too.

Tip for the Year
Look to build on your skills and strengths. You have a good future ahead of you and effort made now can prepare you for the opportunities that await. Also, be attentive to others and ensure you communicate clearly. Extra effort can make an important difference this year.

Famous Goats

Jane Austen, Lord Byron, Vince Cable, Coco Chanel, Nat 'King' Cole, Jamie Cullum, Robert de Niro, Catherine Deneuve, Charles Dickens, Vin Diesel, Ken Dodd, Sir Arthur Conan Doyle, Douglas Fairbanks, Will Ferrell, Jamie Foxx, Bill Gates, Robert Gates, Mel Gibson, Whoopi Goldberg, Mikhail Gorbachev, John Grisham, Oscar Hammerstein, George Harrison, Billy Idol, Julio Iglesias, Sir Mick Jagger, Steve Jobs, Norah Jones, Nicole Kidman, Sir Ben Kingsley, Christine Lagarde, John le Carré, Matt LeBlanc, Franz Liszt, James McAvoy, Tim McGraw, Sir John Major, Michelangelo, Joni Mitchell, Rupert Murdoch, Randy Newman, Sinead O'Connor, Michael Palin, Aaron Paul, Eva Peron, Pink, Keith Richards, Flo Rida, Julia Roberts, Philip Seymour Hoffman, William Shatner, Ed Sheeran, Queen Silvia of Sweden, Gary Sinise, Jerry Springer, Lana Turner, Mark Twain, Rudolph Valentino, Vangelis, Barbara Walters, John Wayne, Justin Welby, King Willem-Alexander of the Netherlands, Bruce Willis, Shailene Woodley.

20 February 1920 to 7 February 1921 — *Metal Monkey*

6 February 1932 to 25 January 1933 — *Water Monkey*

25 January 1944 to 12 February 1945 — *Wood Monkey*

12 February 1956 to 30 January 1957 — *Fire Monkey*

30 January 1968 to 16 February 1969 — *Earth Monkey*

16 February 1980 to 4 February 1981 — *Metal Monkey*

4 February 1992 to 22 January 1993 — *Water Monkey*

22 January 2004 to 8 February 2005 — *Wood Monkey*

8 February 2016 to 27 January 2017 — *Fire Monkey*

The Monkey

The Personality of the Monkey

The more open to possibility,
the more possibilities open.

The Monkey is born under the sign of fantasy. He is imaginative, inquisitive and loves to keep an eye on everything that is going on around him. He is never backward in offering an opinion or trying to sort out the problems of others. He likes to be helpful and his advice is invariably sensible and reliable.

The Monkey is intelligent, well read and always eager to learn. He has an extremely good memory and there are many Monkeys who have made particularly good linguists. The Monkey is also a convincing talker and enjoys taking part in discussions and debates. His friendly, self-assured manner can be very persuasive and he usually has little trouble in winning people round to his way of thinking. It is for this reason that he often excels in politics and public speaking. He is also particularly adept in PR work, teaching and any job that involves selling.

The Monkey can, however, be crafty, cunning and occasionally dishonest, and he will seize any opportunity to make a quick profit or outsmart his opponents. He has so much charm and guile that people often don't realize what he is up to until it is too late. But despite his resourceful nature, he does run the risk of outsmarting even himself. He has so much confidence in his abilities that he rarely listens to advice or is prepared to accept help from anyone. He likes to help others, but prefers to rely on his own judgement when dealing with his own affairs.

Another characteristic of the Monkey is that he is extremely good at solving problems and has a happy knack of extricating himself (and others) from the most hopeless of positions. He is the master of self-preservation.

With so many diverse talents, the Monkey is usually able to make considerable sums of money, but he does like to enjoy life and will think nothing of spending his money on some exotic holiday or luxury he has had his eye on. He can, however, become very envious if someone else has what he wants.

The Monkey is an original thinker and despite his love of company, he cherishes his independence. He has to have the freedom to act as he wants and any Monkey who feels hemmed in or bound by too many restrictions will soon become unhappy. Likewise, if anything becomes too boring or monotonous, the Monkey will soon lose interest and turn his attention to something else. He lacks persistence and this can often hamper his progress. He is also easily distracted, a tendency that he should try to overcome. By concentrating on one thing at a time, he will almost certainly achieve more in the long run.

The Monkey is a good organizer and even though he may behave slightly erratically at times, he will invariably have a plan at the back of his mind. On the odd occasion when his plans do not work out, he is usually quite happy to shrug his shoulders and put it down to experience. He will rarely make the same mistake twice and throughout his life he will try his hand at many different things.

The Monkey likes to impress and is rarely without followers or admirers. Many are attracted by his good looks, his sense of humour, or simply because he instils so much confidence in those around him.

Monkeys usually marry young and for it to be a success their partner must allow them time to pursue their many interests and indulge their love of travel. The Monkey has to have variety in his life and is especially well suited to those born under the sociable and outgoing signs of the Rat, Dragon, Pig and Goat. The Ox, Rabbit, Snake and Dog will also be enchanted by his resourceful and outgoing nature, but he is likely to exasperate the Rooster and Horse, and the Tiger will have little patience with his tricks. A relationship between two Monkeys will work well – they will understand each other and be able to assist each other in their various enterprises.

The female Monkey is intelligent, extremely observant and a shrewd judge of character. Her opinions are often highly valued and, having such a persuasive nature, she invariably gets her own way. She has many interests and involves herself in a wide variety of activities. She pays great attention to her appearance, is an elegant dresser and likes to take particular care over her hair. She can be a doting parent and will have many good and loyal friends.

Provided the Monkey can curb his desire to take part in everything that is going on around him and concentrate on one thing at a time, he can usually achieve what he wants in life. Should he suffer any disappointment, he is bound to bounce back. He is a survivor and his life is usually both colourful and eventful.

The Five Different Types of Monkey

In addition to the 12 signs of the Chinese zodiac there are five elements and these have a strengthening or moderating influence on the signs. The effects of the elements on the Monkey are described below, together with the years in which they were exercising their influence. Therefore Monkeys born in 1920 and 1980 are Metal Monkeys, Monkeys born in 1932 and 1992 are Water Monkeys, and so on.

Metal Monkey: 1920, 1980

The Metal Monkey is very strong-willed. He sets about everything he does with dogged determination and often prefers to work independently rather than with others. He is ambitious, wise and confident, and is certainly not afraid of hard work. He is very astute in financial matters and usually chooses his investments well. Despite his somewhat independent nature, he enjoys attending parties and social occasions and is particularly warm and caring towards his loved ones.

Water Monkey: 1932, 1992

The Water Monkey is versatile, determined and perceptive. He also has more discipline than some of the other Monkeys and is prepared to work towards a particular goal rather than be distracted by something else. He is not always open about his true intentions and when questioned can be particularly evasive. He can be sensitive to criticism but also very persuasive and usually has little trouble in getting others to fall in with his plans. He has a very good understanding of human nature and relates well to others.

Wood Monkey: 1944, 2004

This Monkey is efficient, methodical and extremely conscientious. He is also highly imaginative and is always trying to capitalize on new ideas or learn new skills. Occasionally his enthusiasm can get the better of him and he can get very agitated when things do not quite work out as he had hoped. He does, however, have a very adventurous streak and is not afraid of taking risks. He also loves travel. He is usually held in great esteem by his friends and colleagues.

Fire Monkey: 1956, 2016

The Fire Monkey is intelligent, full of vitality and has no trouble in commanding the respect of others. He is imaginative and has wide interests, although sometimes these can distract him from more useful and profitable work. He is very competitive and always likes to be involved in everything that is going on. He can be stubborn if he does not get his own way and he sometimes tries to indoctrinate those who are less strong-willed than himself. He is a lively character, attractive to others and loyal to his partner.

Earth Monkey: 1968

The Earth Monkey tends to be studious and well read, and can become quite distinguished in his chosen line of work. He is less outgoing than some of the other types of Monkey and prefers quieter and more solid pursuits. He has high principles, a very caring nature and can be most generous to those less fortunate than himself. He is usually successful in handling financial matters and can become very wealthy in old age. He has a calming influence on those around him and is respected and well liked. He is, however, especially careful about whom he lets into his confidence.

Prospects for the Monkey in 2016

The Year of the Goat (19 February 2015–7 February 2016) will have been a variable one for the Monkey and in its remaining months he will need to exercise care.

With increased spending likely, he will need to watch his outgoings and be wary of risk or succumbing to too many impulse buys. Spending could easily become greater than allowed for and result in possible economies later. Monkeys, take note.

At work, surprising developments are possible and some Monkeys will have the chance to move to new duties or benefit from training or other initiatives. With excellent opportunities awaiting in the Monkey's own year, the progress he makes now could be significant later on. November could see encouraging developments.

Both socially and domestically, there will be a lot happening. Again there could be surprises in store, including opportunities to spend time with people the Monkey has not seen for a long time. However, while he will enjoy himself, he does need to be diplomatic. A remark could be misconstrued, a difference of opinion arise or a person let the Monkey down in some way. The Monkey is generally adept in handling personal relationships, but there could be occasions in the closing months of the Goat year which test his patience.

With this being a busy time, the Monkey should also give some consideration to his own well-being. To push himself too hard without adequate rest may leave him susceptible to colds and minor ailments. With travel well aspected, if he is able to take a break in the closing months of the year, this could do him considerable good.

As millions around the world celebrate the start of the Monkey year on 8 February, many a Monkey will glory in the spectacle as well as look forward to his own year. And it is a year of considerable promise. For many Monkeys, particularly those who have been disappointed with recent progress or are feeling unfulfilled, it will represent a turning point.

To get the best from his year the Monkey does, though, need to decide on what he wants to see happen. With plans to work towards, he will not only be better able to direct his energies but also more alert to possibilities.

He will also be helped by the support he receives. However, to benefit fully, he does need to be open and receptive. Co-operation is an important factor this year and Monkeys should not act in isolation.

At work, this is a year of considerable possibility. Long-awaited promotion opportunities could arise and for some Monkeys there could be the chance to relocate. Some Monkeys will detect developments which they feel have exciting potential. By keeping themselves informed, many can spot an opportunity or gain skills which they can build on. Monkey years are dynamic and, for the keen and enterprising, *rich in possibility*.

For Monkeys who are unhappy in their current role, as well as those seeking a position, this is a year for reappraisal. By considering different ways of using their skills and keeping alert for vacancies, many of these Monkeys will obtain the opportunity they have been hoping for. In some instances, there will be considerable adjustment involved, but the doors that open for many Monkeys this year can prove significant. Also, by showing commitment in their new role, these Monkeys could find other opportunities soon becoming available. Monkey years are encouraging, and February, April, May and September will see some particularly exciting developments.

There will also be some Monkeys who, in view of their knowledge and experience, will be keen to start their own business. These Monkeys should take professional advice as well as find out about government schemes that may be of assistance. With good support, many will be able to set their ideas in motion.

Progress made at work will help financially, and some Monkeys will find ways to supplement their income through an enterprising idea. This upturn will persuade many to go ahead with plans and purchases they have been considering for a while. Here the Monkey's canny nature can be to his advantage and he may be able to identify several attractive offers. Also, if he is able, he should consider making provision for the longer term, perhaps adding to a pension policy or starting a savings scheme. In years to come, he could be grateful for action taken now.

In so many respects, the Monkey will welcome the wealth of opportunity his own year offers, including the variety of recreational pursuits. For the sporting and outdoor enthusiast, there can be thrilling times. Some Monkeys will also regard this as a year for personal improvement and start exercise programmes, introduce dietary changes or set time aside for personal study. By following through their ideas, these Monkeys will not only be satisfied with what they do but may be able to reap considerable benefits.

There will also be travel opportunities, and if there is a particular destination the Monkey is keen to visit or a special event that appeals to him, he should make enquiries. By planning ahead, he will find his hopes have a good chance of being realized.

He will also find himself in demand socially. Not only will many seek out his company, but some close friends could share certain confidences. Here the Monkey's empathy and ability to consider situations from different perspectives can help. However, support does need to be reciprocal, and the Monkey should be prepared to discuss his own ideas and seek advice where necessary.

At most times of the year there will be people to see and places to go, but May, June, September and December could see the most social activity.

For the unattached, a chance meeting could quickly blossom into significant romance, and for Monkeys who have had recent personal upset, new activities and new people can put meaning back into their lives.

The Monkey's home life can also see considerable activity. The Monkey may have ambitious home improvements in mind and discussion and co-operation will be needed. This is a year favouring collective effort.

The Monkey may also suggest activities for everyone to enjoy and his input can make a special difference this year. With this being his own year, he could have a special milestone or occasion to celebrate too. April, August and October can be particularly active months domestically.

The Year of the Monkey is one of great possibility for the Monkey himself. It is a time to act on ideas, build on strengths and make the most of chances. The Monkey has much in his favour this year and his commitment and resourcefulness can be well rewarded. His own year is a time to make things happen. And many Monkeys will succeed admirably.

The Metal Monkey

There is a Chinese proverb which reminds us, 'He who comprehends the times is great,' and the perceptive Metal Monkey will sense that this Monkey year has the potential for being significant. Not only is his animal sign ruling the year, but he will feel ready in himself to move forward.

However, to get most from the year the Metal Monkey does need to liaise well with others, talk over his ideas and build support. To keep his thoughts to himself (as some Metal Monkeys tend to do) or do too much single-handed could reduce his effectiveness. This year there is strength in numbers, and with others helping and rooting for him, he can be far more successful.

Important developments can take place in his work. Many Metal Monkeys will be keen to make more of their strengths and chance can offer a helping hand. Almost as soon as the Monkey year starts, if not shortly before, there could be opportunities for the Metal Monkey to move his career forward. Senior staff may move on, creating new openings, or he may identify an attractive vacancy elsewhere. By signifying interest, he could set important wheels in motion. Also, as others become aware of his desire to progress, influential colleagues could offer support. The input of others can aid the Metal Monkey considerably throughout the year.

Many Metal Monkeys will take on a more extensive role with their current employer, but for those who feel they can better themselves by moving elsewhere or who are seeking work, the Monkey year can hold significant possibilities. By keeping alert for vacancies and considering other ways in which they could use their skills, these Metal Monkeys could obtain a foothold in a different and often thriving sector. In their quest, they should also seek advice from experts. They could be helped in important ways. February, April to early June and September could see significant developments.

Progress made at work will lead to many Metal Monkeys increasing their income over the year and some will also benefit from a special bonus or gift. However, while improvement is indicated, the Metal Monkey will need to be disciplined, otherwise anything extra could quickly be spent, and not always in the most advantageous way. Ideally, the Metal Monkey should plan his major purchases carefully and compare terms and options. Also, if he is able, he should set sums aside for specific requirements or for his future. In this favourable year, he does need to use his resources well.

The Metal Monkey has wide interests and will delight in the wealth of ideas and activities the Monkey year offers. For creative Metal Monkeys in particular, this can be an inspiring time. By developing their talents, they could enjoy unexpected results. Some Metal Monkeys may also become intrigued by a new fitness programme. Monkey years encourage personal development of all kinds.

The sociable Metal Monkey will also find himself with various events to attend. May, June, September and December could be especially lively. Any Metal Monkeys who have had some recent personal difficulty will find that by going out and taking advantage of what is available locally, they can put a sparkle back into their lives. For some, life-changing romance can beckon.

The Metal Monkey's home life will also be busy. There will be achievements to mark and a celebratory feel to parts of the year. By sharing hopes and talking over decisions, the Metal Monkey and his loved ones will find that mutual support can make home life very special this year.

However, while a lot can go well, at times the Metal Monkey will need to temper his zealous nature and resist the temptation of starting too many undertakings at the same time. He may be eager to launch ideas and carry out improvements, but if he is to avoid putting himself under pressure, he has to prioritize. Quality time could also be jeopardized by too much activity. Maintaining a good lifestyle balance will help.

Overall, the Year of the Monkey is a time of great possibility for the Metal Monkey. He does need to seize his opportunities, but with drive, determination and the support of others, he can make important (and deserved) headway. Personal interests can bring him considerable pleasure and he will also have the chance to develop his skills and strengths. The one proviso is that he should not spread his energies too widely. If he watches this tendency, he can make this a pleasing and successful year.

Tip for the Year
Seek support. You have the resolve and abilities to succeed this year, but cannot do it all single-handed. Also, enjoy your good relations with those around you.

The Water Monkey

As the Year of the Monkey starts, the Water Monkey is likely to have high expectations – and some very definite plans. He will often be keen to build on recent developments and make more of his potential. And his personality and drive will lead to a great deal happening in this significant and often special year.

The Water Monkey's relations with others are particularly well aspected, and for those enjoying romance, there will be much to plan and share. Some Water Monkeys will settle down or marry over the year. For these Water Monkeys, this can be an exciting year. Not only will there be individual successes to enjoy but also joint plans to consider. The Water Monkey will often take great pleasure in seeing these take shape and in some instances luck can play a part as well.

For Water Monkeys who start the year alone, changes in their situation can lead to opportunities to meet new people and in some cases build a new social circle. Exciting developments may be in store. For any

Water Monkey who has had a recent personal upset, perhaps a relationship failing, the Monkey year is a time to draw a line under the past and focus on the present. New interests, new possibilities and new people can beckon, and by immersing themselves in the many activities and events of the year, these Water Monkeys can enjoy a considerable improvement in their situation.

May to early July, September and December could be significant months both for meeting others and enjoying some lively times. However, such are the aspects that Cupid's arrow could strike at almost any time. Monkey years are renowned for their surprises.

In addition, some of the Water Monkey's close friends could have reasons to celebrate and the Water Monkey will help with arrangements and enjoy what takes place. On a personal level, he may find himself in demand.

He may also be inspired. New ideas, equipment and opportunities can encourage him to develop his personal interests, and interesting results can follow on.

Certain interests can also lead to travel, and whether the Water Monkey is attending events, seeing sights or visiting places of interest, he will frequently be surprised and delighted by what he is able to do. August and September could be particularly active months.

At work, this is a year of important developments. Water Monkeys who are established in a position will often feel ready to take on greater responsibilities and senior personnel could encourage them, arrange training or give them the chance to widen their experience in another way. Chances *will* arise, either in the Water Monkey's existing place of work or elsewhere, and by the end of the year many Water Monkeys will have made important advances as well as considerably extended their experience.

For Water Monkeys who are discontent in their present line of work, as well as those seeking a position, the Monkey year can open up new possibilities. Again, some who know the Water Monkey and recognize his potential could be of assistance, either in alerting him to openings, suggesting possibilities or putting in recommendations on his behalf. Employment advisers may also provide useful information, and by being active and alert, many of these Water Monkeys will secure an opening which offers potential for development. February, April to early June and September could see encouraging possibilities.

Progress at work will help financially, but this will be an expensive year for the Water Monkey. With an active lifestyle, plus purchases he will be keen to make and items he will want to save towards, he will need to control his spending. If entering into new agreements, he should also check the terms and conditions carefully. This is a year to be thorough and to manage his resources well.

Overall, the Year of the Monkey will be a full and interesting one for the Water Monkey. In his work, there will be good opportunities to learn and progress and this can also be an inspiring time for personal interests. The Water Monkey's keenness and inventiveness can spur him on and there will be successes to enjoy. On a personal level, he will benefit from the support of those around him and affairs of the heart can make this a special time. The Water Monkey will have much in his favour and it rests with him to use his strengths and special talents to advantage.

Tip for the Year
Believe in yourself. Much is possible, but you need to take charge and follow through on your ideas. With resolve, you can make this a successful and enjoyable year, and its rewards can be far-reaching.

The Wood Monkey

The Wood Monkey has an enquiring nature and this Monkey year will offer him ideas, activities and opportunities to delight in.

As the Monkey year starts, the Wood Monkey born in 1944 should give some thought to the plans he would like to carry out over the year. Whether these involve home modifications, personal interests or visits to somewhere special, by having aims to work towards, these Wood Monkeys will find that not only can more be accomplished but strokes of luck can move their plans along as well.

The Wood Monkey's alert nature can also help. Sometimes when considering possibilities, he may chance upon the very information he needs or identify a special offer. He will also benefit from being open and receptive. If he talks over his ideas, others may make useful suggestions or offer assistance in some way.

In his home, he could have definite ideas about what he would like to see happen. It may be that certain household items need replacing, and by investigating options, the Wood Monkey will be very pleased with the purchases made and benefits gained. Many Wood Monkeys will also derive satisfaction from the projects they carry out, perhaps decluttering certain areas, reorganizing some rooms or altering décor. Here the Wood Monkey's sense of style will be to the fore. A few Wood Monkeys may even decide to move. Despite the considerable upheaval, they will welcome the advantages their new home offers. As many Wood Monkeys will find, this is very much a year for following through ideas and making improvements.

Throughout the year the Wood Monkey will be well assisted by those around him and their input can give important impetus to ideas he has in mind. His often infectious enthusiasm will also help get many a plan underway.

As well as the considerable practical activity of the year, the Wood Monkey will enjoy spending time with those who are dear to him. Shared interests could be particularly delightful, as will visits to local events and places of interest. The Monkey year offers a variety of things to do and the Wood Monkey will often enjoy participating.

As always, he will also follow the activities of family members with fond interest and, in view of the decisions and ambitious plans some younger relations will have in mind, will be keen to offer support. Here his ability to empathize could be appreciated and his words carry considerable weight.

The Wood Monkey will also enjoy the opportunities the Monkey year will bring. Travel could be particularly tempting. He will also have various interests he will be keen to pursue. In some instances, one idea or project will lead to another and the Wood Monkey be kept pleasingly occupied. Some Wood Monkeys may be tempted by local courses or interest groups. By making the most of what is available, the Wood Monkey can make this a richly rewarding time.

In view of his larger purchases and plans and, for a few, moving expenses, however, he will need to keep close track of spending and be aware of any obligations he takes on. Should he have questions or doubts, he needs to get these addressed before proceeding. While this is a favourable year, it is not one to make assumptions or proceed on an ad hoc basis. Also, if the Wood Monkey becomes concerned by any matter, he should seek advice. This is no time for keeping anxieties to himself.

For the Wood Monkey born in 2004, this Monkey year can be a full and interesting one. As they move forward in their education, these Wood Monkeys will welcome the chance to develop their knowledge and skills. New aptitudes can also be highlighted and the young Wood Monkey's efforts may allow him to make impressive headway.

With the year so rich in possibility, these Wood Monkeys do, though, need to be forthcoming. Whenever they have ideas or concerns, they should let these be known. Family members and tutors will be glad to give support and advice. Also, while the young Wood Monkey may sometimes feel out of his comfort zone and bewildered by the expectations placed on him, it is by being stretched that he will learn more and discover personal strengths. Wood Monkeys, take note.

Whether born in 1944 or 2004, the Wood Monkey will find the Year of the Monkey is one for acting on ideas and taking opportunities. Once plans are started, support – and luck – can add useful impetus and lead to a lot being accomplished. Shared activities and interests can also develop well and, with many a Wood Monkey feeling on inspired form, there will be ideas aplenty. If anxieties do arise at any time, the Wood Monkey should be forthcoming and seek advice, but generally this is a favourable year and the Wood Monkey will participate in a wide range of activities and enjoy the rewards that will so often follow.

Tip for the Year
Set your plans in motion. This can be a fulfilling year for you. Be open to opportunity and use your special talents well.

The Fire Monkey

This is the Fire Monkey's own year and it will be a significant one for him. Not only does it mark his sixtieth year but it will contain many important developments. There will be keynote decisions to make, plans to carry through and some very special times to enjoy.

Almost all aspects of the Fire Monkey's life will see important developments and throughout the year he will need to involve others in what is happening. Although as a typical Monkey he likes to keep his own counsel, if he shares his thoughts, he can benefit from the assistance and support of those around him. The process of dialogue can also spark other ideas. The Fire Monkey's mind will sometimes be working overtime this year as new ideas emerge or he discovers other possibilities to explore. The Year of the Fire Monkey offers great opportunities to the Fire Monkey himself, but to benefit he does need to be active, aware and involved.

One area which will be the focus of much attention will be work. A few Fire Monkeys will now decide to retire or reduce their working commitments. This may be something they have been considering for some time and they will welcome the additional free time they now have and the easing of recent pressures.

For those who remain in their present position, the year can again be significant. In view of the expertise many now have, there will often be the opportunity to focus on specific assignments and concentrate their efforts in particular ways. With Monkey years being innovative ones, there could also be new projects to oversee. The Fire Monkey's skills will be appreciated in many a workplace this year.

There are also Fire Monkeys who have an entrepreneurial streak and some may decide to offer their skills on a more freelance basis or proceed with an enterprising idea. With good advice and careful thought, they could see their plans developing in an encouraging manner.

For Fire Monkeys seeking work there can also be interesting chances to pursue. Contacts and employment experts could prove helpful, and with support and resolve, these Fire Monkeys can secure new positions which will often suit their skills and requirements perfectly. The start of the Monkey year, April, May and September could see important opportunities and decisions being made.

Finances are also favourably aspected and some Fire Monkeys will benefit from the fruition of a policy, an additional payment or a gift. This will tempt many to go ahead with a variety of plans, including travel, that they may have been contemplating for some time. However, while this is a favourable year financially, the Fire Monkey does need to think through more expensive transactions and be wary of rushed decisions, otherwise anything extra could quickly be spent, and not always in the best way. Fire Monkeys who do retire should also spend time carefully considering their budget, their requirements and any modifications they may need to make. This is a time for good planning and control. In addition, while irksome, forms and paperwork warrant close attention.

With Monkey years being rich in possibility, some Fire Monkeys could become intrigued by new activities or set themselves a personal challenge. Especially for those who retire or have neglected recreational activities of late, this is very much a year for 'me time' and pursuing personal interests. Not only can this add valuable balance to the Fire Monkey's lifestyle but other benefits could follow on as well, perhaps additional exercise or the Fire Monkey's natural talents being recognized and rewarded.

Travel, too, is well aspected and many Fire Monkeys will take a special holiday to mark their sixtieth year. By giving early thought to possible destinations, they can see some exciting plans taking shape. In addition, many Fire Monkeys will enjoy some short breaks, including some occurring late in the year.

Although the Fire Monkey knows many people, he usually has a very close circle of friends, many of whom he has known for a long time. Over the year he will once again enjoy meeting up with them and exchanging news, as well as value their support. If he has concerns at any time, he could particularly value the listening ear of a friend.

Also, any Fire Monkey who is feeling lonely, perhaps as a result of a recent change in circumstances, should aim to go out more over the year. Joining a local group, becoming more involved in their community or giving time to a cause can all help.

Positive action can have important personal value as well as introduce the Fire Monkey to like-minded people. Some Fire Monkeys could make important new friends this year, and for the unattached, their own year can be made even more exciting by romantic possibilities. May, June, September and December could see good social opportunities.

The Fire Monkey's home life is well aspected and his loved ones will often be keen to celebrate his sixtieth birthday in style. The Fire Monkey may be surprised by some of the arrangements and touched by the tokens of affection he is given. In addition to his own birthday, he could be thrilled by the progress of some younger relations and their news over the year will often give rise to further celebrations. The Fire Monkey's own year will contain some very special family times.

With his interest in new technology, he could also decide to update some of his equipment at home, buying more efficient and economical appliances or carrying out some maintenance. Although keen, he should avoid rush and take the time to investigate options and costs. With care, some important decisions can be made and changes implemented.

Overall, the Year of the Fire Monkey can be a special one for the Fire Monkey himself. He will feel more inspired than of late and be better able to determine what *he* wants to do. Important opportunities will arise and he will also be helped by some moments of good fortune. When he has made a decision or started on a plan, circumstances will often assist in a meaningful way. And in his sixtieth year, the love and friendship of those around him will mean a great deal. Many Fire Monkeys will thoroughly enjoy their year – the experiences it brings and the opportunities it opens up.

Tip for the Year
You have an enquiring nature: embrace what your year offers. Follow up ideas, and if new interests tempt you, find out more. Enjoy yourself, give time to yourself and use your strengths. Also, value those who are close to you. They will not only be keen to support you but can help make your year even more special and successful.

The Earth Monkey

There is a Chinese proverb that states, 'Those who accumulate good deeds will prosper,' and this is particularly apt for the Earth Monkey in 2016. Over recent years he will have experienced a lot, and although he will have enjoyed some good results, he will also have had some disappointments. In this auspicious year, the experience, reputation and goodwill he has accumulated will allow him to prosper.

In addition, with this being a Monkey year, many Earth Monkeys will feel inspired and be keen to develop their ideas and further their situation. Once they start to explore possibilities, helpful developments will quickly follow on.

At work, the aspects are particularly encouraging. With the experience many Earth Monkeys now have behind them, there will be chances to progress and take on a more specialist role. Particularly for those who work for a large employer or are in a specific sector of an industry, there will be several opportunities to pursue, and by keeping alert for openings and talking to contacts, many of these Earth Monkeys will find or be trained up for what will be an ideal next position. In 2016 quite a few will find themselves in the right place at the right time *and* with the right experience behind them. It is accumulated deeds that will enable many to prosper.

While the majority of Earth Monkeys will further their career where they are, there will also be those who feel ready for a new challenge. For these Earth Monkeys, as well as those seeking work, again the Monkey year can hold important developments. One of the Monkey's strengths is his versatility, and by being prepared to consider different types of work, many Earth Monkeys will find themselves taking on a new role and relishing the opportunity. Events this year may take some curious courses, but it will seem as if what arises was meant to be. February, April, May and September could see encouraging developments.

Progress at work will often lead to a rise in income and some Earth Monkeys may benefit from an additional payment or gift. For many, this can be a financially improved year. As a result, the Earth Monkey will often decide to proceed with ideas and purchases he has been considering for a while. To get the best value, however, he should take the time to review different options and seek advice. Also, he should not be dilatory with paperwork and should aim to keep key policies up to date and file receipts and guarantees carefully. Mistakes or losses could be to his disadvantage. Earth Monkeys, take note.

The Earth Monkey has wide interests and over the year new recreational pursuits could appeal to him. Being creative, he could also have ideas he is keen to pursue. Monkey years favour the development of skills, and the Earth Monkey could enjoy some notable successes.

The Monkey year can also bring some good travel opportunities, and if the Earth Monkey is attracted by an event related to his interests or there is a place he is keen to visit, he should make enquiries. Some of his trips could be particularly delightful.

He will also appreciate the contact he has with his friends and can gain a great deal by running his ideas past them. The year will also be marked by some key social events. A close friend may enjoy a special celebration and shared interests can also lead to some lively times. May to early July, September and December could see much social activity, and the lonely and unattached Earth Monkey could meet someone who could soon become significant.

The Earth Monkey's home life will also be busy, and ideas and plans need to be fully talked through and sufficient time allowed for practical undertakings. With many commitments and some interruptions, it could be that some projects take longer than anticipated.

Amid all the activity, there will also be a lot to appreciate. The Earth Monkey and other family members could enjoy some well-deserved successes, and travel and shared interests could also bring meaningful occasions. Monkey years can be rich in things to do and places to go, and April, August and October are likely to be particularly busy months.

Overall, the Year of the Monkey can be a very rewarding one for the Earth Monkey, but the initiative does rest with him. With drive, enthusiasm, his individual strengths and the support of others, he can accomplish a great deal and make deserved headway. Both present and accumulated deeds will help his progress this year. Personal interests can develop in interesting fashion and new ideas and activities will often be inspiring. Key to so much, however, will be the good relations the Earth Monkey enjoys with those around him. Family and friends will be delighted to help him make this a successful and pleasing year.

Tip for the Year
Be forthcoming. With input and support, so much more can happen for you. You have much to offer, but you cannot do it all by yourself. Take note, and enjoy this rewarding and encouraging year.

Famous Monkeys

Gillian Anderson, Jennifer Aniston, Christina Aguilera, Patricia Arquette, J. M. Barrie, Kenny Chesney, Colette, John Constable, Patricia Cornwell, Daniel Craig, Joan Crawford, Miley Cyrus, Leonardo da Vinci, Timothy Dalton, Bette Davis, Danny De Vito, Celine Dion, Michael Douglas, Mia Farrow, Carrie Fisher, F. Scott Fitzgerald, Ian Fleming, Paul Gauguin, Ryan Gosling, Eva Green, Jake Gyllenhaal, Jerry Hall, Tom Hanks, Harry Houdini, Charlie Hunnam, Hugh Jackman, P. D. James, Katherine Jenkins, Julius Caesar, Buster Keaton, Alicia Keys, Gladys Knight, Taylor Lautner, George Lucas, Bob Marley, Kylie Minogue, V. S. Naipaul, Lisa Marie Presley, Lou Reed, Debbie Reynolds, Little Richard, Diana Ross, Tom Selleck, Sam Smith, Wilbur Smith, Rod Stewart, Jacques Tati, Elizabeth Taylor, Dame Kiri Te Kanawa, Justin Timberlake, Harry Truman, Ben Whishaw, Venus Williams.

8 February 1921 to 27 January 1922 — *Metal Rooster*

26 January 1933 to 13 February 1934 — *Water Rooster*

13 February 1945 to 1 February 1946 — *Wood Rooster*

31 January 1957 to 17 February 1958 — *Fire Rooster*

17 February 1969 to 5 February 1970 — *Earth Rooster*

5 February 1981 to 24 January 1982 — *Metal Rooster*

23 January 1993 to 9 February 1994 — *Water Rooster*

9 February 2005 to 28 January 2006 — *Wood Rooster*

The Rooster

The Personality of the Rooster

With a clear destination
and firm will,
I raise my sails
to the winds of fortune.

The Rooster is born under the sign of candour. He has a flamboyant and colourful personality and is meticulous in all that he does. He is an excellent organizer and wherever possible likes to plan his various activities well in advance.

The Rooster is usually highly intelligent and very well read. He has a good sense of humour and is an effective and persuasive speaker. He loves discussion and enjoys taking part in any sort of debate. He has no hesitation in speaking his mind and is forthright in his views. He does, however, lack tact and can easily damage his reputation or cause offence by some thoughtless remark or action. He has a very volatile nature and should always try to avoid acting on the spur of the moment.

He is usually very dignified in his manner and conducts himself with an air of confidence and authority. He is adept at handling financial matters and organizes his financial affairs with considerable skill. He chooses his investments well and is capable of achieving great wealth. Most Roosters use their money wisely, but there are a few who are the reverse and are notorious spendthrifts. Fortunately, the Rooster has great earning capacity and is rarely without sufficient funds to tide himself over.

Another characteristic of the Rooster is that he invariably carries a notebook or scraps of paper around with him. He is constantly writing himself reminders or noting down important facts lest he forgets – the Rooster cannot abide inefficiency and conducts all his activities in an orderly, precise and methodical manner.

The Rooster is usually very ambitious, but can be unrealistic in some of what he hopes to achieve. He occasionally lets his imagination run away with him and while he does not like any interference from others, it would be in his own interests to listen to their views a little more often. He also does not like criticism, and if he feels anybody is doubting his judgement or prying too closely into his affairs, he is certain to let his feelings be known. He can also be rather self-centred and stubborn over relatively trivial matters, but to compensate for this he is reliable, honest and trustworthy, and this is appreciated by all who come into contact with him.

Roosters born between the hours of five and seven, both at dawn and sundown, tend to be the most extrovert of their sign, but all Roosters like to lead an active social life and enjoy attending parties and big functions. The Rooster usually has a wide circle of friends and is able to build up influential contacts with remarkable ease. He often belongs to several clubs and societies and involves himself in a variety of different activities. He is particularly interested in the environment, humanitarian affairs and anything affecting the welfare of others. He has a very caring nature and will do much to help those less fortunate than himself.

He also gets much pleasure from gardening, and while he may not spend as much time in the garden as he would like, his garden is invariably well kept and productive.

The Rooster is generally very distinguished in his appearance and if his job permits, he will wear an official uniform with great pride and dignity. He is not averse to publicity and takes great delight in being the centre of attention. He often does well at PR work or any job which brings him into contact with the media. He also makes a very good teacher.

The female Rooster leads a varied and interesting life. She involves herself in many different activities and there are some who wonder how she can achieve so much. She often holds very strong views and, like her male counterpart, has no hesitation in speaking her mind or telling others how she thinks things should be done. She is supremely efficient and well organized and her home is usually very neat and tidy. She has good taste in clothes and usually wears smart but very practical outfits.

The Rooster usually has a large family and takes a particularly active interest in the education of his children. He is very loyal to his partner and will find that he is especially well suited to those born under the

signs of the Snake, Horse, Ox and Dragon. Provided they do not inter-
fere too much in his various activities, the Rat, Tiger, Goat and Pig can
also establish a good relationship with him, but two Roosters together
are likely to squabble and irritate each other. The rather sensitive Rabbit
will find the Rooster a bit too blunt for his liking, and the Rooster will
quickly become exasperated by the ever-inquisitive and artful Monkey.
He will also find it difficult to get on with the anxious Dog.

If the Rooster can overcome his volatile nature and exercise tact, he
will go far in life. He is capable and talented and will make a lasting –
and usually favourable – impression almost everywhere he goes.

The Five Different Types of Rooster

In addition to the 12 signs of the Chinese zodiac there are five elements
and these have a strengthening or moderating influence on the signs. The
effects of the elements on the Rooster are described below, together with
the years in which they were exercising their influence. Therefore
Roosters born in 1921 and 1981 are Metal Roosters, Roosters born in
1933 and 1993 are Water Roosters, and so on.

Metal Rooster: 1921, 1981

The Metal Rooster is a hard and conscientious worker. He knows
exactly what he wants in life and sets about everything in a positive and
determined manner. He can at times appear abrasive and he would
almost certainly do better if he were willing to reach a compromise with
others rather than hold so rigidly to his beliefs. He is very articulate and
most astute when dealing with financial matters. He is loyal to his
friends and often devotes much energy to working for the common
good.

Water Rooster: 1933, 1993

This Rooster has a very persuasive manner and can easily gain the co-operation of others. He is intelligent, well read and enjoys taking part in discussions and debates. He has a seemingly inexhaustible amount of energy and is prepared to work long hours in order to secure what he wants. He can, however, waste a lot of valuable time worrying over minor and inconsequential details. He is approachable, has a good sense of humour and is highly regarded by others.

Wood Rooster: 1945, 2005

The Wood Rooster is honest, reliable and often sets himself high standards. He is ambitious, but also more prepared to work in a team than some of the other types of Rooster. He usually succeeds in life but does have a tendency to get caught up in bureaucratic matters and attempt too many things at the same time. He has wide interests, likes to travel and is very caring and considerate towards his family and friends.

Fire Rooster: 1957

This Rooster is extremely strong-willed. He has many leadership qualities, is an excellent organizer and is most efficient in his work. Through sheer force of character he often secures his objectives, but he does have a tendency to be very forthright and not always consider the feelings of others. If he can learn to be more tactful he can often succeed beyond his wildest dreams.

Earth Rooster: 1969

This Rooster has a deep and penetrating mind. He is efficient, perceptive and particularly astute in business and financial matters. He is also persistent and once he has set himself an objective, he will rarely allow himself to be deflected from achieving his aim. He works hard and is held in great esteem by his friends and colleagues. He usually enjoys the arts and takes a keen interest in the activities of the various members of his family.

Prospects for the Rooster in 2016

A hallmark of the Rooster is his determination. He sets about his activities with considerable resolve. And his efforts in the Goat year (19 February 2015–7 February 2016) will have resulted in some interesting times. Admittedly, there will have been parts of the year which will have frustrated the Rooster and brought uncertainty, but overall it will have been a satisfying time and the closing months will be full and varied.

At work, many Roosters will face an increased workload, and although the pressures will be great, these can highlight the Rooster's efficient approach and enhance his reputation. September and January could be significant months, with opportunities arising for some Roosters.

With a lot happening towards the end of the year, the Rooster will need to keep a close watch on spending and, ideally, budget ahead. Outgoings could be greater than anticipated, especially as many Roosters will have additional travel opportunities at this time.

There will also be an increase in social activity, with August and December particularly busy months. The Goat year can inject some spontaneity into proceedings, with some surprise occasions taking place. The sociable Rooster will greatly enjoy himself.

In his home life, flexibility will be needed, as the Rooster and his loved ones contend with various commitments as well as many arrangements. Someone close could have exciting news to share during the festive season.

The Year of the Monkey starts on 8 February and will be a demanding one for the Rooster. Some situations could be volatile and the Rooster could be ill-at-ease with certain developments. He likes to make his own decisions, but at times he may find himself in an uncharacteristic quandary over what best to do. Monkey years tend not to be the easiest for the Rooster, but they can leave a significant legacy. Next year is the Rooster's own year and what he accomplishes now can prepare him for the considerable opportunities that lie ahead.

Being well-organized, the Rooster likes to keep tabs on what is happening and work to a plan. There will, though, be situations during the year which concern him. However, he should not automatically think the worst. Instead, he should check the facts and wait for matters to become clear. Developments in this Monkey year may not always be straightforward, but can nevertheless bring opportunities for the Rooster.

This is particularly the case in his work situation. Many workplaces will be affected by swift-moving developments. Reorganization, changes in staff and management, and new policies or products can all result in considerable volatility. At such times, the Rooster should remain focused on his role and adapt as required. By showing himself willing to embrace change, he could benefit from the openings that arise. Also, if additional training is available, transfer opportunities occur or the Rooster sees an opening elsewhere, he should follow it up. Extending his experience now can increase his options for later.

For Roosters who are unfulfilled in their present situation and those seeking a position, the Monkey year can also open up some interesting possibilities. By keeping alert for vacancies and not closing their mind to something different, many of these Roosters could secure a position in a new type of work. Considerable adjustment could be involved and the early weeks may be demanding, but this can be an important stepping-stone to future opportunities.

May, June, September and December could prove important months work-wise, but throughout the year the Rooster should take full advantage of any ways of furthering his experience and skills. He can also help his situation by networking and working closely with colleagues. With his talent for putting himself across, he can impress many this year, including some who have considerable influence.

Progress at work can bring a modest improvement in income, but financial vigilance is important this year. Not only will many Roosters face additional expenses, including family requirements and equipment repairs, but the Rooster needs to be careful when entering into any agreements. Terms should be checked, concerns addressed and, if appropriate, professional advice obtained. In matters of finance, this is a year for thoroughness and good control.

Another area which requires increased mindfulness is the Rooster's home life. The Rooster needs to make sure that his many commitments do not start to impinge on family life. A good lifestyle balance is particularly important this year.

Also, with changes occurring in his own work situation and other family members similarly busy, it is important there is openness and a willingness to assist one another. The better the communication, the more easily situations (and changes) can be addressed.

It is also important that the more pleasurable aspects of family life do not suffer due to general activity. Shared interests, special occasions and chances to travel can be much appreciated, with the summer seeing some often lively occasions.

Problems may arise, however, with equipment breaking down, maintenance issues requiring attention or practical activities being delayed. Here again, difficulties need to be talked through. Annoying though they may be, once repairs or replacements have been made and solutions found, they will have brought some benefits. Some problems could be blessings in disguise, prompting action or purchases which would not otherwise have taken place.

As well as giving some attention to his home, the Rooster should give some to himself this year. Being conscientious, he drives himself hard and needs to allow time to relax and enjoy himself. Here, interests and recreational pursuits can be akin to a tonic, and in some cases have the added advantage of additional exercise. Monkey years can also open up new possibilities. Fitness programmes will often appeal. By following up his ideas, the Rooster can enjoy and potentially benefit from what he does.

Another important aspect of the Monkey year is the way it brings the Rooster into contact with others. Many a Rooster will find his social circle widening this year and some new people will particularly warm to him. For the unattached, there can be romantic possibilities. April, May, August and September could see much social activity.

Overall, the Year of the Monkey will challenge the Rooster. Pressures and expectations will be placed upon him, but by rising to the challenge and seizing any opportunities to further his experience, he can impress others and improve his prospects, particularly for next year. Work-wise, the year will be demanding but instructive. In financial matters, the Rooster will need to remain disciplined, and he also needs to ensure his general busyness does not impinge on his home life or affect his lifestyle balance. Fortunately the Rooster is usually very aware of his responsibilities, and with his usual good skill, he can emerge from the year with much to his credit.

The Metal Rooster

There is a Chinese proverb which reminds us, 'A long journey will not deter one with high aspirations,' and this is very applicable to the Metal Rooster. Determined, ambitious and full of self-belief, he works hard, building steadily on his experience. Over the year he will continue to make progress and, in the process, gain valuable new insights into his capabilities.

However, while this will be a constructive year, it will not necessarily be easy. The resolute Metal Rooster likes to set about his activities in his own style, but in the Monkey year, greater flexibility would be advised. To be wedded to certain ways of doing things could deny the Metal Rooster opportunities. In 2016 he needs to be alert to developing situations and embrace change.

For the many Metal Rooster who are established in a particular line of work, the Monkey year can mark an important juncture in their career. There will be the chance for many to take on new duties, and if in a large organization, move to another section. In either case, there will be a lot to learn. However, the duties many Metal Roosters take on now can highlight particular strengths which they will be encouraged to develop in following years. For many, what occurs now can be a contributory factor in later success.

This also applies to Metal Roosters who feel they have achieved all they can in their present situation and are ready for more substantial change, as well as those seeking a position. The job-finding process will take time, but will give these Metal Roosters the chance to consider their strengths and explore different employment possibilities. If eligible, some may be able to take advantage of training or refresher courses. With persistence, many will find important doors opening. As these Metal Roosters settle down in a new role, the pressures can be considerable, but with commitment, they can secure a platform they can build on. May to early July, September and December could see encouraging developments, but this is a fast-moving year and once the Metal Rooster sees an opening, he should act before the chance slips away.

Also, this is an excellent year for personal development, and if the Metal Rooster feels it could be useful to acquire a skill or additional qualification, he should set time aside to do this. It could prove a useful investment in his future.

The Metal Rooster can also benefit from his personal interests. Not only can these help him relax and be good for his general well-being, but he will also enjoy the chance to explore ideas.

Some attention to well-being and lifestyle can also be useful this year. Whether improving the quality of their diet or getting advice on appropriate forms of exercise, many Metal Roosters can benefit from introducing positive lifestyle changes.

In financial matters, the Metal Rooster will need to be careful. Over the year, commitments could increase and additional expenses and repair costs arise. As a consequence, the Metal Rooster needs to keep track of spending and remain disciplined. He should also check the terms of any new agreement he enters into and attend to paperwork promptly. This is no year for risk or making assumptions.

Another area where he needs to be attentive is his home life. Sometimes work pressures and other commitments could preoccupy him and make increased incursions into his time. He does need to be aware of this and if he is feeling stressed or has a lot to do, he should tell others. That way, those around him will be better able to understand and assist.

Striking a good lifestyle balance can make an important difference this year and if possible the Metal Rooster should try to take a holiday with his loved ones. Even if not travelling too far, he will find a change of scene very welcome. The summer and end of the year could see some attractive travel possibilities.

Although the Metal Rooster may be selective in his socializing this year, he will welcome contact with his friends and the chance to share views with some who are in similar positions to his own. Certain friends could prove of particular value this year. April, May, August to early October could see good social opportunities.

For the unattached Metal Rooster, an existing or new friendship could blossom over the year. Romance will brighten the lives of quite a few Metal Roosters.

Overall, the Year of the Monkey will be an important one for the Metal Rooster, as it will give him the chance to add to his skills and experience. 'A long journey will not deter one with high aspirations' and the Monkey year will, in many ways, equip the Metal Rooster for his journey and assist him along his ambitious path. In view of his busy lifestyle, he does, though, need to make sure quality time with his loved ones does not suffer. Their support can be valuable in many ways in this constructive year.

Tip for the Year

Keep your lifestyle in balance. You can accomplish a lot this year but do preserve some time for yourself and those around you. Enjoy your interests and value your loved ones and you will be well rewarded.

The Water Rooster

Monkey years are active and fast-moving, and over the next 12 months the Water Rooster will experience a great deal. And what he accomplishes now can determine the shape of the next few years. The importance of this Monkey year should not be underestimated.

Some Water Roosters will be in education and often reaching the final stages of their courses. For these Water Roosters, this can be an exacting time, with dissertations to complete, final exams to sit and much to learn. However, while the pressures will be considerable, by remaining disciplined, many Water Roosters will secure (and often better) the results they have been hoping for. Another motivating factor will be the possibilities certain qualifications can open up. As the Chinese proverb reminds us, 'Follow proper procedures and enjoy success in whatever you do.' By studying hard, the Water Rooster will find rewards will follow.

For Water Roosters in work, this can also be a significant year. Often, having proved themselves in one capacity, these Water Roosters will be looking to further their skills and better their remuneration. Monkey years can open up important opportunities, but it will be up to the Water Rooster himself to make things happen.

Water Roosters in large organizations will find their in-house knowledge can stand them in excellent stead as some staff move on. If they put themselves forward, even if they are not initially successful, their desire to move ahead will be noted and in some cases lead to offers of training and additional duties. Many Water Roosters will be able to help their situation by participating more in their workplace and networking. As has often been found, the more people you know, the more opportunities tend to open up, and this can be very true for the Water Rooster this year.

The majority of Water Roosters will make important headway in their present place of work, but for those who feel there are better prospects elsewhere or are currently seeking work, the Monkey year can hold important developments. Although the job-seeking process may be difficult and competitive, by keeping alert for openings and stressing their skills and experience, many Water Roosters will secure an important opportunity. And once they have had the chance to establish themselves and show their capabilities, they will often be encouraged to go further. What the Water Rooster does now can be instrumental in the exciting possibilities that lie ahead, especially in 2017.

In view of the busy nature of the year it is, however, important that the Water Rooster gives some consideration to his own well-being. A balanced diet may help energy levels, as will regular and appropriate exercise.

Interests and recreational pursuits can also often help the Water Rooster unwind as well as be a good outlet for his talents and ideas. Some interests can also give rise to travel opportunities, and for the music and sports enthusiast, there could be events this year that they will particularly enjoy. Personal interests can add an important and beneficial element to this often demanding year.

The Water Rooster will also appreciate his social life. There will be parties and other celebrations (including his own) to enjoy, and for Water Roosters enjoying romance, there will be wonderful moments to share. For the unattached, the Monkey year can bring a meeting with someone new, often in circumstances which seem destined to be. For affairs of the heart, this can be a remarkable year. April, May and late July to September could see the most social activity.

For Water Roosters who are settled with a partner, this can also be an exciting time. However, the Water Rooster will need to be attentive and take care that other commitments do not leave him preoccupied or encroach too far into home life. Good communication is also vital this year. If the Water Rooster talks over his concerns and hopes, it will enable those close to him to be more aware of his situation and better able to assist.

More senior relations, too, will be keen to offer support and this can be of particular help with certain decisions or plans under consideration this year.

In money matters, this will be an expensive time and the Water Rooster will need to watch spending levels. Also, if taking on new agreements, he should check the obligations and take advice if necessary. This is a year for exercising good control.

Overall, the Monkey year will be an exacting one. The Water Rooster will be keen to do well and a lot will ride on his many activities. This can bring moments of pressure, but by remaining focused, many Water Roosters will be pleased with what they are able to achieve. The Monkey year can give many the skills and platform needed for further progress. On a personal level, many Water Roosters will enjoy the social and romantic opportunities this lively year can bring, as well as benefit from the encouragement of those around them. With a lot happening, the

Water Rooster will, though, need to balance out all he does and set aside time for himself. This will be a very full but potentially significant year.

Tip for the Year
Believe in yourself. This year will give you the chance to develop skills that can take you far. Put in the effort, for what you do now will often be a solid investment in your future.

The Wood Rooster

The practical Wood Rooster prides himself on being well-organized and efficient, and during the Monkey year he will need to keep his wits about him. Some undertakings could be problematic and certain decisions cause anxiety. However, while the Monkey year will have its challenging moments, with support and his usual good judgement, the Wood Rooster can emerge from it satisfied with the results of his efforts.

Of key importance this year is the need for consultation. Although the Wood Rooster has very definite views, he does need support in his undertakings and should take heed of the views of those around him. If not, some may feel aggrieved that they were not adequately consulted. Particularly in the Wood Rooster's home life, the year favours a collective approach.

Over the year many Wood Roosters will be keen to carry out improvements on their home, including replacing failing equipment as well as smartening up certain areas. Once the Wood Rooster has ideas, he will be keen to implement them, but costs and choices will need careful consideration. Original plans are apt to change in the Monkey year, and if options are compared, the eventual decisions can often be that much better. This particularly applies to purchases of equipment.

For Wood Roosters who decide to move or have major renovations carried out on their home, again plans may not always proceed in the way or to the timescale intended. With help and good advice, however, substantial benefits can be gained.

In addition to drawing on the support of others, the Wood Rooster will have many chances to reciprocate. Younger relations could have important decisions to make and be glad of the Wood Rooster's opinions and assistance. Wood Roosters who are grandparents will again find the time they give will be appreciated as well as strengthen their bonds with their loved ones. The summer and closing weeks of the year could see some special family occasions taking place.

With his enquiring mind, the Wood Rooster will also enjoy following up his own interests. If he is a member of a local group or decides to join one, certain skills he has could be encouraged and lead to him doing more. Creative activities are especially well aspected and could develop in exciting fashion.

In addition, the Wood Rooster should keep himself informed about events happening in his area as well as amenities and resources he could use. Local activities can also be an excellent way to meet others, especially for Wood Roosters who are feeling lonely. Late March to May, August and September could see the most social activity, although at most times of the year there will be a variety of activities to enjoy.

Travel, too, can be pleasing, although while the Wood Rooster likes to plan ahead, some trips could be decided on at the last moment as special offers are taken up or invitations received. Nevertheless, many Wood Roosters will enjoy their travels, including some quite late on in the year, and see some impressive sights.

With travel possibilities, however, plus expensive home purchases and other outgoings, the Wood Rooster will need to manage his resources well this year. With any major purchase or new agreement, he should check the terms carefully. Paperwork, too, needs care. A lapse could lead to protracted bureaucracy. Wood Roosters, take note.

For the Wood Rooster born in 2005, the Monkey year will be eventful, especially as the Wood Rooster may change school and start a new level of his education. This can be a daunting time, but by making the most of his opportunities, the young Wood Rooster will not only gain valuable new knowledge but also fresh insights into his strengths and abilities. This is a year to be open-minded and receptive to what is available.

With expectations high, however, and sometimes new environments and subjects to get used to, the young Wood Rooster could at times be anxious or feel he is struggling. Rather than keep his concerns to himself, it is important he talks to those who are close to him and gets support.

On a personal level, the young Wood Rooster can make some significant new friendships this year, some of which will become long-standing. His lively nature can make him popular company.

Whether born in 1945 or 2005, the Wood Rooster can find the Monkey year demanding. There will be problems and challenging situations to address, and plans will sometimes take different courses from those envisaged. But by drawing on support, seeking advice and being flexible, the Wood Rooster may not only find solutions but also realize the problems were opportunities in disguise. Throughout the year, it is important that he consults others and is mindful of their views. Without sufficient communication, differences of opinion may arise and support not be so forthcoming. This is a time to liaise with others rather than take an independent stance. However, with care, the Wood Rooster can make this a rewarding and interesting year.

Tip for the Year
Be aware of what is happening around you and adjust accordingly. With support and flexibility, you can achieve more. Also, use the resources available to you and enjoy developing your skills and interests. Encouraging results can follow.

The Fire Rooster

The element of fire strengthens a sign's resolve and the Fire Rooster certainly possesses a determined nature. Always keen to make the most of himself, he is a doer, has good judgement and uses his skills well. However, in 2016 he will need to keep his wits about him. Uncharacteristic lapses, assumptions or lack of communication may cause difficulty.

Throughout the year it is also important that the Fire Rooster keeps his lifestyle in balance. Neglecting one area of his life could have repercussions in others. The Fire Rooster does need to manage his time well, including, during busy periods, preserving quality time for others as well as looking after his own well-being.

This need for attention also applies to his domestic life. Although he will often be juggling many commitments, he should make sure these do not impact on family life. If he gives time to others and shares matters on his mind, those around him can often ease certain pressures. Home and family life can be rewarding this year, but mindfulness is required. Particularly busy Fire Roosters, take note.

If possible, the Fire Rooster should aim to take a holiday over the year. A rest and change of scene can do him a lot of good. Some especially interesting travel possibilities could arise during the summer months.

Over the year the Fire Rooster will also be keen to assist younger relations, and by spending time talking over the decisions and options they have, he can encourage them in significant ways. Many have a high regard for his judgement and will be grateful for his words.

It is also important that the Fire Rooster does not allow his social life to fall away during the year. Social occasions will not only give him the chance to share news but also to relax and have some fun. April, May and August to early October could see good social opportunities. Fire Roosters who are alone or find themselves in a new environment should make the most of chances to meet others. Their actions can be rewarding and for some this Monkey year can have romantic possibilities too.

The Fire Rooster should also give some consideration to his own well-being. In view of his demanding lifestyle, he should try to ensure his diet is well-balanced and, if lacking regular exercise, seek medical advice on a fitness programme.

Time set aside for personal interests can also give him the chance to unwind. For the keen gardener and outdoor enthusiast, the Monkey year can be especially satisfying.

At work, this will be an eventful year. Although many Fire Roosters will have experienced change recently and would prefer just to concentrate on their existing role, new developments could impact on this. Senior colleagues could leave and the Fire Rooster be well placed to take over, or new initiatives, products and ideas could be introduced and the Fire Rooster could be called upon to implement the changes. Some weeks could be very busy and the Fire Rooster will need to ensure his work pressures do not start to impinge on other areas of his life. However, while this may be a demanding year, many Fire Roosters will move their career forward, often progressing to a more specialist role.

Fire Roosters seeking a position will also find that by acting quickly when they see an opportunity, they can often succeed in taking on a new and ultimately important position. Late April to the end of June, September and December could see key developments.

In money matters, the Fire Rooster will need to be attentive and thorough. Though he may have many matters on his mind, giving scant attention to important paperwork or (uncharacteristically) mislaying some documents could work to his disadvantage. He needs to keep tabs on his situation, watch his budget and follow up anything which is unclear. This is not a year for risk.

Overall, the Monkey year will give the Fire Rooster the chance to use his talents to advantage. At work, many Fire Roosters will find their skills in demand. The pressure may be considerable, but these Fire Roosters will have the opportunity to make progress. Throughout the year, despite the various demands on his time, it is important the Fire Rooster keeps his lifestyle in balance and sets time aside not only for himself but also for his loved ones. With care, this can be a satisfying year, but so much depends on managing his time well. Fortunately, being organized and adept, many Fire Roosters will cope well with the rigours of the Monkey year and emerge from it with some significant achievements to their credit.

Tip for the Year

Enjoy your relations with others. Participation can make your year more rewarding. Value your loved ones and give consideration to your own well-being too. Above all, keep your lifestyle in balance in this busy year.

The Earth Rooster

A lot can happen in the Monkey year and for the Earth Rooster, who likes certainty and to follow carefully laid plans, there could be some difficult moments. However, while the Monkey year will bring its challenges, it will give rise to some very good opportunities as well as prepare the Earth Rooster for the substantial successes that await in 2017.

Throughout the year the Earth Rooster needs to keep himself informed of developments taking place around him. To immerse himself so much in his own activities that he is unaware of events and opportunities can put him at a disadvantage. In addition, he should pay close attention to the views of others. Too independent an approach could lead to problems. In the Monkey year, awareness and good liaison are so very important.

This is especially the case because the Earth Rooster will have the chance to further his knowledge and skills this year. This will often come through his work, but if there is a particular skill or qualification he feels it would be helpful to acquire, he should follow it up. One possibility may soon lead to another.

Personal interests can also be gratifying this year, and if the Earth Rooster joins others, he can be encouraged in his activities as well as enjoy himself. In addition, interests and recreational pursuits can be good ways for him to unwind and balance his lifestyle. In this busy year, spending time with others and striving for a good lifestyle balance are important.

Domestically, this will be a year of much decision-making. For the Earth Rooster and his partner, there could be work-related choices as well as major purchases to consider for the home. Younger relations, too, may be making decisions about subjects, courses and places of further education. With a lot happening, good communication will be of particular value. The Earth Rooster's reasoned judgement and talent for thinking ahead will be appreciated.

However, preoccupation, competing demands and busy work schedules could all impact on family life this year and lead to possible tension. Whenever possible, the Earth Rooster should preserve time for shared interests and other enjoyable pursuits. These can do everyone good.

In addition, he will welcome the travel opportunities that arise, and visits to places of interest may be particularly appealing. Again, the Earth Rooster needs to bear in mind that all-important lifestyle balance – and enjoy the rewards he works so hard for.

He should also keep in regular contact with his friends. For quite a few Earth Roosters, there could be celebrations and special parties to attend. For the unattached and those enjoying courtship, affairs of the heart are favourably aspected and may add sparkle to this already full year. Late March to May, August and September could see the most social opportunities.

At work, the Earth Rooster prides himself on his efficiency and organizational skills, but despite his best endeavours, the Monkey year could bring its challenges. Staff shortages, changes in personnel, the slow workings of bureaucracy and annoying delays could all be exasperating. However, it is at such times that the Earth Rooster's skills are highlighted, and by doing his best and showing resourcefulness, he can impress many and do his prospects a lot of good. As a result of what he does in often challenging situations, he could be rewarded with greater responsibilities and better remuneration as the year progresses. The Monkey year will require effort, but it does encourage career development.

In addition, if training is available, the Earth Rooster should take advantage of it. By adding to his skills and keeping himself informed of developments in his industry, he could be alerted to other possibilities to consider in the near future.

For Earth Roosters who are seeking a position elsewhere, as well as those looking for work, the Monkey year can give rise to some interesting opportunities. By considering different ways in which they could use their skills and keeping alert for openings, many of these Earth Roosters could secure a position offering a fresh challenge. Sometimes the first few weeks will be daunting, but once settled, many Earth Roosters will relish the chance to prove themselves in a new capacity. Much more substantial progress is likely in 2017. This year, May, June, September and December could see encouraging developments.

In view of the progress made at work, the Earth Rooster's income will often increase, but he will need to keep a close watch on outgoings and make ample allowance for more substantial purchases. He should also be thorough when dealing with paperwork. Monkey years are not ones for risk or rush. Careful financial management will be required.

Overall, the Year of the Monkey will be demanding and the Earth Rooster will have to deal with changes and many competing demands on his time. Being conscientious and thorough, he could be concerned by the pace of developments. However he is farsighted and can add to skills and prepare himself for opportunities in the future. Developing his skills can have considerable future benefit. Throughout the year, he should also liaise closely with others and set quality time aside to share with his loved ones as well as give himself the occasional respite from all the activity. With a good lifestyle balance, this can be a full and potentially significant year for him.

Tip for the Year
Seize any chances to add to your skills and knowledge. Also, be sure to give your loved ones your full attention. Share ideas and enjoy time together. Your thoughtfulness will be valued and make a real difference this year.

Famous Roosters

Tony Abbott, Fernando Alonso, Beyoncé, Cate Blanchett, Barbara Taylor Bradford, Gerard Butler, Sir Michael Caine, the Duchess of Cambridge, Enrico Caruso, Eric Clapton, Joan Collins, Rita Coolidge, Daniel Day-Lewis, Minnie Driver, the Duke of Edinburgh, Gloria Estefan, Paloma Faith, Roger Federer, Errol Flynn, Benjamin Franklin, Dawn French, Stephen Fry, Joseph Gordon-Levitt, Melanie Griffith, Josh Groban, Goldie Hawn, Katherine Hepburn, Paris Hilton, Jay-Z, Catherine Zeta Jones, Quincy Jones, Diane Keaton, Søren Kierkegaard, D. H. Lawrence, David Livingstone, Matthew McConaughey, Jayne Mansfield, Steve Martin, Paul Merton, Bette Midler, Ed Miliband, Sienna Miller, Van Morrison, Willie Nelson, Kim Novak, Yoko Ono, Dolly Parton, Matthew Perry, Michelle Pfeiffer, Natalie Portman, Priscilla Presley, Eddie Redmayne, Kelly Rowland, Paul Ryan, Jenny Seagrove, Carly Simon, Britney Spears, Johann Strauss, Verdi, Richard Wagner, Serena Williams, Neil Young, Renée Zellweger.

28 January 1922 to 15 February 1923 — *Water Dog*

14 February 1934 to 3 February 1935 — *Wood Dog*

2 February 1946 to 21 January 1947 — *Fire Dog*

18 February 1958 to 7 February 1959 — *Earth Dog*

6 February 1970 to 26 January 1971 — *Metal Dog*

25 January 1982 to 12 February 1983 — *Water Dog*

10 February 1994 to 30 January 1995 — *Wood Dog*

29 January 2006 to 17 February 2007 — *Fire Dog*

The Dog

The Personality of the Dog

I have my values
and beliefs.
These are my beacon
in an ever-changing world.

The Dog is born under the signs of loyalty and anxiety. He usually holds very firm views and beliefs and is the champion of good causes. He hates any sort of injustice or unfair treatment and will do all in his power to help those less fortunate than himself. He has a strong sense of fair play and will be honourable and open in all his dealings.

The Dog is very direct and straightforward. He is never one to skirt round issues and speaks frankly and to the point. He can be stubborn, but he is prepared to listen to the views of others and will try to be as fair as possible in coming to his decisions. He will readily give advice where it is needed and will be the first to offer assistance when things go wrong.

The Dog instils confidence wherever he goes and there are many who admire him for his integrity and resolute manner. He is a very good judge of character and can often form an accurate impression of someone very shortly after meeting them. He is also very intuitive and can frequently sense how things are going to work out long in advance.

Despite his friendly and amiable manner, the Dog is not a big socializer. He dislikes having to attend large functions or parties and much prefers a quiet meal with friends or a chat by the fire. He is an excellent conversationalist and is often a marvellous raconteur of amusing stories and anecdotes.

The Dog is also quick-witted and his mind is always alert. He can keep calm in a crisis and although he does have a temper, his outbursts tend to be short-lived. He is loyal and trustworthy, but if he ever feels badly let down or rejected by someone, he will rarely forgive or forget.

The Dog usually has very set interests. He prefers to specialize and become an expert in a chosen area rather than dabble in a variety of different activities. He usually does well in jobs where he feels that he is being of service to others and is often suited to careers in the social services, the medical and legal professions and teaching. He does, however, need to feel motivated in his work. He has to have a sense of purpose and if ever this is lacking he can quite often drift through life without ever achieving very much. Once he has the motivation, however, very little can prevent him from securing his objective.

Another characteristic of the Dog is his tendency to worry and to view things rather pessimistically. Quite often his worries are totally unnecessary and are of his own making. Although it may be difficult, worrying is a habit that all Dogs should try to overcome.

The Dog is not materialistic or particularly bothered about accumulating great wealth. As long as he has the money necessary to support his family and to spend on the occasional luxury, he is more than happy. However, when he does have any spare money he tends to be rather a spendthrift and does not always put it to its best use. He is also not a very good speculator and would be advised to get professional advice before entering into any major long-term investment.

The Dog will rarely be short of admirers, but he is not an easy person to live with. His moods are changeable and his standards high, but he will be loyal and protective to his partner and will do all in his power to provide a comfortable home. He can get on extremely well with those born under the signs of the Horse, Pig, Tiger and Monkey, and can also establish a sound and stable relationship with the Rat, Ox, Rabbit, Snake and another Dog, but will find the Dragon a bit too flamboyant for his liking. He will also find it difficult to understand the imaginative Goat and is likely to be highly irritated by the candid Rooster.

The female Dog is renowned for her beauty. She has a warm and caring nature, although until she knows someone well she can be both secretive and very guarded. She is highly intelligent and despite her calm and tranquil appearance can be extremely ambitious. She enjoys sport and other outdoor activities and has a happy knack of finding bargains in the most unlikely of places. She can also get rather impatient when things do not work out as she would like.

The Dog usually has a very good way with children and can be a doting parent. He will rarely be happier than when he is helping someone or doing something that will benefit others. Providing he can cure himself of his tendency to worry, he will lead a very full and active life, and in that life he will make many friends and do a tremendous amount of good.

The Five Different Types of Dog

In addition to the 12 signs of the Chinese zodiac there are five elements and these have a strengthening or moderating influence on the signs. The effects of the elements on the Dog are described below, together with the years in which they were exercising their influence. Therefore Dogs born in 1970 are Metal Dogs, Dogs born in 1922 and 1982 are Water Dogs, and so on.

Metal Dog: 1970

The Metal Dog is bold, confident and forthright and sets about everything he does in a resolute and determined manner. He has a great belief in his abilities and no hesitation about speaking his mind or devoting himself to some just cause. He can be rather serious at times and can become anxious and irritable when things are not going according to plan. He tends to have very specific interests and it would certainly help him if he were to broaden his outlook and become more involved in group activities. He is extremely loyal and faithful to his friends.

Water Dog: 1922, 1982

The Water Dog has a very direct and outgoing personality. He is an excellent communicator and has little trouble in persuading others to fall in with his plans. He does, however, have a somewhat carefree nature and is not as disciplined or as thorough as he should be in certain matters. Neither does he keep as much control over his finances as he should, but he can be most generous to his family and friends and will make sure that they want for nothing. He is usually very good with children and has a wide circle of friends.

Wood Dog: 1934, 1994

This Dog is a hard and conscientious worker and will usually make a favourable impression wherever he goes. He is less independent than some of the other types of Dog and prefers to work in a group rather than on his own. He is popular, has a good sense of humour and takes a keen interest in the activities of the various members of his family. He is often attracted to the finer things in life and can obtain much pleasure from collecting stamps, coins, pictures or antiques. He prefers to live in the country rather than the town.

Fire Dog: 1946, 2006

This Dog has a lively, outgoing personality and is able to establish friendships with remarkable ease. He is an honest and conscientious worker and likes to take an active part in all that is going on around him. He also likes to explore new ideas and providing he can get the necessary support and advice, he can often succeed where others have failed. He does, however, have a tendency to be stubborn. Providing he can overcome this, he can often achieve considerable fame and fortune.

Earth Dog: 1958

The Earth Dog is very talented and astute. He is methodical and efficient and is capable of going far in his chosen profession. He tends to be rather quiet and reserved, but has a very persuasive manner and usually secures his objectives without too much opposition. He is generous and kind and always ready to lend a helping hand when it is needed. He is also held in very high esteem by his friends and colleagues and is usually most dignified in his appearance.

Prospects for the Dog in 2016

The Dog likes order and consistency and may have felt ill-at-ease with some of the developments of the Goat year (19 February 2015–7 February 2016). This can be a time of volatility, and changing situations may have brought the Dog worrying moments. However, while he may have faced many challenges, he will also have achieved a considerable amount. The remaining months will continue to be busy.

In his home, the Dog is likely to have undertaken quite a few ambitious projects, and for some this could have included a move. As the year draws to a close, many Dogs will be keen to finish off practical activities, including making what will be major purchases. The canny Dog could be fortunate in finding the right items on often favourable terms. End-of-year sales could yield additional bargains.

However, with the considerable practical activity and the many arrangements that will need making at this time, the Dog does need to liaise well with his loved ones.

There will also be an increase in social activity and the Dog will appreciate spending time with friends and catching up with some he has not seen for some while. December and early January could see a flurry of activity, with some surprising occasions and news concerning a friend.

At work, the Dog may find the pressures considerable and his objectives challenging. However, by doing his best, he can achieve some notable successes. October could see important developments.

Overall, although the Goat year will have been demanding, many Dogs will have benefited from the support of others as well as experienced events which will have meant a lot personally.

The Year of the Monkey, which starts on 8 February, will be an encouraging one for the Dog. His judgement can serve him well this year and if he acts with determination, he can secure some key objectives. As Virgil noted, 'Fortune favours the bold,' and in this Monkey year, fortune *will* favour the bold and enterprising Dog.

One of the Dog's characteristics is that he relies a lot on his instinct, and as the Monkey year begins, he will sense his prospects are improving. Dogs who are feeling unfulfilled or nursing disappointment in particular should view the Monkey year as a time for positive change.

At work, the Monkey year will give the Dog more opportunity to use his strengths, and his skills and loyalty *will* be recognized. Dogs who have been with the same employer or in the same type of work for some time will now have the chance to move on to greater responsibilities. Suitable openings for promotion can also arise and, for those employed in large organizations, transfers to other positions could be tempting.

Dogs who are currently feeling unfulfilled and staid in their work should take advantage of the favourable aspects and look for a position elsewhere. Once they start to make enquiries and register with employment agencies, they could be alerted to several openings worth considering. These could involve a considerable change of duties but be just what these Dogs need.

This also applies to Dogs seeking work. By widening their search, many could be offered the opportunity to establish themselves in a new role. For some, this may mean leaving their comfort zone, but Monkey years are encouraging.

March, April, September and November could see interesting developments, but opportunities can arise quickly at any time and need to be seized without delay. The Dog's instinct can serve him well this year and he will often sense which openings are right for him.

Another factor in the Dog's favour will be the support he receives, including from unexpected quarters. Colleagues, some influential, could put in recommendations for him (sometimes without his knowledge) and his reputation and references will also help his prospects. He should seize any chances to network, as his manner and qualities will impress many this year.

Progress at work will help financially, but the Monkey year will be an expensive one. Much spending is again likely on the home, and for some Dogs who considered or started moving plans last year, relocation is now possible. Travel is also strongly indicated this year and in view of all these outgoings, the Dog will need to budget ahead. With care, however, he will be pleased with the many plans he is able to carry out.

It is also important that he gives some consideration to his own well-being this year and, if necessary, reviews the quality of his diet and his level of exercise. To drive himself hard without adequate rest may leave him susceptible to colds and other niggling ailments. In this encouraging year, he should do his best to remain on top form. Dogs, take note.

Personal interests can help keep the Dog's lifestyle in balance and the Monkey year will provide a variety of ideas. Should something new appeal to the Dog, he should aim to find out more. Some Dogs will also be keen to take certain skills further and set themselves a new challenge or project. This can be an inspiring time.

There will also be good travel opportunities, and if possible, all Dogs should aim to take a holiday. This could give them a much-needed rest as well as the chance to visit some interesting locations. Late summer could see good possibilities.

Although the Dog is often selective in his socializing, an increase in activity is indicated this year and he could receive invitations to parties and other celebrations as well as enjoy contact with his close circle of friends. February, March, June and December could be busy, and for Dogs who are lonely or have had some recent personal difficulty, someone they meet now could restore some sparkle to their life. Socially, this can be a rewarding and pleasing time.

In his home life, the Dog will continue to have ambitious plans and one idea will often lead to others. However, ample time does need to be allowed for practical activities and ideally they should be spread out over the year rather than attempted all at once.

With personal and career successes, good travel possibilities and plans being implemented, the year can be marked by several domestic high points. The Dog's input will once again be valued, and May and September could be particularly busy and pleasing.

Overall, the Monkey year holds good prospects for the Dog, but a lot rests with him. If he is determined, good progress can be made. The Dog will be well supported and his home and social life busy and often special, but in view of all the activity, he does need to look after himself, including setting time aside for personal interests and to enjoy the good travel opportunities that will arise. If he seizes the initiative and balances his lifestyle, he can make this both a pleasing and progressive year.

The Metal Dog

The Metal Dog is determined and conscientious and puts a great deal of effort into his many activities. In 2016 his commitment is set to reward him well. This will be a progressive and often lucky time for him.

Over the year the Metal Dog will be encouraged by those around him. Particularly when making decisions or considering ideas, he will value the help that loved ones and those with expertise can offer. During the Monkey year, he will have many rooting for him and keen for him to secure the success he deserves. As he meets new people, too, his straightforward manner will impress and he can build some useful connections. Both in his work and personal interests, this is an excellent year to network and raise his profile.

The Metal Dog is not the biggest socializer, but he will frequently be surprised and delighted by the social opportunities of the Monkey year. By participating in what is happening, he can look forward to some lively times. February to early April, June and December could see the most social activity.

Metal Dogs who are feeling lonely should immerse themselves in local activities and take up any chances to go out. Positive action can reward them well. For some, affairs of the heart can add excitement to the year. For personal relationships, this can be a busy and often special time and it would benefit the Metal Dog to go out more rather than keep himself to himself.

In his home life, a lot is set to happen, including a move for some. In addition, the Metal Dog and his loved ones could face changes in routine. Adjustments will need to be made, but with good co-operation, much can be gained from the changes taking place. Here again, support from loved ones can be an encouraging factor in the Metal Dog's year.

While often busy with practical undertakings, he will also find shared interests and trips can be enjoyable and do relationships a lot of good.

May, September and the end of the year could be active and possibly celebratory times in the Metal Dog household.

The Metal Dog can also look forward to making progress in his work. When new openings arise, he will often be well qualified to apply and his loyalty and commitment will stand him in good stead. Monkey years favour enterprise and there will also be the opportunity for many Metal Dogs to contribute ideas and take on fresh objectives. Many senior colleagues think highly of the Metal Dog's abilities and his involvement this year can be of increasing value. March, April, September and November could see potentially significant developments.

For Metal Dogs who feel limited where they are and would welcome a position offering greater scope, as well as those seeking work, the Monkey year offers interesting prospects. By keeping alert for vacancies and talking to friends and contacts, these Metal Dogs could be alerted to new possibilities or think of different ways in which they could use their strengths. Monkey years can open interesting doors, and by being willing to adapt, the Metal Dog may secure a position which will turn out to be a significant development in his working life. However, he needs to be quick in making applications and stress his experience. Monkey years reward giving that little bit extra.

Progress made at work will help financially, but with the Metal Dog's existing commitments, plus ideas for his home and good travel possibilities, he will need to watch his spending and plan ahead. This is a time for good financial management.

Although the Metal Dog will be kept busy this year, he should allow some time for recreational pursuits. These can help him unwind and provide a break from other activities and concerns.

Also, if lacking regular exercise, he should try to remedy this and take advice on activities that may help. Similarly, if he has concerns about his well-being at any time, he should get these checked out. He does need to ensure he is in good form and able to enjoy the fruits of his labours.

The Monkey year is in many ways a rewarding one for the Metal Dog. In his work there will often be the chance to make more of his talents, and the success he enjoys now will not only be well deserved but often mark an important stage in his career. He will be encouraged by the belief, support and assistance of those around him, and will value his home life and close circle of friends. Travel and new friendships can add interest to this rewarding year, and with initiative and resolve, the Metal Dog can do well.

Tip for the Year
Be active. Explore possibilities and look to move forward. With the support you enjoy and the chances that will become available, this is a year of considerable possibility. Seize the moment.

The Water Dog

The Monkey year is one of great possibility for the Water Dog. It can see some personally significant events and there will be special times to enjoy.

Water Dogs who are following a specific career should use this year to further their experience and move on to greater responsibilities. Often openings will become available in their existing place of work, and by being active team members and adding to their working knowledge, many of these Water Dogs will make impressive headway.

The Water Dog can also help his prospects by taking advantage of any training that may be available, meeting others connected in his industry and, if applicable, joining a professional organization. By being involved and raising his profile, he will be noticed and his talents recognized.

There will also be some Water Dogs who feel they could better their prospects by moving to another employer. By keeping alert for openings within their industry, many will make what can be a significant transfer. Admittedly, there could be considerable adjustment involved, but with commitment and the desire to do well, many of these Water Dogs will reach a new level in their career.

Those seeking work should also keep alert for developments in their area, including recruitment drives of large employers. By being active and informed, many will have the chance to establish themselves in an often different capacity. Work-wise, the Monkey year is encouraging, and late February to April, September and November could be key months.

Progress made at work will also help financially, with many Water Dogs increasing their income and sometimes benefiting from an additional payment or gift. However, the Water Dog will have considerable commitments to meet, plans to realize and (sometimes) deposits to make. To do all he wants, he will need to remain disciplined.

Travel is favourably aspected and if possible the Water Dog should aim to go away over the year. For some, a special offer could be tempting. The Water Dog will enjoy any breaks he is able to take this year.

Despite his many commitments, he should also allow time for his personal interests. These cannot only help him relax but sometimes allow him to use his talents in other ways.

In addition, if sedentary for much of the day, he could benefit from activities that offer the chance of additional exercise. In this full year, the Water Dog does need to pay some attention to his own well-being. Should he feel below par or lacking his usual energy at any time, he should seek medical advice.

With water as his element, the Water Dog is a great communicator and many people enjoy his company and interesting repartee. During the year he will be in demand, with events to attend and friends to meet. He may also be involved in helping with a delicate personal matter. He will meet quite a few new people this year, some of whom will, in time, become part of his social circle. For Water Dogs who are unattached, significant romance can unexpectedly but gloriously arise this year. February to early April, June to early July and December could see the most social activity.

This will also be an important year domestically. In many Water Dog households there will be a cause for celebration, possibly a birth, a change of residence or a personal or career success. Whatever takes place, the Monkey year will see the realization of some of the Water Dog's dreams. Admittedly, there will be pressures, too, with some weeks hectic as plans are implemented, but in the main, the Monkey year will be exciting and often meaningful. May and September could see much domestic activity.

With such a lot happening, the Water Dog's ability to communicate well and enthuse others will help, and the more activities that can be undertaken jointly, the better. Sometimes more senior relations may be able to assist, including in giving time.

Overall, the Year of the Monkey will be a busy and sometimes demanding one for the Water Dog, but it will also be one of opportunity. Work prospects are favourably aspected, and by developing his skills and following up possibilities, the Water Dog can make important headway. Commitment will be required, but he will be helped by the good relations he enjoys with many of those around him, and by being involved in what is going on and communicating in his usual effective way, he will be able to move many of his plans forward. There will be many factors in his favour this year. With his busy lifestyle, he does need to give some consideration to his well-being, however. Recreational pursuits can help him unwind. Many Water Dogs will have celebrations and successes to enjoy and the Water Dog's often special qualities can be both recognized and rewarded in this encouraging year.

Tip for the Year
Add to your skills. New knowledge and capabilities can open important doors. This is a year to develop and advance. Use it well and enjoy the fruits of your efforts, both now and in succeeding years.

The Wood Dog

The Wood Dog can look forward to a full and pleasing year. With characteristic drive, he can accomplish a considerable amount and his achievements will help shape the next few years. The importance of this lively year should not be underestimated.

In addition to the encouraging aspects, there will also be several factors in the Wood Dog's favour. One will be his sense of purpose and desire to prove himself. By working steadily towards his goals and seizing his opportunities, he can do well. Another factor is his ability to relate well to so many people. The Wood Dog is alert and aware and makes good company, and this can win him not only good but also influential support this year. In 2016 he will learn a lot about himself and his capabilities.

For Wood Dogs in education, this can be a demanding time, with coursework to complete and exams to sit. Although this may be daunting, there will be good opportunities for the Wood Dog to prove what he can do, and by working consistently, many Wood Dogs will be pleased with the results they obtain. The Monkey year will require great effort, but the rewards can be significant.

The Monkey year can also have important consequences for some Wood Dogs. Through their studying, they may discover a vocation or specialism that particularly attracts them. Tutors and other professionals may also offer suggestions to consider for the future. By being aware and following up the possibilities that feel right, these Wood Dogs can set significant wheels in motion.

For Wood Dogs in work, the Monkey year can also hold major developments. Unexpected openings may occur as staff leave and/or workloads increase. There will be the opportunity for many Wood Dogs to take on additional duties over the course of the year. Significantly, the responsibilities some now take on, or the training they undertake, could indicate areas to concentrate on in the future. Developments this year can be timely and far-reaching.

For Wood Dogs seeking work, there also can be interesting openings to pursue, but with competition likely to be fierce, the Wood Dog will need to be persistent and show initiative, including emphasizing his skills to prospective employers. Commitment will be required, but once these Wood Dogs get their feet on the employment ladder, they will have the chance to prove themselves and the positions they take on now will often have a bearing on their future career. March to early May, September and November could see encouraging developments.

The Wood Dog will also enjoy the way he can develop his interests this year. Monkey years have vibrancy and encourage creativity and the exploration of talents. The expert guidance some Wood Dogs receive this year concerning an interest or skill could open up fresh possibilities and be well worth heeding.

The Monkey year also favours travel and there will be the chance for many Wood Dogs to enjoy new places as well as have a good time with those they go with. For the outdoor enthusiast, the Monkey year can give rise to some exciting occasions.

With such a busy lifestyle, the Wood Dog will need to keep a close watch on his financial situation, however. With discipline, he will be pleased with the considerable amount he is able to do, but he needs to guard against too many spur-of-the-moment indulgences. These can easily mount up. Also, if taking on a new financial commitment, he should check the terms and question anything that is unclear. Similarly, if he is ever in a dilemma and would welcome advice, he should remember that senior relations will often be keen to help.

The Wood Dog often drives himself hard and would also do well to give some consideration to his own well-being, including making sure his diet is healthy and adequate and he gives himself the chance to rest after busy times. If he has any concerns or feels lacklustre at any time, he should seek advice.

His social life is wonderfully aspected this year and he will enjoy many different occasions and the company of good friends. Having known some of these for a long time, he will value the trust and rapport he enjoys and the advice that can be shared. With some Wood Dogs changing their location, perhaps as study courses end or work opportunities arise, there will also be the opportunity to meet others this year, and new friendships and in some cases significant relationships can be forged. February to early April, June to early July and December could be particularly lively months.

For Wood Dogs with a partner, there will be exciting plans to follow through and hopes to share. There may be sudden opportunities, too, including invitations to attend celebrations (of which there could be several this year), to travel, or to do something connected to a shared interest. Some major purchases could also delight the Wood Dog. A lot is set to happen this year, although the Wood Dog should resist the temptation of committing himself to too many undertakings (or costs) at the same time. This is a year to pace himself and to enjoy what is possible.

Overall, the Monkey year has considerable potential for the Wood Dog. This is a time to have fun, to appreciate friends and close relationships – and to put in the effort. Results, qualifications and work positions will all need to be worked for. However, the Wood Dog has the ability to do well and carve out a successful future, and his achievements now can pave the way.

Tip for the Year
Work hard and heed the advice you are given. This can be more important than you may realize. Also, enjoy your relations with those around you. Many will be keen to encourage you and their input can make a difference.

The Fire Dog

The Fire Dog will not only be celebrating the start of a new decade in his life but will also see the realization of some hopes and ambitions this year. This will be a rewarding and constructive time for him.

One of the most pleasing aspects of the year is how the Fire Dog will be drawn into certain activities. This can be especially the case in his own interests. Many Fire Dogs will have interests they are particularly fond of and they will enjoy the way these develop during the Monkey year. For the creative Fire Dog, new thoughts or projects could be particularly inspiring. There could be techniques to experiment with and encouraging results to celebrate. Monkey years favour inventiveness and many Fire Dogs will be on inspired form.

With this also being a year for participation, any Fire Dogs who would welcome the chance to try a new activity or go out more should find out about interest groups and activities available in their area. By doing something positive, they could discover a new pursuit which brings them pleasure as well as possibly an additional outlet for their talents. Some Fire Dogs may like to keep themselves to themselves, but this is a time to be involved and enjoy what is available. Lonely and perhaps dispirited Fire Dog, do take note *and engage.*

Similarly, some Fire Dogs may have a long-cherished dream, perhaps about writing a book, recording experiences or visiting a certain place. Now is the time to take this further, including talking it over with loved ones. Much can become possible this year, but those all-important first steps need to come from the Fire Dog himself.

Although many Fire Dogs keep themselves active, they should also give some consideration to their well-being, including the quality of their diet and level of exercise. If the Fire Dog feels either is deficient, it would be worth seeking medical advice on the best way to proceed. Similarly, if he has any concerns, he should get these checked out. Attention to his own well-being can make a difference this year, including to his energy levels.

Travel is well aspected and many Fire Dogs will have the chance to enjoy a special holiday. By planning this in advance and reading up about their destination, they will particularly enjoy their time away. Here again some cherished dreams can be realized this year.

The Monkey year can also give rise to some lively social occasions. New or existing interests can have a good social element and once again the Fire Dog will value his close friends. Pleasingly, for some who may have felt lonely of late, the Monkey year can bring the gift of an important new friend. Monkey years can see many encouraging developments, including personal ones. February, March, June to early July and December could see the most social activity.

The Fire Dog's home life will also be special this year. Loved ones will often be keen to mark his seventieth birthday and may have some thoughtful surprises lined up. In many cases, the love and kindness shown the Fire Dog this year will touch him deeply.

His own love and care for younger relations will also be evident, and whenever he feels someone is under pressure or agonizing over a predicament, his kindly but level-headed approach will be of considerable value. Home life this year can be special and the Fire Dog will be at the heart of so much that goes on.

He will also enjoy the way some plans and hopes can now be advanced, and if he has projects or purchases in mind, this can be a good year to proceed. Involving others will also help his plans come to fruition in this active year.

With travel, personal projects and interests and family activities, however, the Fire Dog will need to keep a close watch on spending levels and ideally make early allowance for more substantial plans. This is a year for good budgeting.

For the Fire Dog born in 2006, the Monkey year offers considerable scope. Many young Fire Dogs will have fun pursuing interests and exploring ideas and capabilities. In their education, new subjects or equipment they get to use can make them more aware of their skills. In this respect, the Monkey year can be both illuminating and enriching.

The young Fire Dog will also enjoy the camaraderie of those around him and a particular interest of his is likely to bring him in contact with someone who is destined to become a long-standing friend.

Whether born in 1946 or 2006, the Fire Dog will find the Monkey year an encouraging one and it will be up to him to make the most of it. Ideas and thoughts should be followed up, as once activities are started, they can quickly gain momentum. On a personal level, the Fire Dog can look forward to some excellent travel possibilities as well as to some special times with his loved ones. There may be some surprises too. An interesting and personally rewarding year.

Tip for the Year
Follow up your ideas. Don't be left wondering in years to come, 'What if?' This is a special year for you with the chance to do the special things you want. Enjoy it.

The Earth Dog

There is a Chinese proverb which recommends, 'Hoist your sail when the wind is fair. Seize the opportunity.' This advice is very apt for the Earth Dog this year. This is a favourable time for him and by seizing the opportunity he can accomplish a great deal.

At work, many Earth Dogs will have seen considerable change in recent years. This year will give them more chance to concentrate on their area of expertise. Some Earth Dogs may be given specific objectives or take advantage of opportunities to move to positions they find more fulfilling. In the Monkey year many will feel more in control of what they do, and in the process be able to make more of particular strengths and enjoy some well-deserved successes.

Earth Dogs who feel ready for more substantial change or are seeking work will find that by seeking out positions that interest them and emphasizing their skills to prospective employers, their determination will ultimately deliver. It may take time, but the positions they take on this year will often give them more chance to use specific strengths. As the Earth Dog has so often shown, it is when he is inspired and content in his role that he produces his best work. March, April, September and November could see encouraging developments.

Whatever his work situation, the Earth Dog will also be helped by colleagues (both present and former) and if he is in need of certain information or would welcome advice, it is important he asks for it. Earth Dogs seeking change or a position could find someone they know alerting them to a possible opening or making the introduction they need. In this Monkey year, the respect and goodwill many Earth Dogs enjoy can make an important difference.

The Monkey year also encourages exploring ideas and talents and the Earth Dog should aim to spend some time enjoying his personal interests. Creative pursuits are particularly highlighted this year and some Earth Dogs could become enthused by a project they set themselves or an activity they take up. Those who lead busy lives or have let their personal interests fall away should aim to set aside some time for themselves this year. They can benefit in many ways.

The Earth Dog should also give some consideration to his well-being, and should he have any concerns, get these checked out.

Giving himself a break from his busy lifestyle will also help, and with travel well aspected, he should try to take a holiday. Some Earth Dogs may also take up a chance to visit a place they have long wanted to see or attend a specific event. The Monkey year can give rise to some interesting travel opportunities.

In view of all his plans and commitments, the Earth Dog will, however, need to keep track of his outgoings and budget carefully. This is a year which rewards good financial management. Fortunately, the Earth Dog's disciplined approach will enable him to proceed with many of his hopes and ideas.

Although the Earth Dog is selective in his socializing, the Monkey year can give rise to some lively occasions and offer a pleasing mix of things to do. The Earth Dog could find certain interests introducing him to new people and useful contacts can be made. For the unattached, the Monkey year can see an increase in social activity. Shared interests and activities can be especially satisfying. February to early April, June and December could be pleasing months.

The Earth Dog's home life is also set to be busy this year. There will be achievements to mark, and whether celebrating his own progress or that of another family member, the Earth Dog will enjoy some special moments, often made all the more meaningful by the effort involved.

He will also often initiate some ambitious home projects. However, although keen, he does need to allow ample time to complete them. Some could be more wide-ranging and disruptive than anticipated. May and September could see considerable domestic activity.

Overall, the Year of the Monkey is a constructive one for the Earth Dog and will give him the chance to make more of his strengths. Whether in his work or personal interests, he should focus on areas he enjoys, as his knowledge and skills are capable of rewarding him well this year. New ideas can also emerge and interesting results follow on. The Earth Dog will be encouraged by the support of those around him and delight in sharing his success. By 'hoisting his sail when the wind is fair', he can look forward to making good and well-deserved progress.

Tip for the Year
With so much happening this year, do give some time to yourself. Enjoy your interests, enjoy sharing your time with others and enjoy the rewards you work so hard to achieve.

Famous Dogs

Brigitte Bardot, Gary Barlow, Candice Bergen, Justin Bieber, Andrea Bocelli, David Bowie, Jimmy Buffett, George W. Bush, Kate Bush, the Duke of Cambridge, Naomi Campbell, Peter Capaldi, Mariah Carey, King Carl XVI Gustaf of Sweden, José Carreras, Paul Cézanne, Cher, Sir Winston Churchill, Bill Clinton, Leonard Cohen, Abbie Cornish, Matt Damon, Charles Dance, Claude Debussy, Dame Judi Dench, Jamie Dornan, Kirsten Dunst, Dakota Fanning, Joseph Fiennes, Robert Frost, Judy Garland, George Gershwin, Anne Hathaway, Barry Humphries, Holly Hunter, Michael Jackson, Jennifer Lopez, Sophia Loren, Andie MacDowell, Shirley MacLaine, Melissa McCarthy, Madonna, Norman Mailer, Barry Manilow, Freddie Mercury, Nicki Minaj, Liza Minnelli, Simon Pegg, Elvis Presley, Tim Robbins, Susan Sarandon, Claudia Schiffer, Dr Albert Schweitzer, Sylvester Stallone, Robert Louis Stevenson, Sharon Stone, Nicola Sturgeon, Donald Sutherland, Mother Teresa, Uma Thurman, Donald Trump, Voltaire, Lil Wayne, Shelley Winters.

16 February 1923 to 4 February 1924 — *Water Pig*

4 February 1935 to 23 January 1936 — *Wood Pig*

22 January 1947 to 9 February 1948 — *Fire Pig*

8 February 1959 to 27 January 1960 — *Earth Pig*

27 January 1971 to 14 February 1972 — *Metal Pig*

13 February 1983 to 1 February 1984 — *Water Pig*

31 January 1995 to 18 February 1996 — *Wood Pig*

18 February 2007 to 6 February 2008 — *Fire Pig*

The Pig

The Personality of the Pig

It's the doing,
the giving,
the playing the part,
that makes life what it is.
And what it can be.

The Pig is born under the sign of honesty. He has a kind and understanding nature and is well known for his abilities as a peacemaker. He hates any sort of discord or unpleasantness and will do everything in his power to sort out differences of opinion or bring opposing factions together.

He is also an excellent conversationalist and speaks truthfully and to the point. He dislikes any form of falsehood or hypocrisy and is a firm believer in justice and the maintenance of law and order. In spite of these beliefs, however, he is reasonably tolerant and often prepared to forgive others for their wrongdoings. He rarely harbours grudges and is never vindictive.

The Pig is usually very popular. He enjoys other people's company and likes to be involved in joint or group activities. He will be a loyal member of any club or society and can be relied upon to lend a helping hand at functions. He is also an excellent fundraiser for charities and is often a great supporter of humanitarian causes.

The Pig is a hard and conscientious worker and is particularly respected for his reliability and integrity. In his early years he will try his hand at several different jobs, but he is usually happiest where he feels that he is being of service to others. He will unselfishly give up his time for the common good and is highly valued by his colleagues and employers.

The Pig has a good sense of humour and invariably has a smile, joke or some whimsical remark at the ready. He loves to entertain and to please others, and there are many Pigs who have been attracted to careers in show business or who enjoy following the careers of famous stars and personalities.

There are, unfortunately, some who take advantage of the Pig's good nature and impose upon his generosity. The Pig has great difficulty in saying 'no', and although he may dislike being firm, it would be in his own interests to say occasionally, 'Enough is enough.' He can also be rather naïve and gullible; however, if at any stage in his life he feels that he has been badly let down, he will try to become self-reliant. There are many Pigs who have become entrepreneurs or forged a successful career on their own after some early disappointment in life. Although the Pig tends to spend his money quite freely, he is usually very astute in financial matters and there are many Pigs who have become wealthy.

Another characteristic of the Pig is his ability to recover from setbacks reasonably quickly. His faith and his strength of character keep him going. If he thinks that there is a job he can do or there is something that he wants to achieve, he will pursue it with dogged determination. He can also be stubborn and no matter how many may plead with him, once he has made his mind up he will rarely change his views.

Although the Pig may work hard, he also knows how to enjoy himself. He is a great pleasure-seeker and will quite happily spend his hard-earned money on a lavish holiday or an expensive meal – for the Pig is a connoisseur of good food and wine – or a variety of recreational activities. He also enjoys small social gatherings and if he is in company he likes he can very easily become the life and soul of the party. He does, however, tend to become rather withdrawn at larger functions or when among strangers.

The Pig is a creature of comfort and his home will usually be fitted with the latest in luxury appliances. Where possible, he will prefer to live in the country rather than the town and will opt to have a big garden, for the Pig is usually a keen and successful gardener.

The Pig is very popular with others and will often have numerous romances before he settles down. Once settled, however, he will be loyal to his partner and he will find that he is especially well suited to those born under the signs of the Goat, Rabbit, Dog and Tiger and also to another Pig. Due to his affable and easy-going nature he can also establish a satisfactory relationship with all the remaining signs of the Chinese zodiac, with the exception of the Snake. The Snake tends to be wily, secretive and very guarded, and this can be intensely irritating to the honest and open-hearted Pig.

The female Pig will devote much time and energy to the needs of her partner and children. She will try to ensure that they want for nothing and their pleasure is very much her pleasure. Her home will either be very clean and orderly or hopelessly untidy. Strangely, there seems to be no in-between with Pigs – they either love housework or detest it! The female Pig does, however, have considerable talents as an organizer and this, combined with her friendly and open manner, enables her to secure many of her objectives. She also has very good taste in clothes.

The Pig is usually lucky in life and will rarely want for anything. Provided he does not let others take advantage of his good nature and is not afraid of asserting himself, he will go through life making friends, helping others and winning the admiration of many.

The Five Different Types of Pig

In addition to the 12 signs of the Chinese zodiac there are five elements and these have a strengthening or moderating influence on the signs. The effects of the elements on the Pig are described below, together with the years in which they were exercising their influence. Therefore Pigs born in 1971 are Metal Pigs, Pigs born in 1923 and 1983 are Water Pigs, and so on.

Metal Pig: 1971

The Metal Pig is more ambitious and determined than some of the other types of Pig. He is strong, energetic and likes to be involved in a wide variety of different activities. He is very open and forthright in his views, although he can be a little too trusting at times and has a tendency to accept things at face value. He has a good sense of humour and loves to attend parties and other social gatherings. He has a warm, outgoing nature and usually has a large circle of friends.

Water Pig: 1923, 1983

The Water Pig has a heart of gold. He is generous and loyal and tries to remain on good terms with everyone. He will do his utmost to help others, but sadly there are some who will take advantage of his kind nature and he should, in his own interests, be a little more discriminating and be prepared to stand firm against anything that he does not like. Although he prefers the quieter things in life, he has a wide range of interests. He particularly enjoys outdoor pursuits and attending parties and social occasions. He is a hard and conscientious worker and invariably does well in his chosen profession. He is also gifted in the art of communication.

Wood Pig: 1935, 1995

This Pig has a friendly, persuasive manner and is easily able to gain the confidence of others. He likes to be involved in all that is going on around him but can sometimes take on more responsibility than he can properly handle. He is loyal to his family and friends and derives much pleasure from helping those less fortunate than himself. He is usually an optimist and leads a very full, enjoyable and satisfying life. He also has a good sense of humour.

Fire Pig: 1947, 2007

The Fire Pig is both energetic and adventurous and sets about everything he does in a confident and resolute manner. He is very forthright in his views and does not mind taking risks in order to achieve his objectives. He can, however, get carried away by the excitement of the moment and ought to exercise more caution in some of the enterprises in which he gets involved. He is usually lucky in money matters and is well known for his generosity. He is also very caring towards the members of his family.

Earth Pig: 1959

This Pig has a kindly nature. He is sensible and realistic and will go to great lengths in order to please his employers and to secure his aims and ambitions. He is an excellent organizer and is particularly astute in business and financial matters. He has a good sense of humour and a wide circle of friends. He also likes to lead an active social life, although he does sometimes have a tendency to eat and drink more than is good for him.

Prospects for the Pig in 2016

The Pig sets great store by his relations with others and in the Goat year (19 February 2015–7 February 2016), many Pigs will have experienced happiness and support. Both the Pig's home and social life will have been busy, and as the year draws to a close, the Pig will find himself with a lot to do, arrange and enjoy. September and the end of the year could be particularly busy times and bring parties and surprise occasions which will delight the Pig. Many Pigs could also give timely advice to a close friend in the closing months of the Goat year.

Goat years are excellent for personal and career development and the Pig should take advantage of any chances to further his skills and knowledge in what remains of this one. What he does now can often help both his current situation and future prospects.

At work, by seizing any chances to extend his remit and prove himself in what could be pressured times, the Pig can move forward. Present commitment can reap future reward.

With the closing months of the year being so busy, the Pig's outgoings will be high, and while he will often be generous and enjoy all the activity, sensible control over the purse-strings would be wise. Too many impulse buys could mount up.

The Pig will have seen a lot happen in the Goat year, and while his progress may have been modest compared to some years, what he has succeeded in doing can be built upon in the Monkey year.

*   *   *

The Year of the Monkey, which starts on 8 February, will be a reasonable one for the Pig, but while he can make good progress at work and his personal prospects are again promising, it will require great effort. Delays, niggles and sometimes situations outside his control will impact on some of what he wants to do, and throughout the Monkey year he will need to keep alert and adapt accordingly. Fortunately the Pig is blessed with a resourceful nature and can often steer his way round the year's trickier aspects, but it is nevertheless a time for care and watchfulness.

At work, the Monkey year can see considerable activity, with new initiatives and working practices and many product launches. As a result, there will be the chance for many Pigs to move ahead. Those who are looking to improve their situation should keep alert for openings as the Monkey year starts and stay informed about developments in their place of work. Once they start to explore possibilities, chances can very quickly start to arise. The Pig's skills and background will often be valuable assets and the Monkey year encourages progress.

For Pigs considering a more substantial change or seeking work, professional bodies or contacts may be able to offer useful advice, and by keeping alert for possibilities, these Pigs could find a position that is just right for them. March, May, July and November could see encouraging developments.

Monkey years are also times of innovation, with many new approaches finding favour. Pigs whose work involves creative thought should make the most of their talents, putting forward their ideas and promoting their strengths. The skills of many will be encouraged this year and some well-deserved successes can be enjoyed. But again this is a year for effort. Pigs, take note, and *make your strengths count*.

As always, the Pig will be keen to forge good relations with his colleagues and generally his working relations will be positive. However, while he will enjoy good support, he should be wary about making assumptions. Some people are not as reliable or as motivated as he is and there could be instances this year when another person slacks or lets him down. It would be wise for the Pig to keep tabs on what is happening and what others are doing. Monkey years can have challenging moments, but it is in overcoming these that the Pig's qualities can be seen and reputation enhanced.

The Pig will also need to be vigilant in money matters. During the year many Pigs could face repair costs and buy new equipment as well as have commitments to meet and other plans and purchases in mind. Careful budgeting will be required. Also, the Pig should be wary of risk. To act (or buy) too hastily could leave him with regrets. In this Monkey year it is better to check, to be sure and to take time over decisions rather than hurry. Pigs, take note.

With personal interests, however, this can be an inspiring time, with ideas occurring, projects starting and some Pigs being inspired by a popular new activity. Creative Pigs should consider putting their talents to greater use and explore ideas and new approaches. Innovation and participation can reward the Pig well this year.

For Pigs who are unattached and those newly in love, affairs of the heart can also make this Monkey year special. Relationships can develop and, for some Pigs, new love be found, sometimes in a fortuitous way. And when in love, the Pig's life – and year – can be so very different.

The Pig will also enjoy the social opportunities that arise over the year. Some people he meets at events connected to his interests can become useful contacts and potentially important friends. Many will warm to the Pig's genial nature this year. April, June, August and September could see the most social activity.

Throughout the year the Pig will, though, be kept busy and he needs to make sure this does not impact adversely on his home life. To be preoccupied or too involved with other commitments could cause difficult moments. His situation may not be helped by additional pressures arising, including equipment breaking or home maintenance issues being problematic. There will be times during the year which frustrate the Pig, but with help, problems can be overcome and the solutions (including new equipment) often turning out for the best.

It is also important that over the year the Pig and others in his household communicate well and quality time is not sidelined due to all the activity. Pigs, take note. Home life is very special to you and, as with all things, it requires care, attention and your own unique contribution. By being aware and mindful, however, the Pig can overcome the more awkward aspects of the Monkey year. The second half of the year will be generally easier than the first, with August and September seeing special occasions in many a Pig home.

The Pig likes to be active and the Monkey year will offer him the chance to be involved in a variety of activities. In his work there will be opportunities to use his skills in more fulfilling ways, while personal interests are favourably aspected and ideas and new activities will often be inspiring. Monkey years also have exciting romantic prospects. Domestically, it is important that the Pig spends time with others, and when problems and pressures arise (as they do in any year), shows patience and fortitude. Monkey years can have their challenges, but by remaining aware of these and putting in the effort, the Pig can make progress in this one.

The Metal Pig

The Metal Pig has great resolve and when he sets out to do something, he invariably gets results. He has willpower and personality, and as the Monkey year starts, he may well find himself looking ahead with specific goals in mind.

In his work, he can see important developments. Many Metal Pigs who have established themselves in their present place of work can look forward to securing an increased role this year. Senior colleagues will often be keen for these Metal Pigs to make more of specific strengths and, whether through offering promotion and/or greater responsibilities, will help move their career forward. Monkey years also favour enterprise and there may be the chance for the Metal Pig to contribute ideas and become more involved in work developments. This is no year to hold back. For the ambitious, this can be an exciting and rewarding time.

For Metal Pigs who feel opportunities are lacking where they are and would welcome a fresh challenge, as well as those seeking work, the Monkey year can also open up interesting possibilities. By keeping alert for vacancies and making enquiries, many of these Metal Pigs will find their initiative and skills yielding results. It will take effort, and what is offered could be surprising and require a certain amount of readjustment, but the Metal Pig will often be given an excellent chance to explore new skills and unlock hidden talents in the process. Work-wise, this is an encouraging year. March, May, July and November could see particularly interesting developments.

Progress at work will help the financial position of many Metal Pigs, but the Monkey year can be made expensive by breakages, repairs and the equipment many Metal Pigs will be keen to buy. In view of the prevailing aspects, the Metal Pig does need to keep a close watch on outgoings and check the terms and obligations when making larger purchases. Also, should he authorize any home repairs, he should compare quotations and check that his requirements are being met. To prevent problems, he needs to be thorough. Metal Pigs, take note.

Domestically, the Metal Pig will again need to be attentive and involved. Sometimes pressures and other commitments could eat into his time and whenever possible he needs to compensate for this. Shared interests and occasional treats can make an important difference. In this busy year, the Metal Pig does need to strive for a good home/work lifestyle balance. Also, at times during the year, he (and/or his family members) could face heavy workloads or be concerned about forthcoming changes and it is important that thoughts are discussed openly so others may better help and understand. Sometimes, too, there will be additional problems to address, including home maintenance issues. Here all need to be involved and decide together on the best solutions.

If possible, the Metal Pig should try to take a holiday with his loved ones over the year. A rest and a change of scene can do everyone good.

He should also make sure that his social life does not suffer due to his various commitments. He will appreciate the chances to talk to his friends, exchange views and seek advice. However, he must be careful not to make assumptions. An issue could arise which troubles him or about which a friend has reservations. He does need to take note of this and be aware.

April, June and mid-July to September could be lively months with much domestic and social activity.

For unattached Metal Pigs, the Monkey year can have exciting romantic possibilities in store, while those currently enjoying romance could see their relationship growing stronger. Many of these Metal Pigs will decide to settle down with another during the year.

The Metal Pig will also benefit from preserving time for his interests. These can again do him much good, including giving him the chance to unwind. Creative activities could be particularly satisfying. Some Metal Pigs may decide to take an interest in a new direction or set themselves a personal goal (sometimes with a keep-fit element) and again their enthusiasm can lead to some pleasing results.

Overall, the Year of the Monkey will be a busy one for the Metal Pig. At work, there will be opportunities to make greater use of specific strengths, and personal interests, too, can develop well. However, while this is an encouraging year, the Metal Pig does need to maintain a good lifestyle balance, including sharing time with others. This can be an interesting and rewarding year, but the Metal Pig does need to manage his time well.

Tip for the Year
Value your relations with those around you. Consult, listen and share. Your efforts can make an important difference. Also, seize opportunities to move forward and make greater use of your abilities.

The Water Pig

Monkey years are action-oriented and the Water Pig will respond well to the variety and scope of this one. He is set to do well, too, although it will require considerable effort on his part.

At work, many Water Pigs will have made progress in recent years, often establishing themselves in a specific area and gaining important skills. In the Monkey year they will have the chance to take this further, especially as promotion opportunities arise or new initiatives open up new responsibilities and roles. The Water Pig will often be ideally positioned to benefit, with his in-house knowledge an asset. For Water Pigs pursuing a particular career, there may also be the chance of additional training or a move to duties which will give them a wider understanding of their industry. What happens this year can be an important stage in their development. Water Pigs who are reserved, this is a time to believe in yourselves and put yourselves forward.

For Water Pigs who are seeking a fresh challenge or who feel they could better their prospects and remuneration by changing employer, the Monkey year can also hold significant developments. Almost as soon as they start to make enquiries, ideas and possibilities can arise. These Water Pigs should not be too restrictive in the type of positions they consider. Their strengths can be developed in many ways and skills gained now can be built upon later.

A feature of the Monkey year is that it favours new approaches and creative thinking, and for Water Pigs whose work or personal interests are in any way creative, this is an excellent time to develop and promote their talents. Frequently inspired and with ideas aplenty, they can make this an exciting time.

For Water Pigs seeking work, again the Monkey year can bring up some excellent opportunities. By keeping informed of developments in their area, many will secure a valuable foothold and the chance to prove themselves.

Late February, March, May, July and November could see some interesting chances, but openings and offers could occur at almost any time and the Water Pig needs to respond quickly.

Headway made at work can also improve income, but this can be an expensive year. Many Water Pigs could face repair and replacement costs as well as extra home, travel and commuting expenses. As a result, the Water Pig will need to be disciplined and keep track of spending. He should also be wary of risk or haste and check the terms of any new agreement he takes on. This is a year to be vigilant and thorough.

With his genial manner, the Water Pig gets on well with many people and enjoys an active social life. The Monkey year can give rise to a good mix of social occasions and new acquaintances can be made as the Water Pig develops his interests or changes his work. Others will appreciate his company and warm to his personality, but the Water Pig could be concerned by the attitude of another person. If troubled, he should exercise care and, while generally so trusting, be discriminating. Water Pigs, take note, for Monkey years can pose problems for the unwary. April, June, August and September could see the most social activity.

For the unattached, the year can be rich in romantic possibility, while for those enjoying love, this can be an exciting year with significant personal decisions likely.

The Water Pig's home life will also see considerable activity, although busy lifestyles will often need to be reconciled. Good communication and quality time will be of especial value. The Water Pig's suggestions for activities all can share can be particularly appreciated. Also, the more undertakings can be tackled together, the better, particularly with home maintenance or equipment issues requiring sometimes swift attention.

Short breaks or weekends away will also add interest to this full year. Some travel opportunities could arise quite unexpectedly.

Overall, the Year of the Monkey will be a busy one for the Water Pig. In his work there will often be chances to further his role and/or take on something new and so develop his skills. Personal interests, especially if creative, can also develop in an encouraging manner. Romantic prospects are promising and there will be many good times for the Water Pig to enjoy in his home and social life, although he should take careful note of the views and feelings of others. In this active year, he does need to maintain a good lifestyle balance.

Tip for the Year
Give time to those who are important to you. Not only will this benefit rapport but it can also lead to more of your plans coming to fruition.

The Wood Pig

There is a Chinese proverb which reminds us, 'There is no limit to learning,' and these words hold very true for the Wood Pig this year. Monkey years favour personal development and the knowledge the Wood Pig can gain in this one can be significant, both for the present and the longer term. Also, Monkey years have vitality and can often broaden the perspective of the Wood Pig.

For the many Wood Pigs in education, there will be much to study and some will be of a complex nature. However, by focusing on what needs to be done, not only will many Wood Pigs make good progress but also gain the skills and qualifications needed for certain vocations. The effort the Wood Pig makes now is an investment in himself and his future.

The young Wood Pig may also have the chance to decide on certain specialisms, choose assignments related to what he wants to do or gain work experience. By making the most of his opportunities, he can gain insights into careers he may wish to pursue as well as highlight certain aptitudes. Monkey years can be illuminating and instructive.

These Wood Pigs will also value their camaraderie with other students. Not only will there be a good level of mutual support, especially when the pressure is on, but a lot of fun can also be had.

For Wood Pigs in work or seeking it, the Monkey year can again hold important developments. Those in work will often be encouraged to learn more about different aspects of their industry. Also, once they have proved themselves in one capacity, other possibilities can begin to open up. The skills the Wood Pig gains now can be an important part of his development.

For Wood Pigs who are unhappy in their current line of work and those seeking work, the Monkey year can bring interesting opportunities. By registering with employment agencies and getting more information about the types of work that interest them, many could be alerted to possibilities they had not considered before. What many secure this year can be the all-important foothold they need. It will take time, but tenacity will prevail. March, May, July and mid-October to the end of November could see encouraging developments.

With a busy personal and social life and possibly expensive interests, the Wood Pig will, however need to manage his money carefully and ideally set himself a budget for certain activities. To be spendthrift or succumb to too many temptations could curtail some plans later on. Also, if he takes on new commitments or is attracted to a financial venture, he should check the details and implications.

The Wood Pig will, though, take pleasure in his personal interests and often delight in the way he can use his talents. By spending time on activities he enjoys, he may not only feel enthused but also find the energy filtering through to other areas of his life.

In so much this year, he will be encouraged by those around him and helped by the good rapport he enjoys with so many. Over the year many Wood Pigs will find themselves in demand, with a lot of socializing to look forward to. April, June, August and September could be busy and often special months.

Wood Pigs enjoying romance could find this strengthening over the year, while for the unattached, the Monkey year can be rich in romantic possibility. Exciting times are ahead for many. However, the Wood Pig does need to be attentive and take careful note of the feelings of others. Misreading situations could cause difficulty. Monkey years can have awkward moments for the unwary. Wood Pigs, take note.

With the Wood Pig being faced with important decisions this year, he should also draw on the willingness of senior relations to assist. By being forthcoming, he could be helped in unexpected ways. He will often have the chance to reciprocate, including with decisions some family members have or problems (sometimes of a technical nature) they need to address.

Overall, the Year of the Monkey will be a demanding one for the Wood Pig, and whether studying or in work, he will need to show commitment and be ready to learn. In the process, however, he can not only gain the skills needed for future progress but also discover more about his strengths. The ambitious Wood Pig will have many hopes for the future and what he does now can help. During the year he will be glad of the support of those around him and his social life and personal interests can bring much pleasure and variety to this active time. Romantic prospects, too, are promising. The Wood Pig can do well and enjoy this year, but it is important that he puts in the effort. There is no limit to learning ... or what learning can open up.

Tip for the Year

With much happening, including good times, you need to keep your various activities in balance and, when work or studying needs to be done, remain focused. There is much to be gained this year and it can be to your long-term advantage. Good luck.

The Fire Pig

'Variety is the spice of life' and the Monkey year can offer the Fire Pig a variety of activities and opportunities. He will often have a satisfying mix of things to do. However, to help give the year some direction, as it starts, he should give careful consideration to his objectives for the next 12 months. He could also find it helpful to discuss his hopes with those close to him. Sometimes, as ideas are aired they can also inspire, and plans can quickly take shape as a result.

Some of the Fire Pig's attention will be focused on his home. In some instances, there will be problems that need addressing, including equipment which breaks or has become unreliable, and some areas which the Fire Pig considers have become drab. By working out how best to proceed, he can find his actions making a surprising difference. The first quarter of the year in particular can see much practical activity.

The Fire Pig will value the support of his loved ones, especially as some may have specialist knowledge or a deft way with arrangements. He will also be keen to reciprocate and over the year will give considerable time to family members. This could include spending time with grandchildren or great-grandchildren as well as advising a close relation over a tricky decision. Here his wise counsel may be particularly appreciated.

He will also enjoy the varied social and family occasions that arise, and the more that can be shared, the better. There may be invitations to visit friends and attend social gatherings as well as some of the local events being held. There could also be interesting travel opportunities, some occurring at short notice. April, June and mid-July to September could be particularly active months both for socializing and travel.

Fire Pigs who are feeling lonely or dispirited will find that by going out more and perhaps joining a local interest group, they can make some important new acquaintances. Monkey years favour personal relations. However, a word of warning: when in company, the Fire Pig needs to be attentive to others. An unguarded comment or difference of opinion could prove awkward. Fire Pigs, take note and avoid *faux pas*!

Personal interests can bring the Fire Pig great pleasure and by setting himself some projects, he will enjoy developing his ideas and using his skills. Fire Pigs who enjoy research could become engrossed in what they discover. Creative projects can also be particularly satisfying. Some Fire Pigs may be interested in locally run courses and by taking advantage of these can benefit in many ways (including social).

In view of the equipment many Fire Pigs will buy, possible repair and maintenance costs and family activities, the Fire Pig will, however, need to keep a close watch on his financial situation. When entering into any new agreement, he should check the terms carefully. Paperwork should also be dealt with thoroughly and kept safely. This is a year for giving important matters extra attention.

In general, the Year of the Monkey can be a rewarding one for the Fire Pig. Interesting possibilities can arise, and whether involving himself in ongoing activities or trying out something new, by making the most of his time the Fire Pig will be pleased with what he is able to do. Family and friends will encourage him and he in turn will offer time, advice and assistance. The Fire Pig likes to be busy and involved, and the Monkey year will, for many, be an especially gratifying one with a lot to do and appreciate.

Tip for the Year

Take action. To make things happen and secure results, you need to be the driving force. Set your plans in motion and draw on the support of those around you. This can be an interesting and fulfilling year for you.

The Earth Pig

There is a Chinese proverb which is appropriate for many an Earth Pig this year: 'Diligence is a priceless treasure and contains a talisman for survival.' The Earth Pig recognizes the need for effort but he is also cautious, preferring to think things over and take one step at a time. This approach will continue to serve him well in this active, interesting and often lucky year.

An encouraging feature of the Monkey year is that it will give the Earth Pig greater chance to use his strengths. Whether in work, his personal interests or another sphere, there can be good opportunities for him and his diligence will again prove its worth.

In many workplaces there will be changes taking place, possibly new working practices, product launches or shifts in responsibility. The Earth Pig will often play an increasing part and have the chance to bring his experience to bear. Some Earth Pigs could become involved in implementing change, training junior staff or taking over new responsibilities, and many will have the opportunity to use their strengths in new and telling ways. As many an employer recognizes, the Earth Pig has an important contribution to make.

He also has a talent for ideas, and when suggestions or solutions are needed, his resourceful thinking can be valued. His contribution this year can be considerable.

The majority of Earth Pigs will welcome the opportunities they will have with their present employer, but for those who consider their prospects can be bettered by a move elsewhere or who are seeking work, the Monkey year can have interesting developments in store. To benefit, these Earth Pigs could find it helpful to talk to friends, contacts and others connected with their industry. Word-of-mouth recommendations can play an important part in what opens up this year. The Earth Pig should also follow up any ideas he may have. His instinct can guide him well, and if he senses a possibility or sees a vacancy that appeals to him, he should take action. March, May, July and November could be important months for emerging opportunities.

The encouraging aspects also extend to the Earth Pig's personal interests. Many Earth Pigs will be inspired by both existing and new activities, and their interest will often have been aroused by a friend or by something they have read. Again, many will take pride in what they do.

Some will also find their interests can lead to travel opportunities, and if there is an event or attraction the Earth Pig would like to go to, he should investigate and see what is possible. Similarly, if able to take a holiday this year, some early planning can lead to some rewarding experiences.

The Earth Pig will, though, need to manage his finances well. With accommodation costs, travel, family expenses and items he is keen to acquire, including equipment for home and personal use, he should watch his spending and make advance provision for outgoings. This is a year for diligence and good financial management. Also, the Earth Pig should not be lax when dealing with paperwork, as delays or oversights could be to his disadvantage. Earth Pigs, take note.

With his many activities and interests, the Earth Pig knows a great many people and over the year will again value his good friends and contacts. As has often been found, the more people you know, the more chances tend to open up, and this could be the case for the Earth Pig this year. Certain friends could prove especially helpful in alerting him to opportunities, suggesting possibilities or offering advice. In this busy year, it is important that the Earth Pig takes advantage of the help that is available and is forthcoming rather than keeps his thoughts to himself.

The Monkey year can also give rise to some fine social occasions and the Earth Pig will be keen to take part. April, June, August and September could be particularly active months.

For the unattached, affairs of the heart are positively aspected and many Earth Pigs will enjoy newfound romance. For those who have had recent personal difficulty, new people, new activities and new opportunities can help lift the shadows they may have felt under. This is a year to be active and engaged, although when in company the Earth Pig does need to be attentive to others and aware of differing viewpoints. A wrong assumption or minor disagreement could cause some difficult moments. Earth Pigs, take note.

The Earth Pig's home life will be busy, but while there will be family successes to celebrate and plans to implement, the year may not be problem-free. Maintenance issues and mechanical faults could inconvenience the Earth Pig, and some projects he is keen to tackle could be more complex than envisaged. The skills and patience of quite a few Earth Pigs will be tested, but benefits can follow, with new equipment offering advantages, and ideas that are followed through enhancing living areas.

Where possible, it would be helpful for everyone in the Earth Pig's household to be involved in practical undertakings. With good co-operation and support, much more will become possible.

Also, the Earth Pig should ensure that his commitments and often busy lifestyle do not make too many incursions into his home life. Fortunately, most Earth Pigs are aware of this, but quality time together is an important ingredient of home life and should be preserved. The Earth Pig's domestic life can be rewarding and special this year, but increased mindfulness is advised.

In general, the Year of the Monkey is an encouraging one for the Earth Pig and will bring opportunities to use his ideas and skills. However, he does need to put himself forward. This is no year to hold back or let chances slip. In much of what he does he will be assisted by others, and his reputation and contacts can help his progress. The Monkey year can also contain many pleasures and some fine social opportunities. Domestic activities can lead to beneficial outcomes too. In this busy year, the Earth Pig does need to keep his lifestyle in balance, but he will be able to demonstrate his strengths and move forward.

Tip for the Year
Liaise with others. With combined effort, your progress can be much easier. Good opportunities will arise this year. Be proactive and make your presence felt. Remember your diligence is a priceless treasure and can serve you very well this year.

Famous Pigs

Bryan Adams, Woody Allen, Julie Andrews, Marie Antoinette, Fred Astaire, Pam Ayres, Emily Blunt, Humphrey Bogart, James Cagney, Maria Callas, Samantha Cameron, Henry Cavill, Hillary Rodham Clinton, Glenn Close, Sacha Baron Cohen, Cheryl Cole, Alice Cooper, the Duchess of Cornwall, Noël Coward, Simon Cowell, Oliver Cromwell, Billy Crystal, the Dalai Lama, Ted Danson, Dido, Richard Dreyfuss, Ben Elton, Ralph Waldo Emerson, Mo Farah, Henry Ford, Gillian Flynn, Stephen Harper, Emmylou Harris, Ernest Hemingway, Chris Hemsworth, Henry VIII, Conrad Hilton, Alfred Hitchcock, Roy Hodgson, Sir Elton John, Tommy Lee Jones, Carl Gustav Jung, Stephen

King, Kevin Kline, Miranda Lambert, Hugh Laurie, David Letterman, Jerry Lee Lewis, Meat Loaf, Ewan McGregor, Ricky Martin, Johnny Mathis, Queen Máxima of the Netherlands, Pippa Middleton, Dannii Minogue, Morrissey, Wolfgang Amadeus Mozart, George Osborne, Sir Michael Parkinson, James Patterson, Maurice Ravel, Ronald Reagan, Ginger Rogers, Winona Ryder, Françoise Sagan, Carlos Santana, Arnold Schwarzenegger, Steven Spielberg, Lord Sugar, David Tennant, Emma Thompson, Carrie Underwood, David Walliams, the Duchess of York.

Appendix

The relationships between the 12 animal signs, both on a personal level and a business level, are an important aspect of Chinese horoscopes and in this appendix the compatibility between the signs is shown in the two tables that follow.

Also included are the names of the signs ruling the hours of the day and from this it is possible to find your ascendant and discover yet another aspect of your personality.

Finally, to supplement the earlier chapters on the personality and horoscope of the signs, I have included a guide on how you can get the best out of your sign and the year.

Relationships between the Signs

Personal Relationships

Key

1. Excellent. Great rapport.
2. A successful relationship. Many interests in common.
3. Mutual respect and understanding. A good relationship.
4. Fair. Needs care and some willingness to compromise in order for the relationship to work.
5. Awkward. Possible difficulties in communication and few interests in common.
6. A clash of personalities. Very difficult.

	Rat	Ox	Tiger	Rabbit	Dragon	Snake	Horse	Goat	Monkey	Rooster	Dog	Pig
Rat	1											
Ox	1	3										
Tiger	4	6	5									
Rabbit	5	2	3	2								
Dragon	1	5	4	3	2							
Snake	3	1	6	2	1	5						
Horse	6	5	1	5	3	4	2					
Goat	5	5	3	1	4	3	2	2				
Monkey	1	3	6	3	1	3	5	3	1			
Rooster	5	1	5	6	2	1	2	5	5	5		
Dog	3	4	1	2	6	3	1	5	3	5	2	
Pig	2	3	2	2	2	6	3	2	2	3	1	2

Business Relationships

Key

1. Excellent. Marvellous understanding and rapport.
2. Very good. Complement each other well.
3. A good working relationship and understanding can be developed.
4. Fair, but compromise and a common objective are often needed to make this relationship work.
5. Awkward. Unlikely to work, either through lack of trust or understanding or the competitiveness of the signs.
6. Mistrust. Difficult. To be avoided.

	Rat	Ox	Tiger	Rabbit	Dragon	Snake	Horse	Goat	Monkey	Rooster	Dog	Pig
Rat	2											
Ox	1	3										
Tiger	3	6	5									
Rabbit	4	3	3	3								
Dragon	1	4	3	3	3							
Snake	3	2	6	4	1	5						
Horse	6	5	1	5	3	4	4					
Goat	5	5	3	1	4	3	3	2				
Monkey	2	3	4	5	1	5	4	4	3			
Rooster	5	1	5	5	2	1	2	5	5	6		
Dog	4	5	2	3	6	4	2	5	3	5	4	
Pig	3	3	3	2	3	5	4	2	3	4	3	1

Your Ascendant

The ascendant has a very strong influence on your personality and will help you gain an even greater insight into your true personality according to Chinese horoscopes.

The hours of the day are named after the 12 animal signs and the sign governing the time you were born is your ascendant. To find your ascendant, look up the time of your birth in the table below, bearing in mind any local time differences in the place you were born.

11 p.m.	to	1 a.m.	The hours of the Rat
1 a.m.	to	3 a.m.	The hours of the Ox
3 a.m.	to	5 a.m.	The hours of the Tiger
5 a.m.	to	7 a.m.	The hours of the Rabbit
7 a.m.	to	9 a.m.	The hours of the Dragon
9 a.m.	to	11 a.m.	The hours of the Snake
11 a.m.	to	1 p.m.	The hours of the Horse
1 p.m.	to	3 p.m.	The hours of the Goat
3 p.m.	to	5 p.m.	The hours of the Monkey
5 p.m.	to	7 p.m.	The hours of the Rooster
7 p.m.	to	9 p.m.	The hours of the Dog
9 p.m.	to	11 p.m.	The hours of the Pig

Rat

The Rat ascendant is likely to make the sign more outgoing, sociable and careful with money. A particularly beneficial influence for those born under the signs of the Rabbit, Horse, Monkey and Pig.

Ox

The Ox ascendant has a restraining, cautionary and steadying influence that many signs will benefit from. This ascendant also promotes self-confidence and willpower and is especially good for those born under the signs of the Tiger, Rabbit and Goat.

Tiger

The Tiger ascendant is a dynamic and stirring influence that makes the sign more outgoing, action-orientated and impulsive. A generally favourable ascendant for the Ox, Tiger, Snake and Horse.

Rabbit

The Rabbit ascendant has a moderating influence, making the sign more reflective, serene and discreet. A particularly beneficial influence for the Rat, Dragon, Monkey and Rooster.

Dragon

The Dragon ascendant gives strength, determination and ambition to the sign. A favourable influence for those born under the signs of the Rabbit, Goat, Monkey and Dog.

Snake

The Snake ascendant can make the sign more reflective, intuitive and self-reliant. A good influence for the Tiger, Goat and Pig.

Horse

The Horse ascendant will make the sign more adventurous, daring and on some occasions fickle. Generally a beneficial influence for the Rabbit, Snake, Dog and Pig.

Goat

The Goat ascendant will make the sign more tolerant, easy-going and receptive. It could also impart some creative and artistic qualities. An especially good influence for the Ox, Dragon, Snake and Rooster.

Monkey

The Monkey ascendant is likely to impart a delicious sense of humour and fun to the sign. It will make the sign more enterprising and outgoing – a particularly good influence for the Rat, Ox, Snake and Goat.

Rooster

The Rooster ascendant helps to give the sign a lively, outgoing and very methodical manner. Its influence will increase efficiency and is good for the Ox, Tiger, Rabbit and Horse.

Dog

The Dog ascendant makes the sign more reasonable and fair-minded and gives an added sense of loyalty. A very good ascendant for the Tiger, Dragon and Goat.

Pig

The Pig ascendant can make the sign more sociable and self-indulgent. It is also a caring influence and one that can make the sign want to help others. A good ascendant for the Dragon and Monkey.

How to Get the Best from your Chinese Sign and the Year

Each of the 12 Chinese signs possesses its own unique strengths and by identifying them you can use them to your advantage. Similarly, by becoming aware of possible weaknesses you can do much to rectify them and in this respect I hope the following sections will be useful. Also included are some tips on how you can get the best from the year.

The Rat

The Rat is blessed with many fine talents, but his undoubted strength lies in his ability to get on with people. He is sociable, charming and a good judge of character. He also possesses a shrewd mind and is good at spotting opportunities.

However, to make the most of his abilities, he does need to impose some discipline upon himself. He should resist the (sometimes very great) temptation of getting involved in too many activities all at the same time and should decide upon his priorities and objectives. By concentrating his energies on specific matters he will fare much better. Also, given his personable manner, he should seek out positions where he can use his personal relations skills to good effect. For a career, sales and marketing could prove ideal.

The Rat is astute in dealing with finance, but while often thrifty, he can sometimes give way to moments of indulgence. Although he deserves to enjoy the money he has so carefully earned, it would sometimes be in his interests to exercise restraint when tempted to satisfy too many expensive whims!

The Rat's family and friends are important to him and while he is loyal and protective towards them, he does tend to keep his worries and concerns to himself and would be helped if he were more willing to discuss his anxieties. Others think highly of him and are prepared to do a lot to help him, but for them to do so the Rat does need to be less guarded.

With his sharp mind, keen imagination and sociable manner, he does, however, have much in his favour. When he has commitment, he can be irrepressible and, given his considerable charm, often irresistible as well! Provided he channels his energies wisely, he can make much of his life.

ADVICE FOR THE RAT'S YEAR AHEAD

General Prospects

Monkey years favour activity and the shrewd Rat will detect a myriad of opportunities. Speed is of the essence – to delay or hold back could mean chances slipping away. Rats, take note and *seize the moment*.

Career Prospects

The Rat should make the most of his strengths and experience, as there can be good chances for him to advance his career. His prospects can also be helped by training and new positions taken on over the year.

Finance

The Rat will see through some expensive plans, so while income may improve, spending needs to be watched and large outgoings budgeted for in advance.

Relations with Others

The Rat enjoys company and will relish the activities and fun this Monkey year brings. Shared activities are favourably aspected and romance can be special. With a lot happening, the Rat does need to consult others regularly. Loved ones and contacts will assist with certain hopes and plans. An active and pleasing year.

The Ox

Strong-willed and resolute, the Ox certainly has a mind of his own! He is persistent and sets about achieving his objectives with dogged determination. In addition he is reliable and tenacious and is often a source of inspiration to others. He is an achiever, and he often achieves a great deal. However, to really excel, he would do well to try and correct some of his weaknesses.

Being so resolute and having such a strong sense of purpose, the Ox can be inflexible and narrow-minded. He can be resistant to change and prefers to set about his activities in his own way rather than be dependent on others. His dislike of change can sometimes be to his detriment and if he were prepared to be more adaptable and adventurous he would find his progress easier.

The Ox would also be helped if he were to broaden his range of interests and become more relaxed in his approach. At times he can be so preoccupied with his own activities that he is not always as mindful of others as he should be, and his demeanour can sometimes be studious and serious. There are times when he would benefit from a lighter touch.

However, the Ox is true to his word and loyal to his family and friends. He is admired and respected by others and his tremendous willpower usually enables him to achieve a great deal in life.

Advice for the Ox's Year Ahead

General Prospects

Monkey years have energy and vitality, and while the Ox may be uncomfortable with the pace of developments in this one, important new chances can open up. This is a year for developing knowledge and skills. What is gained now can often have important (and beneficial) long-term implications.

Career Prospects

Oxen should take full advantage of training and any other chances to add to their experience. What they can do now can prepare them for openings in the future. New positions taken on now can often be successfully built on later. A potentially significant year.

Finance

Progress at work will often lead to an increase in income and with good control of his budget, the Ox can fare well.

Relations with Others

Oxen have a tendency to be reserved and private, but this year they should join more readily with others. The Ox's home and social life can be a source of considerable pleasure and he can benefit from the support of those who know him well. New friendships and romance are favourably aspected, but to benefit fully, the Ox should engage more and enjoy what this lively year makes possible.

The Tiger

Lively, innovative and enterprising, the Tiger enjoys an active lifestyle. He has a wide range of interests, an alert mind and a genuine liking of other people. He loves to live life to the full. However, despite his enthusiastic and well-meaning ways, he does not always make the most of his considerable potential.

Being so versatile, the Tiger does have a tendency to jump from one activity to another or dissipate his energies by trying to do too much at the same time. To make the most of himself, he should try to exercise a certain amount of self-discipline. Ideally, he should decide how best he can use his abilities, give himself some objectives and then stick to them. If he can overcome his restless tendencies, he will find he will accomplish far more.

Also, in spite of his sociable manner, the Tiger likes to retain a certain independence in his actions, and while few begrudge him this, he would sometimes find life easier if he were more prepared to work in conjunction with others. His reliance on his own judgement does sometimes mean that he excludes the views and advice of those around him, and this can be to his detriment. He may possess an independent spirit, but he must not let it go too far!

The Tiger does, however, have much in his favour. He is bold, original and quick-witted. If he can keep his restless nature in check, he can enjoy considerable success. In addition, with his engaging personality, he is well liked and much admired.

ADVICE FOR THE TIGER'S YEAR AHEAD

General Prospects

An active year, but the Tiger needs to keep his wits about him. This is a time to take careful note of developments and adapt accordingly. To be too independent or single-minded could cause problems. It is a case of making the most of situations *as they are*.

Career Prospects

An excellent year to build on strengths and add to experience. What is accomplished now can prepare the Tiger for future opportunities.

Finance

The Tiger's judgement will be on good form and some pleasing purchases and important plans will go ahead. But to do all he wants, he will need to be disciplined and watch spending.

Relations with Others

In this busy year, the Tiger needs to remain his mindful self, otherwise disagreements could arise and friendships suffer. At work, it is especially important that the Tiger liaises closely with others and builds support. Time spent with loved ones can be valued, but throughout the year the Tiger needs to be aware of awkward undercurrents.

The Rabbit

The Rabbit is certainly one who appreciates the finer things in life. With his good taste, companionable nature and wide range of interests, he knows how to live well – and usually does!

However, for all his *finesse* and style, the Rabbit does possess traits he would do well to watch. His desire for a settled lifestyle makes him err on the side of caution. He dislikes change and as a consequence can miss out on opportunities. Also, there are many Rabbits who will go to great lengths to avoid difficult and fraught situations, and again, while few may relish these, sometimes in life it is necessary to take risks or stand your ground. At times it would certainly be in the Rabbit's interests to be bolder and more assertive in going after what he desires.

The Rabbit also attaches great importance to his relations with others and while he has a happy knack of getting on with most people, he can be sensitive to criticism. Difficult though it may be, he should really try to develop a thicker skin and recognize that criticism can provide valuable learning opportunities, as can some of the problems he strives so hard to avoid.

However, with his agreeable manner, keen intellect and shrewd judgement, the Rabbit does have a lot in his favour and invariably makes much of his life – and enjoys it too!

ADVICE FOR THE RABBIT'S YEAR AHEAD

General Prospects
A reasonable year, but the Rabbit needs to keep alert and respond to changes, unanticipated though these may sometimes be. He should devote some time to himself, develop his interests and attend to his well-being. With care and good use of his time, he can make this a satisfying and constructive year.

Career Prospects
The Rabbit may be concerned about developments and increased pressures, but, uncomfortable though these may be, they will give him the chance to extend his experience and prepare himself for the opportunities to come. A testing year, but with potentially important gains following on.

Finance
While income may improve, spending needs to be watched and financial paperwork managed with care. Not a year for risk or sloppiness.

Relations with Others
The Rabbit will find himself in demand, but he needs to be alert and attentive. A possible disagreement or disappointment could upset him.

Throughout the year openness and good communication will be vital. Also, if any matter is worrying him, he would do well to seek additional advice.

The Dragon

Enthusiastic, enterprising and honourable, the Dragon possesses many admirable qualities and his life is often full and varied. He always gives his best and even though not all his endeavours meet with success, he is nonetheless resilient and hardy, and is much admired and respected.

However, for all his qualities, the Dragon can be blunt and forthright and, through sheer strength of character, sometimes domineering. It would certainly be in his interests to listen more closely to others rather than be so self-reliant. Also, his enthusiasm can sometimes get the better of him and he can be impulsive. To make the most of his abilities, he should give himself priorities and set about his activities in a disciplined and systematic way. More tact and diplomacy might not come amiss either!

However, with his lively and outgoing manner, the Dragon is popular and well liked. With good fortune on his side (and the Dragon is often lucky), his life is almost certain to be eventful and fulfilling. He has many talents, and if he uses them wisely he will enjoy much success.

ADVICE FOR THE DRAGON'S YEAR AHEAD

General Prospects
A busy year with good opportunities. However, to make the most of it, the Dragon should liaise closely with others. This is a year to be involved, to work with others and to look to progress.

Career Prospects
The Dragon can make effective use of his skills this year as well as extend them. Many Dragons can substantially advance their career as well as strengthen their reputation and prospects. Good relations with colleagues will help.

Finance

A year to be thorough and to avoid rush or risk. Major transactions should be carefully considered and, when possible, early provision made for larger outgoings. Financial paperwork also needs close attention.

Relations with Others

A year to liaise with others, build support and be a part of what is going on. The Dragon's go-it-alone tendencies need to be watched! With some often lively occasions taking place, he can enjoy the year but it is a time for sharing and togetherness. New friendships, contacts and, for some, marriage or settling down together can make this active year even more special.

The Snake

The Snake is blessed with a keen intellect. He has wide interests, an enquiring mind and good judgement. He tends to be quiet and thoughtful and plan his activities with considerable care. With his fine abilities, he often does well in life, but he does possess traits which can undermine his progress.

The Snake is often guarded in his actions and sometimes loses out to those who are more action-oriented and assertive. He also likes to retain a certain independence in his actions and this too can hamper his progress. It would be in his interests to be more forthcoming and involve others more readily in his plans. The Snake has many talents and possesses a warm and rich personality, but there is a danger that this can remain concealed behind his often quiet and reserved manner. He would fare better if he were more outgoing and showed others his true worth.

However, the Snake is very much his own master. He invariably knows what he wants in life and is often prepared to journey long and hard to achieve his objectives. He does, though, have it in his power to make that journey easier. Lose some of that reticence, Snake, be more open and assertive, and do not be afraid of the occasional risk!

Advice for the Snake's Year Ahead

General Prospects

A year of considerable possibility, but while the Snake can do well, he does need to pace himself and be alert to developments. With care and support, he can prosper, but he does need to be aware of the year's trickier aspects.

Career Prospects

Opportunities can arise quickly this year and the Snake needs to be responsive. This is a time to move forward, build on skills and fulfil potential. Effort and commitment can be rewarded – very well rewarded.

Finance

A pleasing year with good management allowing many Snakes to improve on their position and realize some key plans, especially accommodation-wise.

Relations with Others

A friendship issue could be troubling and the Snake needs to be careful in delicate and fraught situations. Dialogue and increased awareness are recommended. In many of his activities, however, the Snake will be well supported and he can enjoy many agreeable occasions.

The Horse

Versatile, hardworking and sociable, the Horse makes his mark wherever he goes. He has an eloquent and engaging manner and makes friends with ease. He is quick-witted, has an alert mind and is certainly not averse to taking risks or experimenting with new ideas.

He possesses a strong and likeable personality, but he does also have his weaknesses. With his wide interests he does not always finish everything he starts and he would do well to be more persevering. He has it within him to achieve considerable success, but to make the most of his talents he does need to overcome his restless tendencies. When he has made plans, he should stick with them.

The Horse loves company and values both his family and friends. However, there will have been many a time when he will have lost his temper or spoken in haste and regretted his words later. Throughout his life he needs to keep his temper in check and be diplomatic in tense situations, otherwise he could jeopardize the respect and good relations he so values.

However, the Horse has a multitude of talents and a lively and outgoing personality. If he can overcome his restless and volatile nature, he can lead a rich and highly fulfilling life.

ADVICE FOR THE HORSE'S YEAR AHEAD

General Prospects

The Horse will welcome the vitality of the Monkey year and be keen to go ahead with his plans. However, he needs to focus and be careful not to spread his attention too widely. A good year, but energies need to be channelled.

Career Prospects

Career prospects are excellent and by making the most of his opportunities and following through his ideas, the Horse can make important progress. This is no year to stand still but to reap the benefits of the skills, experience and goodwill he has built up. A year to participate, build and move ahead.

Finance

Accommodation matters will feature prominently, with some Horses moving. With many expenses likely and an often busy lifestyle, the Horse will need to manage his outgoings well.

Relations with Others

Joint activities and initiatives are favourably aspected and the Horse should seek support for some of his ambitious plans. He will enjoy taking part in many of the activities the year brings and new contacts and friendships have the potential to become important.

The Goat

The Goat has a warm, friendly and understanding manner and gets on well with most people. He is generally easy-going, has a fond appreciation of the finer things in life and possesses a rich imagination. He is often artistic and enjoys the creative arts and outdoor activities.

However, despite his engaging manner, there lurks beneath his skin a sometimes tense and pessimistic nature. The Goat can be a worrier and without the support and encouragement of others can feel insecure and be hesitant in his actions.

To make the most of himself he should aim to become more assertive and decisive as well as more at ease with himself. He has much in his favour, but he really does need to be bolder and promote himself more. He would also be helped if he were to sort out his priorities and set about his activities in an organized and disciplined manner. There are some Goats who tend to be haphazard in the way they go about things and this can hamper their progress.

Although the Goat will always value the support of others, it would also be in his interest to become more independent and not be so reticent about striking out on his own. He does, after all, possess many talents, as well as a sincere and likeable personality, and by giving his best he can make his life rich, rewarding and enjoyable.

Advice for the Goat's Year Ahead

General Prospects

An active year with good chances for the Goat to make more of his strengths and move forward. However, *he* needs to be the driving force. This is a year for commitment and initiative. Goats, make things happen!

Career Prospects

A year of fast-moving developments. The Goat will have the opportunity to make important headway, learn new skills and prove his worth. By putting in the effort, he can see results. His creativity and personal skills will be appreciated.

Finance

The Goat needs to keep a close watch on spending and deal with financial paperwork carefully. When considering large purchases, it would be prudent for him to get advice as well as fully consider the options and ranges available.

Relations with Others

The Goat will be in demand this year. However, in all his activities, he needs to communicate well. Misunderstandings or assumptions could lead to problems. Goats, take note, and do be open and forthcoming.

The Monkey

Lively, enterprising and innovative, the Monkey certainly knows how to impress. He has wide interests, a good sense of fun and relates well to others. He also possesses a shrewd mind and often has a happy knack of turning events to his advantage.

However, despite his versatility and considerable gifts, he does have his weaknesses. He often lacks persistence, can get distracted easily and also places tremendous reliance upon his own judgement. While his belief in himself is a commendable asset, it would certainly be in his interests to be more mindful of the views of others. Also, while he likes to keep tabs on all that is going on around him, he can be evasive and secretive with regard to his own feelings and activities, and again a more forthcoming attitude would be to his advantage.

In his desire to succeed, the Monkey can also be tempted to cut corners or be crafty and he should recognize that such actions can rebound on him!

However, he is resourceful and his sheer strength of character will ensure that he has an interesting and varied life. If he can channel his considerable energies wisely and overcome his sometimes restless tendencies, his life can be crowned with success. And with his amiable personality, he will have many friends.

Advice for the Monkey's Year Ahead

General Prospects
The Monkey will have high expectations of his own year and be keen to make the most of himself. And he can deliver, but he does need to have support rather than rely on just his own efforts. This is a year to liaise with others. If the Monkey does this and acts with determination, he can enjoy a great deal of success.

Career Prospects
A year of considerable opportunity, with many a Monkey's strengths recognized and encouraged. This is no time to stand still: in his own year, the Monkey needs to make the most of himself and his often special talents. The enterprising nature of many Monkeys can be rewarded and ideas will often develop well.

Finance
An often lucky year, but with many plans in mind, the Monkey will need to manage his resources well. Early provision for requirements will help.

Relations with Others
The Monkey enjoys company and this can be a pleasing year for him. For the unattached, there are good romantic prospects. With so much happening, the Monkey does, however, need to manage his time well. He also needs to involve others in his plans, even if this means compromising his sometimes secretive Monkey nature.

The Rooster

With his considerable bearing and incisive and resolute manner, the Rooster cuts an impressive figure. He has a sharp mind, is well informed on many matters and expresses himself clearly and convincingly. He is meticulous and efficient in his undertakings and commands a great deal of respect. He also has a genuine and caring interest in others.

The Rooster has much in his favour, but there are some aspects of his character that can tell against him. He can be candid in his views and over-zealous in his actions, and sometimes he can say or do things he later regrets. His high standards also make him fussy, even pedantic, and he can get diverted into relatively minor matters when in truth he could be occupying his time more profitably. This is something all Roosters would do well to watch. Also, while the Rooster is a great planner, he can sometimes be unrealistic in his expectations. In making plans – indeed, in most of his activities – he would do well to consult others. He would benefit greatly from their input.

The Rooster has many talents as well as commendable drive and commitment, but to make the most of himself he does need to channel his energies wisely and watch his candid and sometimes volatile nature. With care, however, he can make a success of his life, and with his wide interests and outgoing personality, he will enjoy the friendship and respect of many.

Advice for the Rooster's Year Ahead

General Prospects

The conscientious Rooster will sometimes despair over the workings of the Monkey year. However, amid the changes, challenges and problematic plans, there can be good opportunities. Also, next year is the Rooster's own year and the lessons and developments of 2016 can be potentially significant.

Career Prospects

A demanding year, but an instructive one. By rising to its challenges, being adaptable and using his skills to advantage, the Rooster can make progress and considerably enhance his reputation. What is achieved this year can be the platform for future success.

Finance

The Rooster will be busy this year, but must not take his eye off financial matters. He needs to watch his budget and spending as well as attend to paperwork with care. Uncharacteristic lapses could be to his disadvantage.

Relations with Others

The Rooster needs to make sure his general busyness does not affect his home and social life. Managing his time well and setting some aside for individual and shared interests can make an important difference to his year. It is a time for mindfulness, awareness and a good lifestyle balance.

The Dog

Loyal, dependable and with a good understanding of human nature, the Dog is well placed to win respect and admiration. He is a no-nonsense sort of person and hates any sort of hypocrisy and falsehood. With the Dog you know where you stand and, given his direct manner, where he stands on any issue. He also has a strong humanitarian nature and often champions good causes.

The Dog has many fine attributes, although there are certain traits that can prevent him from either enjoying or making the most of his life. He is a great worrier and can get anxious over all manner of things. Although it may not always be easy, he should try to rid himself of the 'worry habit'. Whenever he is tense or concerned, he should be prepared to speak to others rather than shoulder his worries all by himself. In some cases, they could even be of his own making! Also, he has a tendency to look on the pessimistic side and he would certainly be helped if he were to view his undertakings more optimistically. He does, after all, possess many skills and should have faith in his abilities. Another weakness is his tendency to be stubborn over certain issues. If he is not careful, at times this could undermine his position.

If the Dog can reduce the pessimistic side of his nature, he will not only enjoy life more but also find he is achieving more. He possesses a truly admirable character and his loyalty, reliability and sincerity are appreciated by all whom he meets. In his life he will do much good and befriend many people – and he owes it to himself to enjoy life too. Sometimes it might help him to recall the words of another Dog, Sir Winston Churchill: 'When I look back on all these worries, I remember the story of the old man who said on his deathbed that he had had a lot of trouble in his life, most of which never happened.'

Advice for the Dog's Year Ahead

General Prospects

A busy year rich in possibility. But the Dog does need to take charge, pursue opportunities and look to progress. With determination, he can enjoy some well-deserved success. A good lifestyle balance can also be to his advantage.

Career Prospects

There will be excellent chances for the Dog to make more of his strengths, and with commitment and involvement, he can make important headway. Looking to raise his profile will help.

Finance

With many ambitious plans and some costly undertakings likely, the Dog needs to control spending. Travel is well aspected and should be budgeted for.

Relations with Others

The Dog attaches great importance to his relations with others and will be encouraged by the support he enjoys. Family, friends and contacts can all help in special ways. This is no year for the Dog to keep himself to himself (as some do), but one to engage with the world – and enjoy it.

The Pig

Genial, sincere and trusting, the Pig gets on well with most people. He has a kind and caring nature, a dislike of discord and often a good sense of humour. In addition, he has a fondness for socializing and enjoying the good life!

The Pig possesses a shrewd mind, is particularly adept at dealing with business and financial matters and has a robust and resilient nature. Although not all his plans may work out as he would like, he is tenacious and will frequently rise up and succeed after experiencing setbacks and difficulties. In his often active and varied life he can accomplish a great deal, although there are certain aspects of his character that can tell against him. If he can modify these or keep them in check then his life will certainly be easier and possibly even more successful.

In his activities the Pig can sometimes over-commit himself and while he does not want to disappoint, he would certainly be helped if he were to set about his activities in an organized and systematic manner and give himself priorities at busy times. He should also not allow others to take advantage of his good nature and it would be in his interests to be more discerning. There will have been times when he has been gullible and naïve; fortunately, he quickly learns from his mistakes. However, he possesses a stubborn streak and if new situations do not fit in with his line of thinking, he can be inflexible. Such an attitude may not always be to his advantage.

The Pig is a great pleasure-seeker and while he should enjoy the fruits of his labours, he can sometimes be self-indulgent and extravagant. This is also something he would do well to watch.

However, though the Pig may possess some faults, those who come into contact with him are invariably impressed by his integrity, amiable manner and intelligence. If he uses his talents wisely, his life can be crowned with considerable achievement and he will also be loved and respected by many.

ADVICE FOR THE PIG'S YEAR AHEAD

General Prospects
An encouraging year, but the Pig needs to make the most of his ideas and go after what he wants. This is a year for putting in the effort. Important benefits can follow on.

Career Prospects
Good opportunities can arise, but a lot will be asked of the Pig. However, he is often at his best when challenged and his enterprise and resourcefulness will take him forward. A year for commitment and building on strengths.

Finance
An expensive year is likely, especially with possible repair and replacement costs and the Pig's busy lifestyle. Spending needs to be watched. This is a time for careful financial management.

Relations with Others
The Pig values his good relations with others and will often revel in the many activities of the Monkey year. However, when in company, he needs to be attentive and aware of the views of others. It is also important that he keeps his lifestyle in balance and preserves some time for himself, his interests and, importantly, others.

A Closing Thought

I hope that having read *Your Chinese Horoscope 2016* you have found it of value and interest.

The Monkey year is one of great potential, offering a chance for us all to make more of our individual talents and the opportunities this interesting year will bring. It is a time when our actions can make a difference, both now and in paving the way for the future.

Within you are the riches of your tomorrow.

I wish you well and all good fortune.

Neil Somerville